Dear Alex,
May this book help you in
your own project of doubting
the devout.

בהצלחה גדולה וניצחון!

Josh Schwartz

DOUBTING *the* DEVOUT

Religion and American Culture

The Religion and American Culture series explores the interaction between religion and culture throughout American history. Titles examine such issues as how religion functions in particular urban contexts, how it interacts with popular culture, its role in social and political conflicts, and its impact on regional identity. Series Editor Randall Balmer is the Ann Whitney Olin Professor of American Religion and former chair of the Department of Religion at Barnard College, Columbia University.

Michael E. Staub, *Torn at the Roots:*
The Crisis of Jewish Liberalism in Postwar America

Amy DeRogatis, *Moral Geography: Maps, Missionaries,*
and the American Frontier

Arlene M. Sánchez Walsh, *Latino Pentecostal Identity:*
Evangelical Faith, Self, and Society

Julie Byrne, *O God of Players: The Story of the Immaculata Mighty Macs*

Thomas E. Woods Jr., *The Church Confronts Modernity:*
Catholic Intellectuals and the Progressive Era

Clyde R. Forsberg Jr., *Equal Rites: The Book of Mormon, Masonry,*
Gender, and American Culture

Andrew C. Rieser, *The Chautauqua Moment: Protestants, Progressives,*
and the Culture of Modern Liberalism

Craig D. Townsend, *Faith in Their Own Color:*
Black Episcopalians in Antebellum New York City

Michael D. McNally, *Honoring Elders: Ojibwe Aging,*
Religion, and Authority

DOUBTING

the

DEVOUT

The Ultra-Orthodox in the
Jewish American Imagination

NORA L. RUBEL

Columbia University Press New York

Columbia University Press
Publishers Since 1893
New York   Chichester, West Sussex

Library of Congress Cataloging-in-Publication Data
Rubel, Nora L., 1974–
Doubting the devout : the ultra-orthodox in the Jewish American imagination /
Nora L. Rubel.
p. cm. — (Religion and American culture (New York, N.Y.))
Includes bibliographical references and index.
ISBN 978-0-231-14186-4 (cloth : alk. paper) —
ISBN 978-0-231-14187-1 (pbk. : alk. paper) —ISBN 978-0-231-51258-9 (e-book)
1. Ultra-Orthodox Jews—United States—Public opinion. 2. Public opinion—
United States. 3. Jews in popular culture—United States. 4. American
fiction—Jewish authors—History and criticism. I. Title. II. Series

BM205.R83   2009
700'.48296832—dc22   2009012413

♾

Columbia University Press books are printed on permanent and durable
acid-free paper.
This book is printed on paper with recycled content.
Printed in the United States of America

c 10 9 8 7 6 5 4 3 2 1
p 10 9 8 7 6 5 4 3 2

References to Internet Web sites (URLs) were accurate at the time of writing.
Neither the author nor Columbia University Press is responsible for URLs
that may have expired or changed since the manuscript was prepared.

The burden isn't either/or, consciously choosing from possibilities
equally difficult and regrettable—it's and/and/and/and/and as well.
—Philip Roth, *The Counterlife*

This work is dedicated to the memory of Moshe Yerushalmi (1917–1999),
whose grandchildren continue to live out the "and/and/and/and/and"
of Jewish possibility.
May his name be for a blessing.

CONTENTS

ACKNOWLEDGMENTS

O ver the past few years I have wondered if this book might be an unconscious act of therapy. Growing up in a Reform Jewish household, I used to envy my Orthodox cousins for their intimate knowledge of Jewish law and practice. I also resented them for their ability to seem "more Jewish" than I. Over the years we made different decisions about our lives, both toward and away from the practices of our parents—perhaps making our journeys more similar than our destinations. I am quite certain that without both the pleasures and pains of our relationship, this book would never have been written. But if this book is therapy for my own ambivalent religious sentiment, it is in many ways a study of a shared pathology, one that runs rampant in the American Jewish community—the anxiety of what it means to be a "real" Jew.

So much of writing is a silent conversation with oneself. If you are lucky, you get to actually speak with real people once in a while. I have been quite fortunate in that respect and therefore owe many thanks to many people. Those with whom my conversations helped shape the direction of this project include Lawrence Baron, Annemarie Brennan, Matthew Brown, Dan Clanton, Jill DeTemple, Marcie Cohen Ferris, Leslie Fishbein, Sylvia Hoffert, Jenna Weissman Joselit, Pam Lach, Shanny Luft, Peter Manseau, Sean McCloud, Mary Ellen O'Donnell,

Leah Potter, Jeff Sharlet, Silvia Tomaskova, and Tom Tweed. Additional fodder for thought came from two of my oldest friends: David Hollander and Rachael Jordan. When it came time to actually write, my dear friends Lesleigh Cushing Stahlberg and Cynthia Gentile carefully reviewed drafts and offered thoughtful suggestions. My writing group, consisting of three very wise and wonderful women, Maryellen Davis, Kathryn Lofton, and Quincy Newell assisted me greatly. I appreciate them for their help on all facets of the project and much, much more. Katie knows that much of the progress on this book is due to her magical midwifery.

As director of my dissertation, Yaakov Ariel was incredibly generous with his time and knowledge, always willing to read drafts and discuss the project. As my advisor, he was equally generous. I consider myself quite fortunate to have been Yaakov's student; all graduate students should be so lucky. In addition to Yaakov, my dissertation committee members, Beth Holmgren, Joy Kasson, Laurie Maffly-Kipp, and Randall Styers, all brought their individual interests and expertise to this project. I am grateful for all their suggestions and support, and I have appreciated their great accessibility.

In the process of revising this manuscript, my colleagues at Connecticut College were of great assistance, particularly Roger L. Brooks and Eugene V. Gallagher. Gene is as close a reader as he is a friend. At my present home at the University of Rochester, I have enjoyed the great support of my colleagues in the Religion and Classics department, as well as inspiration from my students in my seminar "Imagining the Jew."

The process of turning a dissertation into a book was made much easier by the assistance and support of Wendy Lochner, Christine Mortlock, and Michael Haskell from Columbia University Press. Not only were they incredibly attentive and helpful, they never made me feel like I didn't know what I was doing. And I really didn't know what I was doing.

I owe Rebecca Alpert and Stephen Prothero a world of thanks for their generosity and assistance, not only with the completion of this project but for the years of advice that have led me to this present place.

Timing is often everything, and I feel so fortunate to have met them in the right time.

I have always viewed this study of American Jews as the story of a family. As I mentioned earlier, my own family has served as a source of both support and inspiration for this project, and I therefore heartily thank the Edelsteins, Nipes, Rubels, and Yerushalmis. In particular, I would like to thank my parents, Ray and Oria Rubel, who always supported my career choice, despite its occasional lack of clarity. During the writing of this manuscript, my father would always save articles he thought I might find interesting, and he never tired of discussing them with me. I owe much thanks to my mother, who inspired this entire project by giving me a copy of Anne Roiphe's *Lovingkindness* when I was in high school and a copy of Naomi Ragen's *Sotah* when I was in college. I hope we never stop sharing books.

Completing this monograph would have been impossible without the love and tireless support of my husband, Rob Nipe. In the early days of the project, Rob scoured used bookstores for any obscure paperbacks that potentially might have something to do with Orthodox Jews. In the later days, he read drafts, made dinner, cared for our children, and convincingly pretended that he actually enjoyed living with me. For all of these things and more, I will always be grateful. As chance would have it, the completion of the dissertation coincided with the birth of my daughter Zoe Anat, and the final revision of the manuscript just barely preceded the birth of my second daughter, Ruby Emilia. I would like to thank Zoe—whose arrival forced me to finally learn efficiency—and Ruby—whose gestation spurred me along. Their presence gives meaning to everything.

DOUBTING *the* DEVOUT

INTRODUCTION

A FAMILY FEUD

"We are one people—our enemies have made us one without our consent."—Theodore Herzl, *The Jewish State*

"Those people are a freaking embarrassment."—Robert J. Avrech, *A Stranger Among Us*

A JEWISH FEUD

Like many domestic disputes, it began with the sharing of a bathroom. In the late 1990s, a group of Orthodox Jewish students filed a lawsuit against Yale University. Yale's housing policy requires that all unmarried undergraduates live on campus for their first two years; the school has a longstanding mission to create not just dormitories but college communities. There are single-sex floors for first-year students, but anyone of any gender can visit, sleep over, or use the bathroom. In 1998, several Jewish students, subsequently known as the "Yale Five," protested the policy, claiming that Yale's accommodations compromised their modesty.

The lawsuit stirred strong reactions in the Jewish community. In an article in the *New York Times*, Samuel Freedman writes, "In their way, the Yale Five seek nothing less than to reverse the course of Jewish history in America."[1] More than most immigrant groups, Jews historically have embraced American secular education with zeal. For Freedman, the litigious choice of the Yale Five signifies a decisive shift in Orthodox attitudes toward American society, observing that "a dormitory address at Yale has emerged as the signifier of an Orthodox Jew's readiness to engage the larger society."[2] Ultimately, the court decided in favor of Yale, finding that the plaintiff's constitutional rights were not violated since the housing policy had been disclosed at the time of application. Since these Jewish students had the freedom of choice to apply elsewhere, this policy further posed no threat of monopoly.

Although this particular housing conflict only affected five students, the Yale Five fracas is indicative of a far greater intra-Jewish conflict, one that has parallels in the wider American culture.[3] As James Hunter writes in his 1991 *Culture Wars*: "[The] personal disagreements that fire the culture war are deep and perhaps irreconcilable. But these differences are often intensified and aggravated by the way they are presented in public."[4] Like other American conflicts over cultural and religious values, the themes of this contemporary Jewish quarrel have made their way into the public eye not only through high-profile legal battles, such as that of the Yale Five, but also through representation in literary and visual popular culture.

The past two decades have seen a rise in literature and film written and directed by American Jews that purport to describe the inner world of ultra-Orthodox Jewish communities. Prior to the mid-1980s, ultra-Orthodox characters were few and far between in Jewish literature and film. Sometimes positive and sometimes negative, those characters that did exist were likely to be depicted as relics of an earlier period rather than living, breathing Jews of contemporary America. In the 1980s, a new sort of Jewish popular culture began to accentuate Orthodox themes as well as characters, but these images were not always flattering. In contrast to earlier works by writers such as Abraham Cahan and Chaim Potok that emphasize the romantic aspects of an orthodox Jewish past, these recent tales of the Jewish American imagination are laden with suspicion rather than sentiment, nerves rather than nostalgia. Such profiles of the ultra-Orthodox coincide with a rapidly growing cultural polarization among American Jewry. Differing views on how to reconcile Judaism with the general culture have resulted in an at times undeclared culture war, largely between Orthodox and non-Orthodox practitioners of Judaism. Liberal Jews tend to see the uncompromising nature of the ultra-Orthodox as threatening to Jewish claims of Americanness. On the other side, the ultra-Orthodox view liberal movements such as Reform, Conservative, and Reconstructionist Judaism as succumbing to assimilation and therefore as threatening to Jewish survival.

While it is difficult to find a time in modern Jewish history where there has been a consensus among Jews, this particular quarrel has roots which go back as far as Emancipation and the Enlightenment. Emancipation, as the historian Paula Hyman points out, "eliminated the autonomous corporate Jewish community, which had some power to constrain its members and thereby enforce a semblance of unity."[5] Given the freedom to enter the greater society without abandoning their religion, Jews confronted a new reality: the freedom *not* to practice Judaism. Subsequently, Judaism has changed dramatically in the last two centuries. Some Jews welcomed the freedom from religious obligation, choosing to secularize completely. Others chose to adapt their religious practices to their host culture rather than abandon them completely. And some chose to fiercely resist the seductions of modernity as best they could, resisting secularism and retaining a semblance of Jewish continuity. In the free, pluralistic society of the United States, Judaism branched into multiple factions, each with its own response to the challenges of modernity.[6]

According to Freedman, at the core of the confrontations between these splinter groups, "lie the same fundamental questions. What is the definition of Jewish identity? Who decides what is authentic and legitimate Judaism?"[7] One cannot attempt to answer these questions without addressing the underlying ideological conflict between religious pluralism and traditionalism. Central to these disputes are the matters of religious authority and Jewish continuity. Liberal Jewish movements such as Reform, Conservative, and Reconstructionist Judaism attempted to create a contemporary living Judaism that was compatible with modern life. Those who opposed the principles of the liberal movements attempted to reinstate traditional practices that were being rapidly abandoned in the interest of acculturation and modernity. Theirs was a counterreformist version of Judaism, and these traditionalist Jews became known as Orthodox Jews. For some Orthodox Jews, this counterreformation did not go far enough, and because of their increasing efforts to resist all that modernity offered, they became known as *ultra*-Orthodox Jews (or "haredim").

Despite these divisions within Orthodoxy, the line of the Jewish culture war falls primarily between Orthodox and non-Orthodox Jews. While the Jewish religious right rejects the acceptance of intermarriage, women's ordination, homosexuality, and patrilineal descent, the left is angered by what they see as the delegitimization of non-Orthodox movements. A survey in the late 1980s saw a majority of American Jews "very offended" "by Orthodox Jews who show no respect for the way you choose to be Jewish."[8] At the heart of this struggle lies an argument over religious authority. Non-Orthodox Jews tend to demonstrate a relativist attitude toward rabbinic authority. Orthodox Jews do not share this relativism, and it is this uncompromising nature of the Orthodox that fuels the tensions of the contemporary Jewish culture war.

AN AMERICAN FEUD

In William Hutchison's work on the history of religious pluralism in America, he notes:

> Americans had managed to apply their pluralist ideals in very visible ways, and usually in perfectly genuine, committed ways. Just as visibly, however, they had applied limits. They had said, "Thus far, and no farther." . . . [T]ime and again, they drew the line at what they perceived as socially threatening behavior.[9]

The texts pursued in this book emerge therefore in an epoch of cultural contestation, a moment when the dominant group, mainstream American Jewry, consciously or unconsciously believes it is being threatened by an invasion of the marginalized group, the ultra-Orthodox. This pattern of anxious literary production has a long lineage in American religious history, beginning with the seventeenth-century Indian captivity narrative. Over the centuries, anti-Indian tales gave way to anti-Catholic, anti-Mormon, and anti-Muslim stories.[10] The authors of these narratives employ manipulative and potentially slanderous tactics in order to rouse the passions of the reader. One such famous (and false) exposé of a nineteenth-century Catholic convent is Maria Monk's *The Awful Disclosures of the Hotel Dieu Nunnery* (1836). In this captivity narrative, Monk—an innocent young Protestant woman—somehow found herself turning to salvation in the arms of a Catholic convent, only to discover that hidden behind the high convent walls existed a dark, lurking evil. That evil ran the gamut from strict rules and behavioral regulations to outright physical and sexual abuse. Monk's popular exposé told of "unspeakable horrors" that took place in the convent: the sexual solicitation of nuns by priests, infanticide, and murder. Read by many at a time when convents were actually being burned down by angry mobs, these convent tales fueled already existing nativist passions. *The Awful Disclosures the Hotel Dieu Nunnery* was later exposed as a ghostwritten venture, the product of a group of Protestant men eager to warn young women of the dangers of the increasingly visible Catholic Church.[11]

Monk's successful narrative (outsold only by *Uncle Tom's Cabin*) highlighted preexisting anxiety about the nature of power and authority, primarily the power wielded over women. These themes can be seen in similar "nonfiction" exposés of Mormons and Muslims. In each instance, the dominant culture constructs extreme portraits of the marginalized group as an articulation of its own cultural insecurity and anxiety. The anti-haredi writings profiled in this study are no exception, placing this American Jewish culture war in a long line of American ethnic and religious conflict. The narratives replace the lecherous priests in anti-Catholic tales with manipulative rabbis, the abusive convent with the repressive yeshiva, but the formula remains the same: these people are different and threatening, and the public should be warned. Thus far, and no farther.

This sort of culture war is assuredly not specific to Jews alone, although the Jewish feud does have its own distinguishing features. The same liberal Jews who produce or consume these anxious narratives possess a deep ambivalence regarding ultra-Orthodox Jews. In their study of pioneer families of the American West, Lillian Schlissel, Byrd Gibbens, and Elizabeth Hampsten observe, "They are us in other clothes, where we began and where our dreams were given form."[12] Similarly, American Jews have the sense that these Jews in long black coats and long dresses are an earlier version of themselves. One such secular character in Dara Horn's 2002 *In the Image* reflects on ultra-Orthodox Jews:

> "I guess I just don't understand how I'm supposed to feel about them. . . . I mean, I see one of these guys on a bus with a hat and a nice long beard, and I know I'm supposed to be thinking to myself, Yes, you are my brother, we stood at Mount Sinai together. Or something like that. But it doesn't work that way. Instead I just think to myself, Why are you dressed like you're Amish? . . . And why . . . do they make me feel, since I'm Jewish and they're Jewish, but I'm not Super Duper Jew like they are, that everything I'm doing in my life is totally wrong?"[13]

Other Jews reject the principles of these ultra-Orthodox, who may resemble their grandparents or great-grandparents, or, in a recent twist of fate, may resemble their children, newly drawn to the allure of conservative religious practice.

This growing Jewish polarization between liberalism and traditionalism fits into a greater American context. While the second half of the twentieth century has seen a relative decrease in tensions between mainstream religious groups in America, there has arisen a new set of divisions over "values" that transcends denominational and religious lines. These divisions are characterized by a shift to the right within many American religious institutions, which leaves liberals and conservatives battling each other from within. Sociologist Robert Wuthnow writes:

> The major divisions in American religion now revolve around an axis of liberalism and conservatism rather than the denominational landmarks of the past. The new division parallels the ideological cleavage that runs through American politics. It divides religious practitioners from one another over questions of social welfare, defense spending, communism, and the so-called moral politics of abortion, sex education, gender equality, and prayer in public schools.[14]

These social, political, and economic issues can be more divisive than the lines that traditionally separated religious communities. The greatest support the Yale Five received came from evangelical Protestants, conservative Catholics, and even some Muslims. Significantly, the plaintiffs received more opposition than encouragement from their fellow Jews. As Samuel Freedman observed, "some of the most indignant letters to the Yale Daily News opposing the Yale Five have come from other Jewish students, blaming the plaintiffs for everything from misrepresenting Judaism to ruining the admission chances of future Orthodox applicants."[15] One such letter from a classmate of one of the Yale Five concluded, "Thanks to Yale for giving us the opportunity to grow without sacrificing our beliefs."[16]

Another Orthodox Yale student commented on the matter:

> "All the non-Jews on campus support them because it looks like a civil rights issue. And all the Jews on campus oppose them because on a certain level I feel that what's going on is it's not a religious motive, that they're not being more religious than the people who are in the religious community here, what they're being is more separatist. And that's a push and pull you see in the Jewish community today."[17]

Even the Orthodox rabbi affiliated with Yale opposed the lawsuit, indicating a divisiveness within Orthodoxy itself, claiming that the majority of Orthodox Jews happily attending Yale "do not like the implication that they're less religious."[18] Some American Jews went so far as to write in angry letters to the *New York Times* over the nature of lawsuit, and on the whole distanced themselves from the plaintiffs at Yale. Despite the successful acculturation Jews have experienced in America, the Yale Five represent the separatists in their midst, threatening their hard-fought comfort level. They are the Jews in other clothes, refusing to fit in and get along.

THE FAMILY MEMBERS: DEFINING THE PLAYERS

This book is not just about the ultra-Orthodox. It is about contemporary American Jewry and about what the haredim represent to mainstream American Jews. This work would, however, be remiss without a general explanation of who the haredim are and how they fit into the American scene.[19]

Who are the haredim? They are the aforementioned "ultra-Orthodox," those separatist, observant Jews who choose not to acculturate and who adhere to a restorative Eastern European Jewish ideology. They are a minority within a minority within a minority. Jews make up less than 2 percent of all Americans; about 12 percent of American Jews are Orthodox; and of that group, about a third are haredi.[20]

Yet despite its small numbers, this haredi minority is hardly monolithic. Ultra-orthodoxy is a broad, umbrella-like term that includes both hasidic and non-hasidic groups, sometimes referred to as *"mitnagdim"* or *"misnagdim"* (opponents) by hasidim. To outsiders, they are often seen as a monolithic group of religious Jews. Generally speaking, they can be identified on the street by the men's black coats and hats and the women's modest dress and head coverings. Despite being almost indistinguishable to outsiders, this community harbors a great diversity. The hasidim and *mitnagdim* present important differences in historical development, as well as in the social organization of their communities.

Hasidism, which is often seen as the oldest, most traditional form of Judaism, is actually a relatively new movement. Founded in the mid-eighteenth century in Ukraine by Israel ben Eliezer, also known as the Ba'al Shem Tov,[21] hasidism was a movement of religious renewal. Hasidism emphasized mysticism and claimed that "simple faith, inward passion and fervent prayer are as important as Talmudic scholarship."[22] By emphasizing the holiness in everyday life, the Ba'al Shem Tov developed a large and enthusiastic following.[23] His disciples subsequently dispersed to many areas of Eastern Europe, bringing their new devotional religiosity with them and establishing communities of hasidim, separate and independent from local rabbinical authority.

The religious hierarchy of the period did not view the hasidim as threatening at first. However, by the mid- to late eighteenth century, when the movement became more widespread, the rabbinical elite declared the hasidim heretics. The joyous singing and dancing of the hasidim impressed their opponents as the expressions of a simple, nonintellectual people. Additionally, concern was expressed over the teaching of kabbalah to the masses as well as the absolute reverence with which hasidim treated their rebbes, the center of a hasidic community. The rebbe is a religious leader who is considered a *tzaddik*, a righteous man. Most hasidic groups believe "that the rebbe [is] not a mere human, but endowed with superior knowledge, piety, and access to the Divine; thus his statements, opinions, interpretations and answers [are] to be acted upon accordingly."[24] This *tzaddikate* is traditionally a hereditary position, leading to hasidic dynasties.[25] In contrast to the hasidic cult of personality, the *mitnagdim* focus primarily on Talmudic learning and emphasize a more rational and less mystical interpretation of the tradition, dismissing the hasidic emphasis on mysticism as an adherence to frivolous folklore.[26] Given their dedication to scholarship, the *mitnagdim* became known best for their schools, the *yeshivot*.[27]

The haredim were not the first Jews to land on America's shores. They arrived long after the two major waves of Jewish immigration in the middle of the nineteenth century and at the turn of the twentieth century. Until World War II, the haredi leadership fiercely resisted immigration to America. In their eyes, this *treife medina* (unkosher land), represented all that was wrong with modernity and, consequently, all that was dangerous to Judaism. This resistance affected those haredim who immigrated earlier, particularly the hasidim, who had difficulty establishing religious communities without a rebbe.

While the Bolshevik revolution crushed Jewish religious life in Russia and Ukraine, World War II and its Holocaust destroyed haredi communities throughout Europe. Whole villages and towns were wiped out, leaving only a small fraction of Europe's Orthodoxy. In the aftermath, most of those who survived made their way to America or Palestine. The remnants of these European communities attempted to recreate their lives on a smaller scale in America. The hasidic communities retained the names of the small towns in Eastern Europe where their headquarters were located. For example, some brands of hasidism became known by Lubavitch (Russia), Satmar (Romania), or Bobov (Poland).

The differences between hasidim and *mitnagdim* are far less pronounced today. Hasidic Jews now put a great emphasis on providing their children with a thorough Jewish education, including yeshiva studies. Hasidic groups that did not build yeshivas after WWII faltered without the power of youth, considered the "rebbe's soldiers."[28] Those that already had yeshivas were the Lubavitch, Bobov, Radomsk, and Slonim; these were exceptions among the hasidim. And while non-hasidic Jews lack a rebbe as the center of their community, they, too, revere certain rabbis as exceptional scholars. The increased authority of the *rosh yeshivah* (head of the yeshiva) is indicative of this fusion of roles.[29]

Attire is another area where differences between the hasidim and *mitnagdim* have become less evident, as some *mitnagdim* have adopted hasidic dress patterns. While outsiders see only the tell-tale black coats and long skirts, Orthodox feminist Blu Greenberg has remarked, "Perhaps in no other area is there so much diversity among Orthodox Jews."[30] The haredim can distinguish among members of their many factions by minor visual differences in those ubiquitous black coats, especially in the manner of dress for Shabbat and festivals. For example, some haredi men wear short pants with white stockings, and some wear long pants. Some haredi black hats are trimmed with fur, others are not. While religious women cannot be as easily distinguished by affiliation with specific haredi sects in the same way men can by dress, their mode of dress signals identity with the religious community at large. All haredi women follow similar guidelines: sleeves that cover elbows, high necklines, and long skirts with stockings. Pants are considered immodest. While different movements disagree over the issues of the color and opacity of stockings, or whether to wear wigs or headscarves, religious women's clothing expresses the value of *tznius* (modesty), held sacred in the haredi community.

The hasidim and *mitnagdim* also evince far less animosity toward each other now that they have a mutual objective: maintaining Orthodox Judaism as practiced in pre-WWII Eastern Europe. This goal is threatened by contemporary Judaism as practiced by the majority of North American Jews, which the haredim sees as diluted, compromising, and potentially leading to the gradual abandonment of Jewish identity altogether. Such concerns led one European rabbi to warn in 1956: "We face three dangers to the development of a pure and enduring orthodoxy: Reform Judaism, Conservative Judaism, and the modern Orthodox."[31] Given their shrinking differences and mutual concerns for the future, it is easy to see how the hasidim and *mitnagdim*, who make up a very small percentage of American Jews, are lumped together.

The majority of American Jews affiliate with the more liberal and progressive Jewish movements such as Reform, Reconstructionist, and Conservative Judaism, which can be characterized by a willingness to adapt to changes brought on by modernity.[32] Issues central to such modification include the roles of women, the concern over traveling on the Sabbath and festivals, and dietary laws.[33] Orthodox Jews distinguish themselves from their more liberal brothers and sisters by their adherence to Talmudic law as it has been understood and codified at the beginning of the modern era.

Historians have made a distinction between segregationist and integrationist Jews, categorizing the ultra-Orthodox Jews as the former because of their separatist nature.[34] Modern Orthodoxy—a designation that is constantly changing—remains in the latter category despite its recent rightward shift. Both the ultra-Orthodox and the Modern Orthodox consider themselves to be "Torah-true Jews" or "Keepers of the Commandments," but Modern Orthodox Jews and ultra-Orthodox Jews part company over the way they see the outside world.

Modern Orthodoxy as a contemporary movement rejects separatist forms of Orthodoxy as well as those Jewish movements it sees as not fully observant. The goal of Modern Orthodoxy has been to coexist in the world with non-Jews, without the need to compromise on religious principles. Yeshiva College, established in New York in 1928, both cemented Modern Orthodoxy as an official movement and provided it with an educational center. With both secular and Jewish education, one ideally could be both an observant Jew and an acculturated, successful American. The relationship of these Modern Orthodox Jews to the outside American world has been cautiously friendly and optimistic. Drawing on terminology from Mary Douglas, Heilman refers to these "Jews for whom the real meaning of Orthodoxy is the ability to live in and be embraced by several cultures and worldviews at once" as "contrapuntalist Jews."[35]

In contrast, ultra-Orthodoxy sees the secular world as full of corrupting influences. Because of this worldview, the ultra-Orthodox live in insular communities (Heilman calls them "contra-acculturative" or "enclavist").[36] Few haredim attend university since secular education represents the most dangerous of these outside influences. Without university and professional degrees, many haredim work at low-paying jobs. As traditionalist Jews, they have traded material success for what they see as spiritual purity and authentic traditional practice. Their attitudes toward acculturated Orthodox Jews who chose to engage with society is less than favorable, as these Jews fly in the face of haredi insular ideology. According to historian Jenna Joselit, the haredim see these Jews as "at best . . . America's 'modern' Orthodox, a subdivision or possibly even a dissident sect of traditional Jews but certainly not the denomination's authentic standard-bearers."[37] This distinction belongs to the ultra-Orthodox, at least in their own eyes.

Yet even though the haredim profess an unbroken lineage from Sinai, historians of Orthodoxy have pointed out that even ultra-Orthodoxy in its current incarnation is a modern movement, dating back no further than the turn of the twentieth century.[38] Like Modern Orthodoxy, it, too, is a reactionary movement, responding to the increasing liberalization of Judaism. The historian Haym Soloveitchik describes parallels between the emergence of Protestant fundamentalists and ultra-Orthodox Jews:

> Both ultra-Orthodoxy and fundamentalism are responses to the challenges posed by modernity to traditional religion, and therefore both are most likely to exist "where tradition is meeting modernity rather than where modernity is most remote". Both also engage in a struggle with their own coreligionists who are perceived as "agents of assault on all that is held dear".[39]

Indeed, some would use the term "fundamentalist" to refer to these Jews, despite the historical use of this term to describe Protestants. The sociologist Samuel Heilman remarks of the haredim, "Fundamentalists regard themselves as the true heirs of the ancients."[40] And while theirs is a new tradition, the haredi self-perception is of an unchanging lineage of true Jews.

This haredi air of authenticity has had an effect upon those previously (and proudly) known as Modern Orthodox. The sociologist Chaim Waxman has referred to contemporary American Orthodox Judaism as undergoing a period of "haredization,"[41] and Samuel Freedman writes, "The term 'Modern Orthodox' has become so pejorative— it is to observant Jews what 'liberal' is to Democrats—that even its practitioners prefer to call themselves 'centrist' or 'traditional.'"[42] The growing effects of ultra-Orthodox observance on Modern Orthodox life can be seen in more than name; changes are visible in speech, dress, and practice. Marvin Schick called this trend "chassidification" in 1979, and others have called the trend of non-haredi Jews being influenced by haredi behavior as "Boro Park chic," a reference to the observant neighborhood in New York.[43] These rightward trends have succeeded in radically polarizing the spectrum of American Jewry, resulting in what can only be described as an outright culture war.

The rise of the Modern Orthodox Jewish day school has been cited as a major factor in Judaism's move to the right, its haredization. The intention of these day schools was to have a place where Orthodox Jewish children could have both a secular education and an equally strong religious education; Jewish students would not have to choose between God and Harvard.[44] These schools, recognized for their commitment to academics, quickly became feeder schools into the Ivy League and other top-tier institutions.

Herein lies the paradox: the Modern Orthodox movement emphasized professional careers such as law, social work, and medicine. Who would be available to teach the Jewish subjects in these day schools if Modern Orthodox Jews were doctors, lawyers, and MBAs? Approximately two-thirds of Judaica instructors are ultra-Orthodox, whose ideals run counter to the original purpose of the Modern Orthodox day school. These instructors do not believe that secular education is important; in fact, many see it as a detriment to one's spiritual enhancement, one that can wear away both belief and religious adherence, as well as take precious time away from Torah and Talmud study. More and more, students at these day schools defer college for a year in an Israeli yeshiva or include this yeshiva year as part of their college education. The greater emphasis on one-year yeshiva programs has resulted in greater observance and a significant shift to the right. Samuel Heilman refers to these yeshivas as "inoculation yeshivas" and claims that their agendas are to make the students wish to stay for a second year.[45] Students return to the United States after experiencing the ease of religious observance in a world that is geared toward such a lifestyle and become frustrated by the less-than-perfect accommodations at home. They see their increased religiosity as a natural extension of the way they have been educated in schools chosen by their parents. Yet their parents are frustrated because while they may appreciate the knowledge coming from these instructors, they do not necessarily wish to see their children emulate their haredi teachers' lifestyles or worldviews.

While the ultra-Orthodox are critical of Modern Orthodox Jewry, they reserve harsher judgment for non-Orthodox Jews. Haredim often view them as a watered-down version of real Jews and as a people deprived of real meaning in their lives; at best, they are a group to be pitied. Consider the following statement from an Orthodox Jew:

> "If we were to give them [non-Orthodox Jews] a test, use any standard recognized by the most uneducated, uninitiated Gentile as to what would constitute Jewish affiliation—Sabbath observance, eating kosher, frowning on adultery, the Ten Commandments—these people would not match up in any way. So therefore I say that they are practicing a religion that is not Judaism. They certainly are not practicing Judaism as it was practiced by their grandparents."[46]

Among other factors, it is this derisive attitude that fuels much anti-haredi sentiment among American Jews.

For the purposes of this book, it does not matter if the haredim in the narratives I will examine are hasidim or *mitnagdim*, if they are Litvak, Bobov, Satmar, or Lubavitch. It does not matter if the men's black hats are fur-trimmed or plain, or if the women wear wigs or kerchiefs. These details are cues for insiders. In his essay "What a Difference a Difference Makes," Jonathan Z. Smith notes "difference most

frequently entails a hierarchy of prestige and the concomitant political ranking of superordinate and subordinate."[47] In this hierarchy, it
matters only that the haredim are haredim and therefore, according to
these anxiety-laden narratives, "not like us."

LITERATURE, CULTURE, AND READING THE "OTHER"

This book will examine selected literary and cinematic narratives featuring ultra-Orthodox characters written by non-haredi Jews, specifically those narratives that were written in the mid-1980s and beyond.
Before this period, the ultra-Orthodox were rare characters in popular
Jewish American culture. Those narratives that did feature them often
did so with a nostalgic gaze. In the 1980s, a new type of literature and
film emerged, one that depicted these characters in a far harsher light.
The surfacing of these narratives at this time is no coincidence, as it
was a period of rapid social change in American Judaism. In 1985, the
Conservative movement made the choice to ordain women, effectively
drawing a line in the sand between non-Orthodox and Orthodox Jews.
This decision was the final straw after years of social and political disagreements, and this development radicalized the two camps, increasing the hostility on both sides. The post-1985 narratives reflect this
friction, as well as the reasons behind it.

"Our stories order our world," writes Michel de Certeau, and indeed
stories and storytelling form a key point of cultural translation and self-
interpretation.[48] As Angela McRobbie notes in "The Politics of Feminist Research, "representations are interpretations."[49] Representations
therefore offer the scholar a place to view the construction and recep-
tion of popular belief. The choice to examine contemporary fictional
narratives as a way of unearthing this new level of tension among American Jews is therefore deliberate and with precedent. David Weaver-
Zercher, in his work *The Amish in the American Imagination*, analyzes
similar popular representations of the Amish in order to explore the
functions that the *idea* of the Amish served for the broader American
culture. He writes: "Unlike other scholarly treatments of Amish life,

the main characters in this study are not the Amish themselves, but rather outsiders who, for various reasons, took it upon themselves to represent the Amish to other Americans."[50] Through an examination of popular literary and cinematic depictions of the haredim, we can not only extrapolate ideas and opinions important to the author but also glimpse those relevant to the author's audience.

Scholars who have successfully employed fiction as a way of assessing trends in the American Jewish community include the sociologists Marshall Sklare and Sylvia Barack Fishman. In a 1964 article entitled "Intermarriage and the Jewish Future," Sklare warns that sociologists are overlooking the increase of Jewish intermarriage and that contemporary literature is a more accurate reflection of the bigger picture:

> In short, the grounds for the American Jewish community's optimism are by no means as firm as they have been assumed to be by laymen and sociologists alike. Interestingly enough, the present state of Jewish endogamy seems to have been grasped more firmly by the novelists than by the sociologists. Even a hasty rundown of the work of such writers as Bernard Malamud, Saul Bellow, Philip Roth, Leslie Fiedler, Bruce Jay Friedman, Herbert Gold, Jack Ludwig, Myron Kaufmann, Neil Oxenhandler, etc., reveals how much recent American fiction has dealt with marriage or the strong possibility of it between a Jew and a Gentile.[51]

Time obviously proved Sklare correct, as intermarriage has become increasingly prevalent in America in the forty years since the publication of his article. Sylvia Barack Fishman is a contemporary scholar who also uses literature and film in order to shed light upon aspects of women in Jewish life. Culling literary and cinematic motifs, she has clarified shifts in pressing Jewish subjects such as the impact of feminism, education, and intermarriage.[52]

SELECTING MY SOURCES

Despite these efforts to examine Jewish culture, little scholarship has addressed the growing culture war between haredim and non-haredi American Jews, with the notable exception of Samuel Freedman's 2000

Jew vs. Jew. However, my own analysis of the work of such writers as Pearl Abraham, Michael Chabon, Nathan Englander, Allegra Goodman, Rebecca Goldstein, Dara Horn, Tova Mirvis, Eileen Pollack, Naomi Ragen, Tova Reich, Anne Roiphe, and the ubiquitous Philip Roth reflects the growing reality that while the ultra-Orthodox represent only a small segment of American Jews, exposure to Judaism's rightward trend has increased anxiety about the direction of American Jewry and Orthodoxy's visibility in American culture.[53]

The writers and directors in this study show orthodoxy and its disputes as part of the fabric that makes up the greater American Jewish tapestry. It comes as little surprise that the People of the Book would play out their angst in this form. It is more surprising that no one has previously examined these American imaginings of the haredim as a gateway to understanding this newest war among the Jews. While scholarly attention has been paid to the controversial literature surrounding Muslims, Catholics, and Mormons, none has been paid to this new installment of an ethno-religious quarrel.[54]

I selected the narratives for this project with certain criteria in mind. All were released after 1985, therefore reflecting a world where non-Orthodox American Jews have opted for an egalitarian practice in opposition to Orthodox tradition. It should be noted that these works address Ashkenazi Jews primarily—the dominant Jewish ethnic group in the United States. The fictions I have selected all feature haredi characters and are written or directed by non-haredi Jews. In addition, these works have a mainstream appeal; if no one were reading these books or seeing the films, they could not be said to have an influence on the public or reflect general values of the time. *A Price Above Rubies* was a large-scale Hollywood movie with major stars, Renee Zellweger and Juliana Margulies. Pearl Abraham and Anne Roiphe are critically acclaimed writers, at least within Jewish literary circles, who contribute to the *Forward*, a weekly Jewish paper. Naomi Ragen and Tova Mirvis are avidly read by the Modern Orthodox community, as well as by non-Orthodox Jews. Ragen and Mirvis also are both regular speakers at Jewish community centers and Hillels across the country. Erich Segal is the bestselling author of mainstream, commercial successes such as

Love Story (1970), *The Class* (1985), and *Doctors* (1988). His 1992 novel *Acts of Faith* spent almost a year on the *New York Times* bestseller list. I also make mention of several Israeli works, including Ragen's *Sotah*, Amos Gitai's *Kadosh*, and David Volach's *My Father My Lord*; the first, a novel, was written in English by its American-born author—and was a bestseller in the United States—and the two latter films were both screened in American Jewish film festivals and widely reviewed in the United States.

Intentionally, these authors provide a diversity of backgrounds. Pearl Abraham comes from a hasidic background and offers a critique of a community she experienced firsthand, while Erich Segal—a liberal Jew and a professor of classics—offers an academic's perspective on the history of hasidism. Boaz Yakin and Naomi Ragen are both from secular backgrounds but had brushes with the yeshiva/haredi world. Yakin rejected it wholesale, and Ragen abandoned the haredi lifestyle but remains a liberal, Modern Orthodox Jew.[55] Anne Roiphe and Tova Mirvis come from quite different backgrounds—Roiphe's was decidedly secular and Mirvis's was Orthodox. Both, however, articulate concern with the growing rigidity of haredim—and, along with it, Orthodoxy as a whole. Each of these authors has a strong relationship with Judaism and an interest and investment in the future of the Jewish people.

A Note About Terms

As the authors provide a diversity of perspectives, and since the ultra-Orthodox themselves are a diverse community, it should come as little surprise that there are a myriad of terms used to refer to ultra-Orthodox Jews. Israelis commonly use the Hebrew term *"haredi"* (or its plural form, *"haredim"*) to refer to the ultra-Orthodox. This term is becoming more common in the American parlance,[56] partially because scholars have come to prefer this term, seeing it as a more neutral term than "ultra-Orthodox" or "right-wing." Samuel Heilman explains the term in his seminal ethnography of ultra-Orthodox Jews, *Defenders of the Faith*:

In biblical Hebrew, the linguistic point of origin for Jewish experience, the term "haredim" appears in the book of Isaiah (66:5) when the prophet admonished his people with the words "Hear the word of the Lord, you who tremble [haredim] at His word." This text, still recited aloud in the synagogue by the devout on several Sabbaths during the year, depicts haredim as those singular people—along with the poor and contrite of spirit—who defend the faith and keep the law, are neither apostates nor heretics, and therefore share a special, exquisitely mutual relationship with God.[57]

Another term used to describe the haredim is *"frum"* (pious or observant).[58] A purely descriptive term for the haredim is "black hat," used as an adjective, which refers to the brimmed black hats that haredi men wear.[59] Significantly, this androcentric term is used to describe haredi men or women, despite its derivation from male attire.

In Samuel Freedman's article on the Yale Five, one of the plaintiffs relates a new term:

"There is an expression floating around—'yeshivish,'" says [Elisha] Hack, a 20-year-old freshman from New Haven. "It doesn't exist in a dictionary. It's 'yeshiva' made into an adjective. And it connotes a level of observance, a way of thought, a type of dress."[60]

The Israeli equivalent of "yeshivish" may be what is known as *"hardal."* Recently described in a *Forward* Philologos article, it is an Israeli acronym used to describe the growing number of Jews who straddle the fence between religious Zionists, traditionally Modern Orthodox, and the haredim.[61] The acronym spells "mustard" and connotes Modern Orthodox who have taken up black hat rigor but are still religious Zionists.

Zionism at one point was seen as antithetical to haredi sensibilities. The idea of creating a secular Jewish state in the holy land of Palestine was considered sacrilegious to those who believed that Zion should be reestablished only by the messiah, who would rebuild the Temple in Jerusalem. Additionally, most Jews involved with the early Zionist movement were far from observant in the eyes of the haredim. Since 1967, however, some hasidic groups, most notably the Lubavitchers, have changed their tune and support Israel as a means of ushering in the messianic age. Others are more conflicted about Israel. On the far other end of the haredi spectrum remain groups such as the Neturei Karta, who are frequently photographed protesting Israel alongside Palestinians. Because of this diversity, there is a category of religious Zionists currently known in Israel as "*haredim leumiyim*," but previously referred to as "*datim leumiyim*." Religious Zionism influences many of the West Bank and Gaza settlements and therefore receives a lot of press in the United States. Because the Israeli-Palestinian conflict is the most publicized dispute in Israel, these settlers are often seen as "the problem" by many left-leaning American Jews, as well as by many Israelis.

While many terms are used to describe them, the haredim refer to themselves in Yiddish as "*Yidn*," Jews, or "*erlicher Yidn*," true Jews. Not ultra-Orthodox, not haredi, just simply Jews. Samuel Heilman writes, "This insider name implies their conviction that, contrary to what others may suggest, they are *not* a separate sect called 'haredim' nor a subgroup in a new homeland for Hebrews but very simply the true Jews."[62] This identification implies their understanding of themselves as authentic, traditional Jews, unchanging over time. It is this self-understanding that other Jews find so irritating and that fuels a desire to discredit the ultra-Orthodox publicly.

A MAP OF THE WORK

I begin my study of this culture war with a historical introduction to twentieth-century Jewish American fiction and its engagement with Orthodoxy. Chapter 1, "Orthodoxy and Nostalgia in America and in the American Jewish Imagination," describes the way Orthodoxy, specifically ultra-Orthodoxy, has been represented by American Jews on both page and screen. The chapters that follow examine selected narratives as examples of a larger pool of American Jewish literature and film featuring haredi characters. These selections demonstrate different themes that can be seen as core factors in this conflict. As Thomas Friedmann observes: "The evolution of Jewish American Literature in this century can, in fact, be seen as a process that begins in the denial of Orthodoxy and, after an apparent hiatus of nearly forty years, continues to develop by re-examining Orthodoxy."[63] I have similarly structured the following chapters of this study after this pattern of Jewish American literature, beginning with narratives that question Orthodoxy, followed by those that reject it, and finally ending with tales that signal a clear return to Orthodoxy as a central concern.

Chapter 2, "Rebbe's Daughters: The New *Chosen*," considers two coming-of-age narratives featuring daughters of hasidic rabbis: Erich Segal's *Acts of Faith* (1992) and Pearl Abraham's *The Romance Reader* (1995). I examine them both in comparison to Chaim Potok's *The Chosen* (1966), an earlier popular novel with similar themes, in order to explore the shift in perspective on the haredi community. These contemporary narratives highlight gender, reflect egalitarian values, and indicate that one of the most divisive issues in Judaism today remains the position of women.

Chapter 3, "The New Jewish Gothic," explores very different narratives: sensationalized, titillating stories about the captivity and oppression of women by devious and deviant haredi men. Naomi Ragen's novel *Sotah* (1993) and Boaz Yakin's film *A Price Above Rubies* (1998) are examined as examples of a larger genre of haredi escapee tales, in which young, married women find themselves in unsatisfying marriages, choose a path deemed deviant by their haredi community, and are punished for their behavior. Through these two narratives, I will profile the archetypes of ultra-Orthodox men and women that are so prolific within contemporary Jewish fiction and indicative of a deep hostility toward the ultra-Orthodox.

Chapter 4, "Muggers in Black Coats," examines Anne Roiphe's *Lovingkindness* (1987) and Tova Mirvis's *The Outside World* (2004) as reflections of the parallel schisms within American Jewry and Orthodoxy itself. Both novels deal with the friction between children who have embraced ultra-Orthodox lifestyles and their parents, as well as the parental anxiety over potential "brainwashing" and "kidnapping" by haredim. The chapter describes the media's response to one such controversial "true-life" case, and a similar fictional televised case, and analyzes the way that literary examples of parental anxiety over these newly religious children echo greater anxiety over the nature of contemporary American Judaism and haredi threats to Americanization. The conclusion, "They Are Us in Other Clothes," examines the literary conversation that American Jews are conducting in contemporary culture. The prevalence of these anti-haredi writings raises the question: What is at stake for these authors and directors? This conclusion reviews the themes presented in the other chapters in order to assert their significance in the contemporary context of acculturation, Americanization, and concern over Jewish continuity.

In 2004, I attended a symposium in Lincoln, Nebraska, where I gave a lecture on the subject of parental anxiety over newly religious children. The talk was open to the public, and a woman from the local Jewish community approached me afterward. She was quite angry with me and challenged me on my "can't we all get along" conclusion. She practically spat out her words of warning: "My father was kidnapped *and* brainwashed. *These* are terrible people." Her pain at the rifts caused within her family by her father's relationship with a haredi community was deep and raw. My attempt at even-handedness on these relationships did not assuage her grief or bitterness. Her hostility was fueled by what she saw as my apologetic for the haredim.

I therefore do not expect this book to change, soften, or curb the growing polarization among American Jews. These fissures, cracks, and divisions have roots in a long debate that stretches back a number of generations. The study is also not meant to indict either side for their chosen lifestyle; nor is it meant to undermine the objections that liberal or haredi Jews may have to the religious and social behavior of others. It does intend, however, to expose the often formulaic and manipulative representations of the ultra-Orthodox by the dominant American Jewish culture. By highlighting the factors ingrained in this conflict and examining the tensions and passions stirred by true believers on both sides of the battlefield, I hope to raise the possibility of an honest conversation about problematic assertions of Jewish authority and authenticity, as well as the limits of tolerance over such claims.

ORTHODOXY *and* NOSTALGIA *in the* AMERICAN JEWISH IMAGINATION

The lousy fanatics! He was straining hard not to hate them, it was an element of his Zionist creed not to detest his fellow Jews no matter how obdurate, ungrateful, manipulative, disdainful, and uncivilized he found them to be, especially the ones who were consumed by religion, so bloody pious and righteous. He was well aware that, for their part, they—the ultra-Orthodox, that is—made no effort at all not to despise him, that they regarded him as an insignificant lump of impure flesh, with a decayed, unredeemable soul, doomed to eternal punishment and damnation. They alone had the monopoly on the divine, only they had access to the spiritual life. —Tova Reich, *The Jewish War*

The Hasidim spoke the Yiddish of their great-grandparents. Children jabbered it in the street. Baruch wanted to go back in time and rejoin his ancestors who had looked and lived like them. In his family, there was little connection to the past. But these devout Mea Shearim Jews seemed unaware that the cobblestone streets they trod weren't the same as those in their ancestors' villages and shtetls. —Tova Mirvis, *The Outside World*

I n Woody Allen's film *Annie Hall* (1977), Diane Keaton, the quintessential WASP, tells Allen, the classic neurotic Jew, that he is what her Grammy would call "a real Jew." Later in the film, Allen attends an Easter dinner at Keaton's family home. While passing around the "dynamite ham," he imagines the family sees him as an ultra-Orthodox Jew, sporting a black hat, black coat, *payess* (side-locks), and a long beard. Regardless of what Granny Hall may or may not mean by a "real Jew,"[1] Allen uses this ultra-Orthodox Jew as a parody of the "real Jew," the Jew as seen from the outside, the Jew he does not want to be. He is not passively accepting but actively interrogating what it means to be a "real" Jew. For Allen—and many non-Orthodox Jews—"real" or *authentic* Judaism is associated with the world of the ultra-Orthodox.[2] This association has led to a problematic and contentious relationship among contemporary American Jews over the nature of Jewish identity, one that can be observed through popular imaginings of haredim in contemporary culture.

In this chapter, I will discuss the dichotomy present in Jewish American imaginings of the ultra-Orthodox and the manifestation of this conflict within different periods of Jewish American writing. I will examine the shifts in this literature, affected by and reflecting the success of the Six Day War, the revival of Jewish diasporic culture from Eastern Europe, renewed interest in Orthodoxy, and exposure to the present Israeli culture wars. This chapter will be the most general of those in this project, setting the context for the more specifically thematic chapters to follow.

From Nostalgia to Nerves

Currently, many non-haredi Jews harbor both a fascination with and an aversion to the haredi lifestyle. This fascination reveals itself in a variety of attitudes toward the ultra-Orthodox. The appeal of an "authentic," Old World brand of Judaism—the kind one's great-grandparents may have practiced—stems from a nostalgia for a world never encountered. Synagogue-sponsored sightseeing trips to Manhattan's Lower East Side, designed to see remnants of "authentic Jewish life" before returning to the assimilated suburbs, also foster a certain wistfulness for what seems in retrospect to be simpler times. While historians emphasize the poverty and anti-Semitism experienced by these archaic, pious Jews, many in the Jewish community celebrate the musical memories of *Fiddler on the Roof* or storybook shtetl images created by Sholom Aleichem and Isaac Bashevis Singer. In an age of suburban sprawl and social alienation, the perceived warmth of such tightly knit communities is often enticing.[3]

For a contemporary generation more likely to have grown up with a doctor than a dairy farmer in the house, quaint images of women in traditional head coverings and men in black coats with long beards stir up nostalgia for attic-stored, sepia-tinted pictures of a long-lost heritage that, for most Jews, was destroyed in the Holocaust. Svetlana Boym's *The Future of Nostalgia* explains, "Nostalgia (from *nostos*—return home, and *algia*—longing) is a longing for a home that no longer exists or has never existed. Nostalgia is a sentiment of loss and displacement, but it is also a romance with one's own fantasy."[4] Boym also points out that this romance can only be played out from a distance, either in time or space; when one gets too close, the illusion shatters and the nostalgia is gone. Thus, enjoyment of *Fiddler on the Roof* does not include detailed reminders of pogroms—although such fears certainly exist; rather, the emphasis is on singing, cooking, a large and loving family, and a strong sense of continuity and tradition. Such are the yesteryear memories worth preserving.

Contemporary American Jewish nostalgia manifests itself in several ways. First, nostalgia may emerge as a spectator pleasure, the sort that Daphne Merkin observes in " 'revolving-door' Jews, staunch secularists who disdain visible signs of affiliation, suddenly lining up to take a closer look at the quaint religious customs long ago left in the care of tottering relatives in Miami Beach."[5] This sort of nostalgia also revealed itself in the klezmer music revival of the 1970s and 1980s, a renaissance of both the joyful and mournful music of the shtetl. Nostalgia may also manifest through spiritual reflection, goading the individual to renew singular aspects of the tradition. However, the most extreme embodiment of contemporary Jewish nostalgia is the restoration impulse. Here, the Jew longs to restore the shtetl, to return to that sepia-tinted moment. This brand of nostalgia is, according to Boym, "at the core of recent national and religious revivals." Within such nostalgia, Boym continues, two plots prevail: the dreamy return to origins and the fear of an antagonistic conspiracy.[6] With a desire for the old and a fear of the new, this restorative nostalgia is the attempted re-creation of pre-Holocaust Eastern European shtetls in urban Brooklyn or Baltimore. Furthermore, as I will demonstrate in subsequent chapters, this nostalgic fear also engenders increasingly rigid guidelines for haredi attire, diet, and practice.[7] Ironically, the same elements that attract American Jews also serve to feed the aversion that many feel toward the haredim. As Boym further points out, "*Algia*—longing—is what we share, yet *nostos*—the return home—is what divides us."[8] The warmth of the tightly knit community, for example, is predicated upon separatism and the exclusion of others. With the exception of a few haredi groups that proselytize to less observant Jews, these communities are closed to outsiders.[9] Some are even unapologetically disdainful of their non-haredi neighbors, especially those who happen to be Jewish. This disdain goes both ways, with non-haredi Jews' complaining about their bewigged and black-hatted neighbors' changing the character of their neighborhood.[10] The haredim have no problem proudly claiming their "chosen-ness," a concept with which contemporary Jews living in a pluralistic society struggle and in some cases even outright reject. In an ethnographic study about the residents of Crown Heights, one Lubavitcher woman responded to questions about the value of Black-Jewish dialogue with, "We're not interested. We're just insular. You don't like me being insular, that's your problem. It's not my problem."[11] This perceived arrogance, coupled with its lack of tolerance, sits awkwardly with many American Jews, who overwhelmingly view religious tolerance as a virtue.

Sociologist Samuel Heilman, writes of this cultural tension:

> For those who have encountered real Hasidim, hoping to find incarnate the mystic who finds meaning in kabbalah that informs his every movement, or who fills his days and nights singing and dancing to melodic tunes, punctuating them with pithy proverbs filled with the wisdom of Hasidic tales, the result is often a disappointment. Romantics turned on by Buber's *Tales of the Hasidim* often find the Hasidic realities of an Orthodox Jewish community, frequently insular and deeply engaged in a political and cultural war against what they perceive to be the corrosive forces of contemporary secular society, hard to bear.[12]

Those who have absorbed romantic descriptions of hasidic life can often be both surprised and disappointed by the realities of the contemporary hasidic world. This perspective has parallels with media coverage of new religious movements, particularly those "restorationist" models such as fundamentalist Mormons. A scholar of NRMs, Susan Palmer, remarks that the media's responses "range from 'Aren't they quaint and adorable' to 'We must rescue them!'"[13] A similar discrepancy in the view of haredim as either saving remnants or as threatening elements to the Jewish community is prevalent in both popular literature and film, as well as in sociological studies.[14]

One such study, Lis Harris's 1985 ethnography *Holy Days: The World of a Hasidic Family*, demonstrates this dualistic fascination with and aversion to the haredim: "Believing that the Hasidim represented some antique version of myself, I have always felt vaguely bound to them and curious to know who they were—a curiosity that neither my education, my social milieu, nor my reading of Hasidic stories did much to satisfy."[15] She also refers to the strong reactions her Jewish friends (unlike her gentile friends) had to her study of the hasidim, responding either with remarks that demonstrated wistful nostalgia or with angry, disdainful outbursts (summing up the twofold relationship of non-haredi Jews to the hasidim or ultra-Orthodox).

In *Postville: A Clash of Cultures in Heartland America*, Stephen Bloom describes the motivations behind his decision to investigate the hasidic community in Postville, Iowa:

> [The Hasidim] were reminders of where we had come from, of what our people had been like long ago. . . . We were cut from the same cloth. I fantasized that the Hasidic enclave in Postville would be a hermitage of wise men. I imagined that they would brighten my soul with witty talk and warm my belly with nurturing food.[16]

While Bloom experienced both witty talk and gastronomic pleasure, his encounters with the Postville hasidim also led to some disappointments. While he felt at a gut level that "these biblical men were somehow a part of me, part of the viscera that my own ancestors had passed down to me,"[17] his disdain for their approach to gender roles and their overall insularity greatly colors his narrative of competing cultures in Iowa.

Bloom and Harris display both nostalgic and bitter sentiments in their studies—Bloom's examination of the Lubavitcher meat-packing industry and Harris's ethnography of a Lubavitcher hasidic family in Crown Heights—and both writers likely would agree with Heilman that those romanticized old-time Jews of the shtetl are not likely to be found in Boro Park or Crown Heights (or Iowa) today.

Another idealized element of the haredi world is its family life, characterized by clearly defined roles for husbands and wives, fathers and mothers, sons and daughters. Others point out that those clearly defined gender roles that are attractive to some are dependent on a rigidly patriarchal system that allows for little deviance from societal norms.[18] The construction of gender roles and the related issues of gender and religious authority are among the most important issues affecting relations between haredi and non-haredi Jews. The dramatic changes in the religious roles of Jewish women have recently forced American Jews to choose sides. The majority of American Jews prize gender equality and demonstrate that perspective by approving the ordination of women.[19] For those members of liberal Jewish movements, there is little tolerance for a Judaism that does not support a woman's right to publicly read from the Torah. Beyond public religious life, the emphasis on the haredi woman's domestic nature as a wife and mother seems to contradict both contemporary American and Jewish ideals.[20] The haredim break with mainstream American egalitarian values over the position of women, and it is this issue that comes up frequently when haredim are criticized by non-haredi Jews.

And so a dichotomy exists in the Jewish American imagination when it comes to the ultra-Orthodox. This can be seen in the financial support of Chabad-Lubavitch by non-affiliated and Conservative Jews "out of guilt."[21] On one hand, there is respect for defenders of the faith, those who despite all obstacles and influences insist on keeping the flame of observant Judaism alive. But on the other hand, there exists an anger toward those who, while claiming to be the only true Jews, espouse attitudes that the majority of American Jews reject. So while liberal Jews may like the *idea* of the haredim, they may not actually *like* the haredim. Indeed, a parallel can be drawn with certain strains of Christian anti-Semitism, where respect and admiration of the biblical Israelites may awkwardly coexist with distaste for actual Jews. In both cases, the conjured image is perceived as incongruous with reality, and the attempt to embrace the authenticity of the past sits uncomfortably with the present. Paradoxically, the supposed authenticity of the haredim is the very thing that threatens many American Jews. If one accepts the claim that the ultra-Orthodox are the "real" Jews, what does that say about the legitimacy of all other American Jews?

People of the Book
in Jewish American Literature

This is by no means the first intra-Jewish cultural dispute to take place in the United States. The second wave of Jewish immigration, in the late nineteenth century, led to a certain embarrassment and discomfort on the part of the already acculturated German Jewish establishment toward their Eastern European counterparts. Much of this uneasiness was caused by class differences between the "old" and "new" Jews, as members of the older community were well educated and financially solvent. Established German Jews showered goodwill upon the poor new immigrants, both as a philanthropic gesture and as a response to fears that greenhorn visibility would damage the fragile status of American Jews by resurrecting latent—or by invigorating already overt—anti-Semitism. Resident middle-class Jews therefore advocated Americanization: learning the English language and American ways of life. One could be trained out of overly *Jewish* Judaism and "taught" to be an American. The immigrants themselves had to contend with the choices available to them: whether to Americanize or how to Americanize, the latter choice being preferable.

The story of American Jews has primarily been told as a narrative of such Americanization. Fiction and memoir endorsed this generational process of assimilation. The American Jewish expectation, much like that of other immigrant groups, was that children should be more successful—not to mention, more *American*—than the previous generation, and the Jewish literature of the time reflected that hope. Anzia Yezierska's *Bread Givers*, Henry Roth's *Call it Sleep*, and Abraham Cahan's *The Rise of David Levinsky* were particularly well received works of immigrant literature that addressed the lives of tenement dwellers and their desire for acceptance and achievement in the New World. Their success could be measured in terms of social acceptance, financial well-being, and educational achievement. While these works highlighted the painful struggle between Old and New World, the New World always won out (sometimes at a high price), and Orthodox characters always represent the Old World.

Such a high-stakes battle can be seen in *Bread Givers*, when the protagonist, Sara Smolinsky, experiences a final showdown with her father over her desire for education. Sara challenges his belief that a woman needs a man. She announces her desire to leave home and to become a teacher. " 'My will is as strong as yours. I'm going to live my own life. Nobody can stop me. I'm not from the old country. I'm American!' " And when he subsequently strikes her face, she writes, "The Old World had struck its last on me"[22] Yezierska paints Sara's father as a hypocritical tyrant who cares more for his holy books than for his struggling family, an archaic representative of the Old World. In the bittersweet conclusion of *Bread Givers*, Sara considers her aging father: "In a world where all is changed, he alone remained unchanged—as tragically isolate as the rocks. All that he had left was his fanatical adherence to his traditions."[23] For Yezierska—and her contemporaries—the Old World, like Reb Smolinsky, is a sad, aging, tragic figure. But no matter how tragic the loss of the Old World, the choice is clear in these early novels.

While later writers may romanticize such Old World figures, those in the process of upward mobility have little choice but to continue looking up. Svetlana Boym remarks on this generational gap:

> First wave immigrants are notoriously unsentimental, leaving the search for roots to their children and grandchildren unburdened by visa problems. Somehow the deeper the loss, the harder it was to engage in public mourning. To give name to this inner longing seemed to be a profanation that reduced the loss to little more than a sound bite.[24]

Looking back makes little sense for this generation of writers, and the Orthodox Jews who are seen as remnants of the Old World seem destined to be left behind forever.

This extinction would seem to be the case for the generation of American Jewish writers after WWII, including Philip Roth, Herman Wouk, and Saul Bellow. These novelists addressed a different scene— an already acculturated American Jewry encountering the alienation of the suburbs. American Jews had by and large risen beyond the pushcart and sweatshop beginnings encountered by Jewish immigrants in the late nineteenth and early twentieth centuries. These writers saw themselves as fully integrated in the American experience. While they were writing from a Jewish perspective, it served more as a vantage point than an affirmation of religious identity. This period of American Jewish literature is characterized more by the prevalence of Jewish characters than religious Jewish themes. It is here that a distinctly ethnic Jewish presence, rather than a religious Jewish presence, becomes apparent.[25]

Orthodoxy has little place in the writings of this period, and if it exists it does so in narratives like Philip Roth's "Eli the Fanatic," which presents Orthodoxy as a primitive remnant of the Old World.[26] Roth's story features Eli Peck, a Jewish resident of "the progressive suburban community"[27] of Woodenton, an affluent "mixed" suburb of Jews and gentiles. Peck has been asked by the Jewish community to approach a threatening presence in their midst, Leo Tzuref, the head of an ultra-Orthodox orphanage housing eighteen war orphans. More alarming than this home for displaced children is an adult war refugee who insists on flaunting his difference by walking through the streets of Woodenton, dressed defiantly—as the residents see it—in a "black coat that fell below the man's knees. . . . By the round-topped, wide-brimmed Talmudic hat, pushed onto the back of his head. And by the beard, which hid his neck and . . . his sidelocks curled loose on his cheeks."[28] Peck has a series of correspondence and meetings with Tzuref, requesting that the "religious activities" of the yeshiva do not leave yeshiva grounds and, perhaps more importantly, that those folks associated with the yeshiva only enter town "provided that they are attired in clothing usually associated with American life in the 20th century."[29] He even offers to buy the refugee a new suit. Peck's dealings with Tzuref and the yeshiva coincide with the birth of his first child, and both experiences produce ambivalent emotions within him. In the conclusion, Peck finds himself wearing the man's black suit—vowing to buy one for his newborn son—as men in white coats take him away.

A satirical piece, "Eli the Fanatic" is concerned with the artifice of 1950s Jewish suburbia. Roth admonishes the citizens of Woodenton for the short-term memory that seems to have accompanied their newfound wealth and security in America. He sees them as not only masking their Jewishness but concealing any trace of authenticity. This allegation is most clearly asserted in a comical scene where Peck sees his next-door neighbor in the garden, painting her rocks pink. While Roth's commentary on the almost-comfortable suburban Jew suggests an intangible feeling of loss over the denial of an "authentic" Jewish past, this piece nonetheless asserts that Orthodoxy is a remnant of the past. For better or worse, American Jews do not wear black hats and black coats; they are modern.

Despite this seeming relegation of Orthodoxy to the past, Thomas Friedman argues that even in avowedly secular twentieth-century Jewish literature—where Orthodox characters, practice, or issues are absent—the "Rabbi" remains as a stand-in for orthodoxy. For example, this Rabbi often exists as a hypocritical character through which the author can demonstrate his or her antipathy toward the Orthodox.[30] This theme foreshadows the later trend of overtly anti-haredi writings.

FROM SABRAS TO SHADCHANS

Jewish literature shifted yet again in 1967. Following the Six Day War in Israel, a new sense of vitality and confidence surged through the Jewish community. The Israeli army's military success led to a sense of pride among American Jews. Some scholars went so far as to say that Israel became the new religion of Jews in America, although it would be a while before American Jewish literature would fully engage Israel as a setting or a character.[31] Nonetheless, primed by the success of Leon Uris's best-selling novel, *Exodus*, about the founding of the modern state of Israel, as well as the 1960 film version starring Paul Newman as a Jewish resistance leader, the American Jews were ready to openly embrace a Jewish identity.[32]

The great success of Chaim Potok's novel *The Chosen* (1967), the film version of *Fiddler on the Roof* (1971), and the 1981 film adaptation of *The Chosen* can be seen as an understandable reflection of a surge in ethnic pride among American Jews. In the aftermath of the Six Day War in 1967, American Jews began to feel that they had a homeland of which they could be proud. Their legacy was not merely that of the defenseless Jews who had perished at Auschwitz, but of living Jews armed with guns, defending themselves (and triumphing) in the Middle East. Ironically, these narratives center not upon the muscled, sunburned Sabras of Israel but upon the traditional Jews of the Eastern European shtetl.

The sociologist Chaim Waxman warns that this sudden boost in Zionism may be somewhat misunderstood:

> One should also be cautious in interpreting the significance of the sharp rise in pro-Israelism among American Jews in 1967. It was probably not as clear a reflection of centrality of Israel in American Jewish identity as some have suggested. It was also a reflection of the *Americanization* of America's Jews, in that many of them felt by then comfortable enough as Americans to express their support for Israel, especially since the United States supported Israel; whereas in earlier times (e.g. 1956, and 1948) they were less comfortable doing so lest they be viewed as less than Americans.[33]

The gusto with which American Jews embraced the Jewish state reflected more than a new Zionist fervor. It signified a comfort in America that the generation before dared not exhibit. As most American Jews had no intention of immigrating to Israel (*nostos*), they played out their enthusiasm (*algia*) for Jewish life in other ways. This enthusiasm for the shtetl, over that of the yishuv, may also indicate a lingering caution on the part of American Jews. It may be seen as safer to reminisce about victims of oppressive regimes than to overtly celebrate the frequently contested nature of Israel, with its Palestinian conflict. Susannah Heschel remarks, "In a sense, too, the romance with East European life was a substitute for Zionism: an inspiring memory that would salvage the Jews from assimilation and disappearance."[34] By embracing *Fiddler on the Roof* as a shared cultural experience, American Jews demonstrated support for Jewish continuity and tradition. Ironically, liberalization is what is being celebrated in the later adaptations of *Fiddler*.

Chaim Potok's images of hasidim and Norman Jewison's interpretation of Sholom Aleichem's Tevye are haredim for American consumption. These are Old World characters who hold fast to their ideology, but we are led to believe that, given the right sort of exposure to modernity, they would adapt to changing ways. Thus the rebbe of *The Chosen* accepts his son's desire to become a psychologist (and shave off his beard and payess), and Tevye accepts his daughters' pleas to marry men through love matches. Tevye's tolerance is tested most with his third daughter, Chava, who performs the ultimate taboo of marrying a Russian non-Jew. He cannot accept this match, but Jewison's 1971 adaptation of this earlier Sholom Aleichem story is far less judgmental of this, signifying the American value of inclusivity. This adaptation, therefore, celebrates liberalism and universalism over parochialism and insularity.

The traditionalist Jews of *Fiddler on the Roof* are attractive and beloved. Shtetl life is romanticized in light of its tragic end. The rebbes in both *The Chosen* and Sidney Lumet's 1992 *A Stranger Among Us* are looked upon favorably, despite their old ways and odd behavior, because they barely managed to get out of Europe alive. So in some ways, the "real Jews" that are acceptable are the "almost dead" real Jews. The haredi communities that formed in America were small and weak at first, and the American Jewish establishment was dominated by Reform-minded Jews. Those acculturated Jews were happy to contribute financially to the few schools and institutions the new haredim wanted to establish; they felt that given the destruction of Jewish life in Europe, it was a small symbolic donation. American Jews were now more comfortable and less paranoid than their German Jewish counterparts of the late nineteenth century. After all, these Jews thought, what could a little charity hurt?

Rumors of the Demise of Jewish American Literature Have Been Greatly Exaggerated

Scarcely a volume on Jewish American literature has been written without responding to Irving Howe's 1977 prediction of the decline of the genre, and mine is no exception.[35] While Jewish literature has not died, it has certainly changed over time. Jews became so successful at breaking into mainstream society that there began to be much anxiety over the preservation of Jewish culture and identity.[36] Thomas Friedman notes in his article "Back to Orthodoxy" that "Jewry and Jewish fiction (in print and on screen), well into the seventies, considered its greatest issue to be intermarriage (the lure of the *shiksa*), assimilation, and a sense of 'otherness' vis-à-vis gentile neighbors."[37] The growing prevalence of intermarriage, itself a sign of acceptance, gave rise to fears over the cultural decline in American Jewish identity as well as the numerical decline in Jewish demographics. Confirming this fear, the 1990 National Jewish Population Survey reported that 52 percent of Jews married since 1985 had married non-Jews, leading some to worry that Christians would succeed in eliminating the Jewish people not through murder but through marriage.

Reflecting this exogamous trend, the literary story of Jews in America was in many ways that of a journey *away* from Orthodoxy, both thematically and with regard to characters.[38] Jews were primarily ethnic characters rather than religious actors. But then something surprising happened. Ultra-Orthodoxy managed to survive despite what many believed to be an increasingly secularized society. And it has not merely survived, it has flourished and, in the words of sociologist Marshall Sklare, "defied the laws of religious gravity."[39] This success did not occur in a vacuum. A major factor encouraging this revival was the American counterculture, which enjoyed involvement with new national political and social movements, as well as the freedom of religious experimentation. The civil rights movement contemporaneously produced an emphasis on black pride, and subsequently many ethnic groups sought to proudly assert their identity. The Jewish Defense

League and Meir Kahane preached a right-wing ideology modeled after the Black Power movement, one that advocated Jewish unity, as well as the militant defense of Jewish rights and Jewish settlements in Israel.[40] Some American Jews embraced Kahane's religious and political agendas and began to make up much of the religious settler movement in Israel, a movement that would later be fictitiously reflected in Philip Roth's 1986 novel, *The Counterlife*.

This generation of seekers experimented with a variety of religious traditions, including new forms of Asian religions and Christianity. Unlike members of the counterculture who chose to embrace Asian religious movements, many young American Jews found themselves embracing Jewish tradition. Some sought a liberal theology, much influenced by the thinking of Abraham Joshua Heschel, a theologian known for his emphasis on the Hebrew Prophets and their calls for social justice. Heschel's followers, including Arthur Green, Michael Lerner, Arthur Waskow, and Zalman Schacter-Shalomi, were instrumental in the development of what could be called progressive Judaism.[41] Others sought what they saw as a return to their roots, to a "traditionalist" Orthodox lifestyle. And new life was breathed into these aging communities. These returnees to tradition (also referred to as "*ba'alei teshuva*")[42] gave vitality to a movement that sociologists of religion saw as destined for obscurity.[43] While the numbers of ba'alei teshuvah remain low, their impact can be measured more by the confidence bolstered among haredim than in community influence. This movement is therefore what Haym Soloveitchik has deemed "phenomenologically significant, not demographically."[44]

While this phenomenon of counter-acculturation had its roots in the 1960s, the move to the right among American Jews did not end in that decade. Today this swing right includes not just secular Jews who became religious but also those in the Modern Orthodox movement who "haredicized." Unlike the "green" Eastern European Jews at the dawn of the twentieth century, this new wave of haredim is quite different. They are not merely traditionalists but activists who are uncompromisingly dedicated to preserving and re-creating pre–WWII Eastern European Jewish Orthodoxy. In 2003, Jason Aronson Press published a study entitled *Paper Plates: When Part of Your Family Keeps Kosher.* This book includes the voices of ba'alei teshuvah, their families, and rabbis. The concluding section lists the top ten things to do if your kid becomes religious and the top ten things to do if you become more religious than your family. Similar guides entitled, *What Do You Mean, You Can't Eat in My Home?: A Guide to How Newly Observant Jews and Their Less-Observant Relatives Can Still Get Along* and *What's Up With the Hard Core Jewish People? An Irreverent Yet Informative Approach to Judaism and Religious Devotion from a Reform Jewish Mother's Perspective* followed in 2005 and 2006, respectively.[45]

Allegra Goodman's 2005 short story "Long-Distance Client" serves as an updated version of Roth's Eli the Fanatic." Mel, a resident of Canaan, Connecticut, becomes aggravated by his new neighbors, the Bialystoker hasidim. While he fancied himself both a "fair-minded" and "unprejudiced" man, these new residents unnerve him.

> When he saw the little Zylberfenig boys running across the slushy front yard, and screaming in Yiddish, their hair long and curling under black velvet yarmulkes as big as soup bowls, their white shirts untucked and fringes flying, he felt only revulsion and embarrassment, mounting anxiety for his neighborhood, his home, and especially his wife. When it came to these fringe members of his own faith, Mel could not remain calm and rational; he could not respect differences, but sped past, silently screaming.[46]

Unlike the displaced persons of Roth's Woodenton, these new haredim are not penniless immigrants, hoping only to put food on the table. They do not need lessons in Americanization; they already know how to be American. They have made different choices, and unlike many of the traditionalist Jews who arrived in America decades before, they proudly and loudly reject American Judaism in its mainstream incarnation.

ONE OF THE GREATEST STORIES OF OUR TIME

Reflecting this newly visible element in American Judaism, the literary trend away from Orthodoxy began to change in the mid-1980s. A new generation of American Jewish novelists began to incorporate overtly religious themes and characters into their work. Some of these authors came from religious backgrounds, such as Pearl Abraham, Rebecca Goldstein, Tova Mirvis, and Tova Reich, and some from more acculturated ones, such as Michael Chabon, Allegra Goodman, Dara Horn, and Myla Goldberg, but embraced religious Jewish material, themes and identity. Donna Riskind, in a 1995 review of three novels with Orthodox subject matter, wrote:

> The way in which the world's oldest faith is surviving in an age of assimilation is one of the greatest stories of our time. It was not an issue for the older cohort of American Jewish writers, who must have imagined that the Jewish future would be a wide, smooth sea of assimilation in which Jewishness could be equated with the language of Yiddish and the embarrassingly backward habits of parents and grandparents.[47]

Even the prolific Philip Roth, perhaps the core member of the Jewish American old-boys' literary club, began explicitly to explore issues of Orthodoxy as they relate to Jewish identity in *The Counterlife* (1986) and *Operation Shylock* (1993).

What was once old became new again in 1998, with the publishing of two novels set in upstate New York's Catskill Mountains, a place once nicknamed "the Jewish Alps" because of its summertime clientele at kosher resorts. Allegra Goodman's *Kaaterskill Falls* and Eileen Pollack's *Paradise, New York* both feature summertime communities of Jews.[48] Goodman's novel includes several interwoven stories featuring ultra-Orthodox Jews in their summer bungalows. Pollack's novel is about a young woman trying to save her family's hotel by restoring the glory of the area and making the most of nostalgic memories of a bygone era. It makes sense that religious Judaism would become important to contemporary Jewish writers since the "ethnic" Jew has been placed in question by intermarriage and the changing ethnic and cultural demographics that result from it. Religious identity is now competing with tribal identity.

Corresponding to this new interest in Orthodoxy, American Jewish literature began to reflect a new parental anxiety: not that their children would "marry out" and no longer be Jewish (although that remained a concern) but that they would become "too Jewish" and embrace haredi values and restrictions. In Anne Roiphe's 1986 *Lovingkindness*, her secular protagonist Annie writes to her daughter who has recently joined a haredi woman's yeshiva in Israel:

> I can understand your interest in things Jewish. I have talked to many of my friends and it seems that a lot of young people are discovering their roots in the cultures and civilizations of the past. However, your grandparents were not the religious sort. They stopped going to synagogue as soon as they were old enough to defy the old man and his old-fashioned expectations. . . . Don't have pictures in your head of a grandpa weaving over the Talmud, shoulders wrapped in tallis, dust on his skullcap. That is somebody else's picture (mine in fact, and I don't go all to pieces over it, either).[49]

Roiphe's Annie knows that her daughter has known no haredi ancestor or traditions and questions why she would "return" to a place she'd never been. That same year, Irving Howe complained of the "upsurge of nostalgia I detect among a good many young people for the immigrant world to which I was already a latecomer and of which they barely know. They aren't nostalgic for anything they themselves experienced, with either joy or anguish; they're nostalgic for the nostalgia of other people."[50] Roiphe and Howe share resentment for a manufactured or generationally removed nostalgia based on sentiment alone.

Similarly, Philip Roth's 1986 novel *The Counterlife* features two brothers, one of whom has embraced a religious Zionist community in Israel. In response to Henry (now known as Hanoch) and his insistence that he is returning to his roots and his people, Nathan reminds him that his "people" watch "double features at the Roosevelt on Saturday afternoons and Sunday doubleheaders at Ruppert Stadium watching the Newark Bears."[51] His "people" were not Talmud scholars, and they were certainly not gun-toting religious zealots. The very nature of ultra-Orthodox Judaism is found by many to be hard to reconcile with the spirit of contemporary American Judaism.

BYSTANDERS IN A CULTURE WAR

As the previous two examples imply, it would be impossible to discuss the growing anxiety among American Jews over Orthodoxy without the background of its parallel conflict in Israel.[52] The visible and tumultuous conflict with Palestinians in many ways masks the severe internal divisions of the world's only Jewish state. While the unease between secular and haredi Jews in Israel and America manifests itself in similar ways, there are critical differences in the Israeli situation. These nation-specific tensions have arisen for economic, political, cultural, and religious reasons.

Following World War II, allowances were made for the few haredim who inhabited Israel. The secular Zionists who founded the Israeli state, like the American Reform and Conservative establishment, felt badly about the events that had plagued European Jewry. Israel has mandatory military service, and in the early days of the state, the haredim were made exempt from this service so they might study in yeshiva. At the time, this exemption affected only a few hundred young men. Additionally, this yeshiva study was financially subsidized by the government, so men could afford to remain within these protected walls far longer than Jews in America. Much as in America, everyone expected the haredi numbers to dwindle and eventually disappear. And much as in America, this did not happen.

Thanks to ba'alei teshuvah, immigration, and disproportionately high birth rates among the haredim, as well as the newly rightist Modern Orthodox and Mizrahi Jewry, the percentage of haredim in Israel has dramatically increased. The end result of this population boom is that these early exemptions, originally meant as a benevolent nod to a disappearing way of life, now affect a much larger number of people than ever intended. For a nation dependent on mandatory military service, this situation has led to much resentment toward the religious communities on the part of secular Israelis. Refusal to serve in the military has resonance in the United States where this sort of objection historically has been met with suspicion (notable objectors have been Shakers, Jehovah's Witnesses, and members of the Nation of Islam).

Additionally, even though most haredim do not serve in the army, their religio-political views affect military operations. Once the vehement anti-Zionist stance was abandoned by some haredi groups, a religious Zionist philosophy began to infiltrate politics. Ironically, among the haredim, a people who historically chose to remain outside the affairs of secular government, a loud call for "Greater Israel" could be heard, greatly influencing the politics over Israel's occupation of the West Bank and Gaza. Parallels can be seen with U.S. evangelical Christians who have demonstrated powerful electoral influence in the last few decades despite earlier eschewals of worldly politics. Similarly, haredi political parties often must be appeased in order for anything to get accomplished in Israel's Knesset.

The haredim also affect the religious lives of Israelis. Orthodox Judaism is the official form of Judaism recognized (although not widely practiced) by Israelis, and in order for a marriage or conversion to be legally recognized in Israel, it must be sanctioned by the Orthodox authority. With a few notable exceptions, many businesses are closed and public transportation is virtually nonexistent on the Sabbath, a situation that greatly annoys non-Orthodox Israelis. Neighborhoods that are primarily haredi block traffic on the Sabbath, making it impossible, and sometimes dangerous, for drivers to pass. Haredi neighborhoods are also notorious for the treatment of "immodestly dressed" women. Women in pants or short skirts are often harassed, usually verbally but occasionally physically. While progressive movements such as Reform and Conservative Judaism are making inroads in Israel, the religious establishment continues to wear a black hat, much to the dismay of a largely secular majority.[53] Cities that once had a sizeable secular population, such as Tzfat and Jerusalem, are seeing increasing migration to other cities—a flight largely blamed on the growing religious population.

All these factors have contributed to a culture of intense hostility that manifests itself in a variety of ways. Politically, this resentment led to the formation of Shinui, a political party that has gained tremendous success from its anti-haredi platform. Tommy Lapid, the party's leader, sums up his distaste for the haredim: "They say that they are the true Jews. If Moses were around today, or Maimonides, they would recognize me as the true Jew, not the ultra-Orthodox."[54] These sentiments resonate with an increasingly bitter secular majority.

Like American Jews who worry that these haredim threaten their legitimacy as Americans, Israelis worry that the haredim, with their tight grip on the past as well as their control over religious life, threaten their image as a progressive people. Culturally, this anxiety makes its way into hostile exposés of the haredi communities, most commonly in newspaper editorials, film, and literature. Since the haredim assume religious, and therefore moral, authority in Israel, secular Israelis delight in divulging any dirty secrets of haredi communities. Sexual misconduct and financial impropriety are favorite themes of these exposés. Those secular Israelis who get their information about the haredim from their morning paper often share a common response: "This kind of thing goes on all the time in the Haredi community. . . . They're just usually slippery enough to get away with it."[55] Similar schadenfreude is on display in the United States when prominent evangelical leaders are caught with their pants down.

Contemporary Israeli film and literature also commonly demonstrate anti-haredi sentiment. According to Noah Efron, a scholar of the Israeli culture war, Yehoshua Bar-Yosef's *Apicores Be'al Korcho* (*A Heretic Despite Himself*) is a popular example. The book claims to expose "Haredi lusts and illicit impulses," and the book jacket describes the author's upbringing in a haredi household, "uniquely qualifying him to accurately portray the emotional and ideological world of the Haredim."[56] The excitement with which readers embrace these "peep show" looks into haredi life is palpable. "It reads like Jackie Collins in a *Shtreimel* and *Kittel*. And all this written by an insider. 'It's got to be accurate,' opined one lecture at Tel Aviv University. 'After all, it's 95 percent autobiographical.'"[57] The works of the best-selling novelist Naomi Ragen also fall into this category of exposé. An American-born Israeli, some call her the second-most popular author in Israel.[58] A very public figure, she commonly speaks of how her writing comes from true experiences among the haredim.

Israelis, like American Jews, also worry about the influence haredim seem to hold over the younger generation, and many narratives regarding the haredim demonstrate fears of conversion. Noah Efron writes: "Uri Zohar, an immensely popular comedian in the 1960s, gave up acting years ago to become Haredi and people still talk about it in hushed tones, like a family tragedy: 'He had everything, *everything*, and still it happened to him.'"[59] As the numbers of haredim steadily increase, so does the anxiety of non-Orthodox Israelis. Efron offers a dark reading of this paranoia.

Nowhere are Haredi Jews as feared and hated as in Israel. Israel is a bastion of a classic sort of anti-Semitism, aimed not against all Jews, but against the ultra-Orthodox, the overly *Jewy* Jews. It is an unsophisticated antipathy that, while not entirely unjustified, is imbued with fantasies of the Haredi faction poised to overrun the helpless secular majority, who are victims of nothing so much as their own tolerance, generosity and good will.[60]

Efron notes that much of the language used by secular Israelis to describe the haredim is eerily reminiscent of classic anti-Semitic rhetoric, attacking their clannishness, greed, and looks. And this quarrel between Israeli Jews has not gone unnoticed by their American counterparts.

Exposure to this Israeli conflict has led to a special American brand of the *kulturkampf*. Despite current studies that show American Jewish levels of attachment to Israel declining, American Jews still keep tabs on the goings-on in the Jewish state through Jewish periodicals, synagogue gossip, and even the mainstream press. Vicious conflicts featuring Orthodox and secular participants cannot help but affect the American Jewish perspective toward Orthodoxy.

While much of the background of the Israeli conflict does not directly affect American Jewry, the ongoing controversy over Israel's Law of Return does. The Law of Return allows Jews to automatically apply for citizenship, and the question of who is *halakhicly* Jewish affects any Jew in the diaspora.[61] Traditional Judaism dictates that in order to be *halakhicly* Jewish, one must be born of a Jewish mother or undergo a conversion. Reform and Reconstructionist Judaism now recognize patrilineal descent. Since Orthodox Judaism is the authority in Israel, Israel recognizes a Jew as someone born of a Jewish mother or having undergone an *Orthodox* conversion. Now, if a convert has undergone a non-Orthodox conversion *outside* of Israel, that person is accepted as Jewish—although this, too, is up for debate.

Mi Hu Yehudi?

While the question of "*mi hu yehudi*" (who is a Jew) began in Israel, this debate has repercussions in America. The issue of the Law of Return was first raised in 1988, and revealed a split between Orthodox and non-Orthodox Jews.[62] It also exposed crucial differences in the American and Israeli perspectives on the issue. Haredim in Israel want to redefine government, while haredim in the United States want to redefine personal status for Jews.[63] An Orthodox rabbi at Yeshiva University proposed a solution to this problem that required "recognizing Reform converts in Israel the same way the law recognizes Moslem and Christian converts, that is as members of a separate religion."[64] Statements such as this only succeed in infuriating non-Orthodox Jews. Most American Jews have no plans to obtain Israeli citizenship, but the idea that the Jewish state that they support—both in spirit and financially—does not view Reform and Conservative Judaism as legitimate is insulting. Regardless of the Israeli outcome, American Jews are fiercely split on this issue.[65]

This intense dispute over membership is also a crucial debate about Jewish identity and is therefore a key point of contestation. It is the liberal Jewish understanding of the haredim—as both unreasonable and arrogant, as Jews who believe that they alone have the monopoly on true Jewish identity—that comes across in much of the American Jewish literature and cinema that feature haredi characters. These narratives challenge the constructed categories of insider and outsider. While the writers are Jewish, they are not haredi. Their Jewishness allows them a certain access, but their worldliness keeps them from truly being one of the community. Authenticity is key in this matter: not only do the haredim command the idea of authentic Jewish experience, but non-haredi authors also claim that their negative depictions are authentic (i.e., from a newspaper; a friend of a friend; or from "living among them").

They are then able to report with authority that they have seen haredi misogyny (for example) "up close and personal."

This hostility is reflected in the growing number of novels and films that specifically address the haredi community as a place that is limiting and, in some cases, even dangerous for women and children, a trope serving as code for an un-American, uncivilized world. These narratives abound with the motifs of haredi repression and oppression of women, the feminized and often deviant nature of the yeshiva scholar, and the coercion and brainwashing of non-haredi children by manipulative rabbis. At the same time, these tales also demonstrate a real ambivalence over the best way in which to relate to the haredi world, as well as an ambiguity regarding the future of liberal Judaism. The chapters that follow examine these themes as they appear in contemporary literature and film.

2

REBBES' DAUGHTERS

The New *Chosen*

"A woman of valor who can find, for her value is far above rubies."
—Proverbs 31:10–31

Women had no brains for the study of God's Torah, but they could
be servants of men who studied the Torah. Only if they cooked for
the men, and washed for the men, and didn't nag or curse the men
out of their homes; only if they let the men study the Torah in peace,
then, maybe, they could push themselves into Heaven with the
men, to wait on them there. —Anzia Yezierska, *Bread Givers* (1925)

While Judaism has hardly remained a static entity since its
conception, the last century has seen a remarkable revolution in Jewish practice. Most significant in this upheaval is the rapidly
changing position of women in contemporary Jewish movements.
Today's American Jews are divided over gender issues such as the
ordination of women (and, recently, homosexuals), reconciliation with
patriarchal practices, and the creation of new rituals and liturgy. And
while current Jewish perspectives on women span a wide spectrum,
from radical egalitarianism to reactionary traditionalism, all have been
affected by this question of the Jewish woman's position.

As earlier generations of American Jewish authors tackled the
issues of assimilation, alienation, and intermarriage, contemporary
Jewish writers similarly pursue issues of gendered identity by religious
adherents. For those who value egalitarian principles, Orthodoxy—
specifically ultra-Orthodoxy—is the embodiment of resistance to these
values. In the last few decades, Jewish literature—traditionally domi-

nated by men—has seen an outpouring of female novelists (as well as a new generation of men sensitive to gender issues). Many of these authors have chosen to situate their characters in orthodox milieus, providing coming-of-age stories in which the characters' questioning of orthodoxy expresses the values of American Jewry's reformist movements. By examining these new woman-centered and -narrated stories, we can see a side of orthodoxy missing from earlier male representations of orthodoxy, the most popular being Chaim Potok's runaway 1967 best-seller, *The Chosen*. The female characters in these contemporary novels pursue personal acts of rebellion and set the stage for institutional change. These novels, featuring young women who pose challenges to their religious upbringing by studying forbidden books both sacred and secular, validate such liberal Jewish movements as Reform, Reconstructionist, and Conservative Judaism, movements that not only value the public participation of women in religious life but also have become fully egalitarian.

This chapter will examine two coming-of-age stories in contemporary Jewish literature: Erich Segal's *Acts of Faith* (1992) and Pearl Abraham's *The Romance Reader* (1995). Both novels feature a young teenage girl, the daughter of a hasidic rabbi, challenging the existing patriarchal religious and social structure. In both cases, the young woman seeks refuge in books. The action of *Acts of Faith* spans the late 1960s to the early 1980s, and *The Romance Reader* is set in the 1970s. Both are witness to a period of great changes in Jewish practice, particularly with regard to the public roles of Jewish women in the Reform and Conservative movements. Both narratives indict the haredi world for their resistance to women's religious and secular education, women's public religious participation, and for the imposed physical and spiritual separation of women from men. Less overt in the narratives, yet still present, is a concern over the insular tribal nature of the haredim and their fierce resistance to outsiders, non-Jews as well as non-Orthodox Jews. Similar themes can be seen in the popular works of contemporary novelists such as Allegra Goodman, Tova Mirvis, and Tova Reich, works that I shall address peripherally in this chapter.

What is significant about these fictional narratives is not that they find fault with the haredi world's rigid lifestyle—for that is not uncommon among secular or acculturated Jews—but that they actually engage with and argue Jewish law rather than merely rejecting *halakha* as archaic tradition passed on by close-minded authorities. These novels specifically target the religious exclusion of women, providing a defense of alternative, non-Orthodox religious movements in Judaism. According to Sylvia Barack Fishman, "For many American Jews, egalitarianism is a sacred principle, and for some it has greater spiritual relevance and power than does rabbinic law."[1] In other words, it might be inaccurate to claim that progressive Jews are by definition less *religious* than Orthodox Jews because they are less bound to ritual observance. Those within the Reform and Conservative movements might even argue that they are promoting the Jewish religion *more* because religious life is accessible to more people through the full participation of women.[2]

While the haredim are a small percentage of an already small group of people, to many Jews they are representative of the opposition to feminism and to women's access to public religious life. Battles over these issues were fought during the 1970s and 1980s in Conservative synagogues, but the line today persists between non-Orthodox and Orthodox Jews. A 1999 study examined a schism within a Conservative community that split into two radically different congregations primarily over the issue of gender, pointing to the centrality of this issue in determining communal divides. The differences between the two resulting congregations in this study were not based on social differences or social ties. They were not based on educational attainment, nor were they based on ethnic, national or racial differences. The division was not predicated upon a congregant's religious upbringing. Social cliques and longstanding friendships were ripped apart, solely on the basis of religious and ideological differences.[3] Therefore, the themes in these narratives reflect a greater conversation about progressive Jewish practice in light of gender. While criticisms of religious orthodoxy are not uncommon in fiction, these selected narratives are significant because they are not promoting secularism but a reinterpreted religious worldview.[4]

"Very Jewish" Books

It is useful to examine Segal's and Abraham's narratives alongside Chaim Potok's *The Chosen*, the novel that the literary critic Sheldon Grebstein referred to as "the Very Jewish Bestseller."[5] Potok's novel was the first to give Americans and American Jews a peek into the hidden world of the hasidim. Set in the 1940s, *The Chosen* tells the story of a friendship between two young men, Danny Saunders and Reuven Malter. Danny is the son of a great hasidic rebbe and heir to his father's spiritual leadership. Reuven is an observant, non-hasidic Jew, and his father is a scholar and Zionist activist. The two meet and begin their journey in a most quintessentially male American event, a neighborhood baseball game. Danny's yeshiva team plays Reuven's in what seems like a battle for legitimacy in the neighborhood. When up to bat, Danny hits the ball with such force that it smacks Reuven in the eye and he lands in the hospital. Danny's awkward attempts at repentance lead to an unlikely friendship that sees the characters through world-altering events such as the end of World War II and the founding of the state of Israel.

Danny—a brilliant Talmudic scholar—reveals to his friend that he has been expanding his studies to include such non-kosher subjects as psychology, even going so far as to learn German (so he can read Freud in the original). The two attend college together, and while Reuven explores the possibilities of becoming a rabbi, Danny is tortured by his desire to become a psychologist, knowing that this choice will devastate his father. In a classic struggle of Old World versus New, Danny's father is ultimately reconciled with his son's choice, claiming that his son will become "a Tzaddik for the world."[6]

The novel is a male story, featuring the friendship between two young men and the relationships of fathers and sons. Women are notably absent from Potok's tale, a stunning feat considering how much of the narrative takes place in domestic contexts.[7] Danny's sister is mentioned once as a way of introducing the tradition of "promising" hasidic children for marriage at a young age. While *The Chosen* is critical of the hasidic world, Potok finds fault primarily with methods of studying the Talmud (he demonstrates a negative view of the hair-splitting yeshiva tradition of *pilpul*) and the anti-Zionist position of many hasidim. Although Reuven is disturbed that Danny's sister was "promised" as a child, for men the status of women is by and large an intellectual problem. For women within the communities, the critique is far more than an academic exercise.

Both *Acts of Faith* and *The Romance Reader* explicitly recall *The Chosen*. Both present a hasidic rebbe as a family patriarch and feature children who cannot conform to the expectations of the parent. While the actual presence of women already marks these narratives as different from *The Chosen*, the more recent novels also demonstrate the emergence of feminist challenges to the patriarchal structure of the haredi world. Significantly, the issues that are addressed in these novels and others like them are ones that non-Orthodox Jewish women have reformed and reinterpreted in order to redefine contemporary American Jewish life. Trading in Potok's sentiment for scorn, the later narratives express dissatisfaction with a Judaism that does not uphold egalitarian principles between the sexes. While these narratives share a rejection of haredi life, it is important to note that this is not a rejection of Judaism but a desire for a radical transformation of tradition.

THE VOICE OF A WOMAN

Acts of Faith is a 1992 best-seller by Erich Segal, the author of *Love Story* (1970). It is an epic story that traces the emotional and spiritual lives of three New Yorkers: the hasidic brother and sister Daniel and Deborah Luria and their Irish Catholic neighbor and *shabbes goy* Timothy Hogan.[8] This exploration concentrates on the story of Deborah Luria. The daughter of a powerful and beloved hasidic rebbe, the Silczer Rav, Deborah is a bright, beautiful, and spiritual sixteen-year-old girl at the beginning of the novel. Despite her love for her family and her faith, she is presented as having problems with some of the more patriarchal Jewish traditions, particularly (and significantly) *kol isha*. Literally "the voice of woman," *kol isha* refers to the Talmudic prohibition against hearing women praying, lest the earthly voice distract men from their more spiritual thoughts. The full phrase that this ban derives from is "*kol b'isha erva*": a woman's voice is lascivious. Deborah's voice is described as "exquisite—so clear and vibrant that [her mother] Rachel often had to caution her to sing softly in the synagogue lest it distract the men."[9] Significantly, the raising of Deborah's voice will have consequences later in the novel.

She also expresses frustration with her education. Deborah attends the "Beis Yakov" school for girls.[10] The Bais Yaakov (literally "House of Jacob") schools were established in Krakow, Poland, in 1917 by Sarah Schnirir.[11] What started out as a school with twenty-five girls grew rapidly throughout Eastern Europe and later took hold in America. It is still the most popular ultra-Orthodox school for girls. At Beis Yakov, Deborah learns that women "were privileged to help their husbands fulfill God's injunction to Adam to 'be fruitful, and multiply, and replenish the earth.' Is that all we are, Deborah thought to herself, baby machines?" (Segal, *Acts of Faith*, 13). A talented and bright student, she is irritated by the simplistic explanations given in answer to her thoughtful questions.

Deborah repeatedly asserts that there must be more to life than being a wife and mother, both esteemed positions in the hasidic, and wider haredi, world. She watches the way her sister is manipulated into a marriage and vows that it will never happen to her. Her father sets her up with a nice young man, Asher Cohen, and while there is nothing disagreeable about him (Deborah actually likes him), she finds herself provoking him into arguments. After speaking of his plans for medical school (an unusual goal in the hasidic world), she politely points out that he has not asked her what she would like to do with her life. He asks what else there is besides being a wife and mother.

> "I'd like to be a scholar."
> "But you're a woman."
> "So I'll be a woman scholar," she replied.   (74)

While Deborah likes Asher, she refuses his proposal. She wants more.

Despite her objections to the position of women in haredi life, it would never have occurred to Deborah to leave the community had she not been exiled by her father over a perceived indiscretion. After she is caught in an innocent but intimate moment with the blond-haired, blue-eyed Timothy Hogan, her father determines that she is in danger of giving in to the "Evil Inclination" (83). Sent to Jerusalem in order to be set back "on the right track" (104), she resides with the Schiffmans, a harsh hasidic family who treat her like a household servant. She wishes to attend school, but they inform her that the law of the land only requires education until the age of sixteen and that she should have better goals, like marriage.

After settling in gloomily with the Schiffmans, Deborah requests, and is granted, the opportunity to observe the Fast of Esther, the day preceding the holiday of Purim, by praying at the Western, or "Wailing," Wall. While it is a solemn holiday, "Deborah always found it a heartening occasion, for no other holiday in her religion celebrated the noble actions of a woman" (120). She travels to the Wall with Leah Schiffman, who fails to see the point of going. "They squash us into a fenced-off corner, and the men pray so loud that you can't even concentrate" (122).

Deborah makes her way to the Wall through the "tiny area of their segregated sanctuary" and begins to pray. Driven by her spiritual enthusiasm, "Deborah's glorious voice had grown in volume and fervor, inspiring the others to follow her example." The men on the other side of the barrier are furious and begin to shout at the women to keep their voices down. "But the women were so caught up in Deborah's zeal that they sang their prayers even more loudly—except for Leah Schiffman, who kept trying to quiet them" (123). Eventually the men throw a wooden chair over the barrier, hitting an elderly woman. The chair is followed by tear-gas canisters. In anger, Deborah picks up a canister and throws it back over the barrier. Other women do the same. Ultimately the guards intervene, hold back the rioting men, and escort the women to a safe place to finish their prayers. Deborah cannot help but observe that the women have been "banished to the Dung Gate—the door of the Old City, which for thousands of years had been used to expel the garbage" (124). Significantly, it is not the attackers who are asked to move; it is the women.

It is likely not an accident that Segal chooses to stage this scene during the Fast of Esther. This incident reflects real clashes between women and the haredi establishment of Jerusalem over access to the Wall, also known as the Kotel. Beginning in the late 1980s, mixed groups of Reform, Conservative, and Orthodox women have attempted to hold women's prayer services at the Wall, and a particularly unpleasant—and well-publicized—confrontation occurred on the Fast of Esther in 1989. Haredi men were so outraged by the women's singing that they broke into the women's section and began hurling chairs at the worshippers. Police eventually intervened by throwing tear gas in order to break up the violence. After the women left the Wall with the police, some of the haredim reportedly began dancing in victory.[12] One participant reported:

> One student got hit on the head with a chair, and I almost got hit with a glass bottle. The violence was terrifying. I have never felt like that in my life! The things we were called were unbelievable, as if, God forbid, we were not Jews, or, God forbid, we were not humans on the same level as the ultra-Orthodox males. It was really sad.[13]

The following day, an op-ed in the *Jerusalem Post* posed the question, "Is the Western Wall an old-style open-air haredi synagogue, or a national monument? Whose Western Wall is it, in fact? The haredi community's, or the Jewish People's?"[14] Similar protests occur over mixed-gender prayer on the plaza of the Wall. While noted in Israel, these incidents receive far more attention in the United States.[15] The main reason for the publicity is that the worshippers drawing ire are disproportionately American.

As this clash on the Fast of Esther was not an isolated incident (or even the first), the female worshippers, who have since formed the organization "Women of the Wall," went to court to argue the right to worship unmolested at the Wall. A fifteen-year-long legal struggle almost came to an end in April of 2003 when the Israeli Supreme Court ruled that women were not allowed to read from the Torah at the Wall. The following year this ruling was overturned. The court did not rule on religious grounds but because the practice was deemed unnecessarily incendiary. The events at the Wall were watched closely by the American Jewish press, especially such public statements as "a woman carrying a Torah (bible) is like a pig at the Wailing Wall."[16] The comparison of a Jewish woman to an unkosher animal and the physical violence that attaches itself to such attitudes offend liberal American Jews. Sylvia Barack Fishman observes, "For many it is this vision of Jew attacking Jew that is the most disturbing element of all."[17] Stories of haredim hurling stones, chairs, and even dirty diapers at women or mixed-sex prayer groups at the Wall cannot help but reach American Jews, most of whom affiliate ideologically with those being attacked.[18]

As such news travels fast, Reb Schiffman has heard about the skirmish by the time Deborah and Leah arrived at home from the Kotel. He calls Deborah a harlot for praying aloud. "The men could hear your voice. Don't you know the Talmud says 'the voice of a woman is a lascivious temptation'?" (Segal, *Acts of Faith*, 125). This episode on a day that applauds the "noble actions of a woman" marks a pivotal moment in Deborah Luria's life.

The morning of her eighteenth birthday, Deborah decides to open a bank account. Her mother had been sending her money, and Leah warned her that it was unsafe to keep money loose in a coffee can. As she walks down the street, she realizes that she is alone, with all her money and her passport. Two hours later, she is on a three-day Egged bus tour of Haifa, Nazareth, and the Galilee. While eating dinner that evening with her traveling companions, primarily Christian pilgrims from the American South, a woman asks her if she isn't too hot, with her heavy long sleeves in the Middle Eastern heat. In response, she deliberately rips off her sleeves, doing away with the imposed modesty of haredi life. "For Deborah, it was a double liberation. She was not only making herself more comfortable physically, she was also tearing away the past" (140).

In addition to its biblical-sight-seeing itinerary, the tour makes a stop at a kibbutz (cooperative farm) named Kfar Ha-Sharon. Deborah is immediately attracted to the egalitarian lifestyle of the kibbutz, amazed by the sight of men and women working side by side. In the Orthodox world, the roles of men and women are carefully prescribed.

And these God-given responsibilities may appear remarkably inequitable, particularly in the eyes of an outsider. Such perceptions receive validation acutely in the matter of the minyan. A minyan is the Jewish community needed to perform a full prayer service, and traditionally this community was a quorum of ten adult men. In 1973 the Conservative movement voted to allow women to be counted in a minyan, ruling that their exclusion was discriminatory. The Reform movement will hold a full service even in the absence of the full ten adult men or women.[19] In *Acts of Faith*, Deborah is frustrated by the omission of women, wondering "why, when a tenth man was lacking to make a quorum needed for prayers, could no Jewish woman be counted as a substitute, although the final place could be filled by a six-year-old boy!" (13–14). As a devout Jew, she was taught that because women are not obligated to participate in communal prayer, they cannot be counted in the minyan. If women know they do not count in the minyan, it is easy to reach the conclusion that they do not count at all.

> Ever since she could remember, Deborah Luria had wanted the privileges bestowed upon her brother at his circumcision. But as she grew up she was obliged to face the painful fact that she could never serve God to the fullest . . . because she has not been born a man. (14)

But here, at the kibbutz, was an opportunity to be valued as much as a man.

Enchanted by the people at Kfar Ha-Sharon, she watches them: "Here were Jews completely different from any she had ever known. If the Torah student was characterized as having cadaverous pallor and stoop-shouldered frailty, the kibbutznicks were at the other extreme—bronzed and bursting with vitality" (141). She speaks with the kibbutz leader, Boaz, who invites her to stay for a while at the kibbutz. When she calls the Schiffmans to tell them that she will be staying at a kibbutz, Leah anxiously asks if the food is kosher. Deborah replies, "No, but the people are" (143). While the chicken may have been served alongside buttered potatoes, the people were good and welcoming of her.

Deborah flourishes at the kibbutz. She makes friends and becomes strong from working outside. As Segal's novel is primarily a love story,

Deborah's Catholic neighbor, Tim Hogan, finds her in Israel, just prior to his ordination. Putting aside the realities of their lives, "in a wooded corner near the Sea of Galilee, the future priest and the rabbi's daughter consummated the passion that had begun one Sabbath eve so long ago" (201). As is the nature of such complicated romances, neither Deborah nor Timothy wishes to ask the other to change his or her life, and they sadly part ways. As fate would have it, Deborah becomes pregnant and gives birth to a son, Elisha. Knowing that she can never tell Tim the truth, she concocts a story with Boaz that Eli's father is Boaz's son, who died while serving in the Israeli Defense Force.

She returns to New York when her father suffers a stroke after hearing that Danny, his only son, does not wish to pursue ordination and will not be his successor. Wishing to pray for her father but unable to do so in her father's hasidic shul, she enters the most profane of sanctuaries—a Reform synagogue. Her half-sister remarks of Reform Jews, " 'They're not real Jews. They have organ music, like a church' " (251). Deborah responds that the Temple had music, an example of Reform Judaism's references to antiquity as a means of legitimizing recent practices in the face of critiques from "more traditional" strains of Judaism.

The rabbi offers to say a prayer for her father's recovery and invites her to read from the Torah on the *bima*.[20] " 'Are you bold enough to defy tradition and taste a little equality?' " he asks (257). While her brother defied tradition by rejecting it outright, Deborah longed to transform—not transgress against—tradition. With this act of public religious participation, Deborah's life is altered.

> In her short lifetime, Deborah had known mighty and apocalyptic moments. But this transcended all of them. It was as if lightning had struck her soul, setting it ablaze. She had performed her filial duty. And believed with all her heart that God had heard the prayer for her father. (260)

This apocalyptic moment does not end with an isolated reading of the Torah, however. Deborah experiences a day of reckoning marking an entrance into Jewish life beyond the woman's gallery.

Likening this day to her brother's bar mitzvah ceremony, Deborah makes it clear that women have no similar rite of passage in her world. The Jewish feminist Alice Shalvi remarks on her first such experience:

> When I went up and made the blessing and gazed at the Torah scroll I realized it was the first time in my life—and I was fifty-three years old then—that I had seen the inside of a Torah, and I just burst into tears. I was so overcome by emotion at the realization that while from the age of thirteen this is, or can be, a weekly experience for a Jewish male, it had taken me fifty-three years to be able to experience it.[21]

Boys have traditionally had a ceremony in the synagogue marking their coming-of-age, but the bat mitzvah is a far more recent affair. While the first American bat mitzvah ceremony took place in 1922, the ceremony didn't become popular until the 1960s. The Conservative movement also took a while longer to allow girls to read from the Torah. Orthodox Jews are beginning to mark the occasion more, but not in the synagogue. Increasingly, Orthodox women hold single-sex services where a girl may read from the Torah, but only in the company of other women, beyond the ears of men. There are also some notable exceptions among several Orthodox minyans in the United States and Israel that are approaching more egalitarian practices.

Steve, the rabbi, befriends Deborah and suggests that perhaps she consider rabbinical school.[22] "Have you ever thought of becoming [a rabbi]? My seminary has already started ordaining women." She realizes that just because Danny does not wish to follow in his father's footsteps, the Lurianic rabbinical line does not have to die out. She is hesitant, however, recalling the prohibitions instilled in her from birth. Rabbi Steve responds to her apprehension about the consequences of such audacity:

> Frankly it offends me that your people look down on me because I won't accept the idiosyncratic ways they've interpreted the Bible. But the Torah belongs to every Jew. God gave it to Moses on Mount Sinai, not to some rebbe in Brooklyn who thinks he has the franchise on holiness. (261)

This Reform rabbi's perspective reflects a sentiment among many American and Israeli Jews who see the strict adherence to minute religious details as missing the spirit of the law. The American-born Israeli writer Hillel Halkin expresses anger over what he perceives as hypocrisy among the haredim, specifically in Israel. He takes issue with the strenuous attention to correct ritual behavior and the less rigorous attention to moral behavior.[23]

The battle over the ordination of women was a bitter one. The Reform movement ordained its first female rabbi, Sally Priesand, in 1972. Reconstructionist Judaism ordained its first female rabbi in 1973 but began accepting female rabbinical students in 1968, at the establishment of its seminary. That same year, Conservative Judaism permitted women to be counted in the minyan and began debating the issue of ordination. In the introduction to her 1983 reader, *On Being a Jewish Feminist*, Susannah Heschel comments on the nature of these deliberations, specifically on Ruth Wisse's stated concerns that the ordination of women will be emasculating for Jewish men. Heschel quotes Wisse:

> "Judaism's ability to create an alternative model of virility, which depended on intellectual and spiritual prowess rather than political and physical might, helped to compensate for the great social dependency of the Jews without undue sacrifice of masculine self-confidence and biological zest."

In response, Heschel suggests that "[Wisse's] argument implies that to protect some degree of self-esteem during the long centuries of persecution and ghetto life, Jewish men were justified in subjugating Jewish women."[24] This alternative model, while allowing for a powerful respect for learning, denied women the same respect as potential scholars. It was not until 1985 that the Conservative seminary ordained a woman, Amy Eilberg. From the start, Reconstructionism allowed for women's ordination. There have been no ordained women within ultra-Orthodoxy; however there is a growing, yet controversial, Orthodox feminist movement that is steadily pushing for this right.[25]

Inspired by this new push toward women's ordination, Deborah follows Rabbi Steve's advice and begins studying at Hebrew Union

College, telling her parents that she will become a teacher. She finds tremendous fulfillment in her studies. Not surprisingly, she is well received when she begins running her own services. Those congregants that don't mind changing tradition view her as a breath of fresh air. And, after all, Deborah gets her wish; she becomes a female scholar and a spiritual leader.[26]

Acts of Faith presents rather obvious parallels to *The Chosen*, featuring a reluctant successor to the office of tzaddik (echoing Danny Saunders). Daniel Luria, his father's only son, discovers a passion for secular education and harbors doubts about the hasidic world. Segal's novel also includes a parallel character for Reuven Malter, but almost three decades later, this character is a woman. Deborah is religiously observant, but, like Reuven, she questions much about hasidic life. Like Reuven, a visitor to the hasidic world, she is an outsider among her own people. Also like Reuven, she becomes a rabbi, a non-hasidic rabbi.

READING AND REBELLING

While it does not span as long a time period as *Acts of Faith*, Pearl Abraham's debut novel, *The Romance Reader* (1995), is the coming-of-age story of Rachel Benjamin, the eldest child of a hasidic rabbi. The novel follows Rachel from the age of twelve, the year when a Jewish girl is considered a woman, to eighteen, when an American child is considered an adult. Rachel, the eldest of seven children, sees her mother's life and knows that she does not want this for herself. "I don't know if I want a family. I'd rather go to the store and buy sandwiches. . . . I don't want to cook. I don't know if I want babies."[27] While the Benjamins live in a religious community in the summer-bungalow community of Ashley, New York, the haredim are not the only people in town. Rachel sees the way others live and the way others dress, and she longs to live the way others do.

Rachel and her sister Leah read voraciously, as much as they can. In this way, Rachel imagines a life beyond Ashley. With whatever money they have, they purchase romance novels at the drug store. These books are forbidden, as they are in English and feature non-Jews in immodest situations. Rachel and Leah concoct a scheme to acquire a library card so that they can read whatever they want for free. The scheme backfires, and their parents find out about their reading habits. After Rachel's disastrous trip to the library, her father scolds her for the sin of assimilation: "'A Jew is never liked by other nations. A Jew reads only Jewish books and must remain separate'" (Abraham, *The Romance Reader*, 34). He warns her, "'If I catch you reading goyishe books, you will stop going to school'" (35). As suspected, her education is dangerous; it has led to the desire for more.

Rachel wonders why she desires these forbidden books. "There are so many books in this small room: prayerbooks stacked on the tables, books for men and boys to study. If I were a boy, studying hard like David, would I still want to read library books?" (35). Her secular education is not encouraged, and her religious education is minimal. She envies her father's bookshelves and the attention her younger brother David receives for his studies. "One day, I will have my own bookcase. On my shelves I'll have at least one book for every letter of the alphabet, with room for more. They'll be my books" (39). She doesn't specify what kind of books they will be, just that they will be hers.

During services she stands alone in the woman's section. Her father comes by to see her later and mentions that he's having trouble with a tune. She helps him, and he smiles, saying "'If you were a boy, I'd keep you near me during services. You could help me.' I don't know how to answer this. I'm a girl. Should I wish I were a boy?" (44). Because of the kol isha prohibition on a woman's voice and the existence of a *mehitza* (literally "partition"), women must remain separate. *Mehitzas* can take various physical forms in different synagogues, but regardless of construction, they exist to separate women from men during prayer.

While the *mehitza* divides men and women, it also divides traditionalists from progressives. In Phil Zuckerman's study on the schism within a Conservative synagogue, he addresses the issue of the *mehitza* as a lightning rod for conflict.

> Since gender is an integral and central aspect of existence, religious issues or symbols that address gender cut to the very core of our being. The *mehitza* is just such a symbol—a symbol of

what I call "gender regulation." Gender regulation is the process by which a community (in this case religious) attempts to define, institute, and justify "masculine" and "feminine" behavior and roles for its members.[28]

In the case of *The Romance Reader*, Rachel is being instructed in feminine behavior. As someone on the other side of the *mehitza*, her knowledge of a prayer's tune is useful to her father, who can practice it. However, while she may teach him the tune, she may not sing it aloud herself. Rachel knows that she is different, that she wants different things, but she doesn't know why and she doesn't wish to change.

She steals paperback books (Harlequins, not holy books) and on Yom Kippur she breaks her fast several hours early.[29] Her behavior leads Leah and David to the conclusion that Rachel must be possessed by a "*dybbuk*," a demon. They decide to exorcise the *dybbuk*, and her brother is quick to state, "But I have to be the rabbi. I'm the boy" (54). This insistence seems comical in context, given David's young age. They also have ascertained that the *dybbuk* is male. "It *is* a he, I think" (55). This gendering of the *dybbuk* implies that Rachel's behavior is not feminine; she is not behaving like a girl or woman is supposed to act. In Jewish folk tradition, this sort of spirit possession is most frequently a male spirit that attaches himself to a woman. This *dybbuk* can be recognized through the transgressive behavior of the woman—in this case, through a young girl's desire for a life other than the one that has been mapped out for her. According to Ruth Bienstock Anolik, these *dybbuk* stories of women possessed by male demons are further evidence of the attempts to suppress rebellious women because "the woman possessed by the *dybbuk*, who appears to vocalize uncontrollably, is in fact silent; the powerful voice actually belongs to the possessing male."[30] In a makeshift exorcism derived from one of their father's tales, the siblings attempt to cure Rachel. This exorcism is partially in fun, partially in earnest, but Rachel knows that nothing has changed.

Segal's *Acts of Faith* also features an exorcism. Rena, half-sister to Deborah and Danny, becomes possessed by the spirit of her mother who died in childbirth (in this case the spirit is a woman). This exorcism, witnessed by Danny, is not the playful performance of the

Benjamin children, but a dark, frightening, sobering event. It is the seriousness with which Danny's father responds to this event that sets in motion Danny's further estrangement from hasidism. If these primitive beliefs and rituals are truly part of the package, "I wondered if I could believe in a God who lets evil spirits fly around the world and has to be propitiated by black candles, spells, and the bleating of rams' horns" (*Acts of Faith*, 166–67). While Danny abandons his community shortly after the exorcism, Rachel sadly wonders how she can ever be herself in the hasidic world, since she knows that the troublesome spirit haunting her family is hers alone.

The Benjamin family goes on a vacation to a seashore community. Rachel regrets going when she learns that she will not be able to swim because men might see her. The family sits in the summer heat by the water. But her father and her brother Levi do swim. Rachel bitterly observes, "It is obvious that they removed all their clothes and went in for a good swim. But they're men, and they're not ashamed of their bodies. They are not the sinning Eves we are" (Abraham, *The Romance Reader*, 85). Rachel wonders what the point of coming to the water is if she can't swim. And she wonders why God would give her a body she has to hide.

The Benjamins' marriage is troubled. Mrs. Benjamin, the harried mother of seven, is worn down and begins pressuring her husband. She threatens to move back to Jerusalem, or she wants to kill herself and leave him with all the kids. Instead, she takes an extended visit to Israel to see her parents. This image of a grown hasidic woman, married with children and fleeing her home, cannot help but color her daughter's perspective on marriage. While she is away, Rachel and Leah run the house. Their father is off traveling too, so they have much freedom. They exercise this by wearing sheer panty-hose, a forbidden item among these hasidim. The women are supposed to wear thick opaque stockings, or better yet, stockings with seams.

The theme of control over women's lives through the monitoring of their appearance appears frequently in narratives regarding the ultra-Orthodox. In Tova Mirvis's *The Outside World*, Tzippy Goldman remarks on the signs, intended for visitors, in Mea Shearim—a haredi neighborhood in Jerusalem—warning against immodest dress for women. "Tzippy worried that the *tznius* police, the self-appointed enforcers of modesty, would see her bare legs. They would chase her down and banish her from the neighborhood."[31] Mea Shearim is notorious for the confrontational behavior of its residents. Women have reported having such things as stones or ink thrown at them for appearing on the streets in shorts, tank tops, or even pants. One sign at an entrance stipulates—in English, French, Russian, and Hebrew—that violating the modesty code "is strictly forbidden." An additional sign in English warns that such violations might "offend our residents and cause . . . unnecessary inconvenience."[32] While these signs are primarily intended for tourists, some seem directly addressed to residents, such as the following: "**Young Girl**: She who wears shameless clothes, woeful are the days of her youth. Her sins are more numerous than the strands of her hair. Cover arms, covered legs, neck and heart covered. **This is modest dress!**"[33] Regardless of audience, these signs provide a constant reminder of the importance of *tznius*, modesty, to members of the community.

These enforcers of *tznius* do not solely reside in Mea Shearim. Hella Winston's 2005 study, *Unchosen: The Hidden Lives of Hasidic Rebels*, features a number of American hasidic women (and men) who complain of the constant gaze of their neighbors upon them. In some cases, this paranoia is confirmed by direct confrontations with fellow residents or, in the case of Winston's subject, Dina, with an anonymous phone call from a man, "telling her that she needed to 'watch' the way she was dressing."[34] Similarly in these fictional narratives, the female protagonist is plagued by the sense that someone is always watching her, judging the length of her sleeves and her skirts, and criticizing the color or thickness of her stockings.

In addition to changes in fashion, Rachel and Leah begin taking life-guarding lessons at the pool. Their instructor is Rikki, a religious girl who has a driver license and attends a Beth Yaakov school (the same religious school system that Deborah attends in *Acts of Faith*). Rikki is also going to attend seminary in Israel the following year. Rachel muses, "I wish I were a Beth Yaakov girl. . . . Away in seminary I could be anyone, do anything" (*The Romance Reader*, 111).[35] Unlike *Acts of Faith*'s derisive attitude toward Beis Yakov, in Abraham's *The Romance Reader* this school is presented as modern in comparison to Rachel's school. The Benjamins (like Abraham's family) come out of the strict Satmar tradition. Bais Rochel, the Satmar girls school, only goes as high as eleventh grade, ensuring that the students will not be able to attend college.[36] While Rachel does not attend a Satmar school, her school is less "modern" than the Beth Yaakov school Rikki attends.

She and Leah pay for the ten-week lifeguarding program out of the money left by their mother. Four weeks into the program, their mother returns. The day after she comes home, Rachel and Leah arrive from school to find their stockings cut up on their bed along with their snorkeling equipment. They are in trouble. Rachel's father lectures to them about modesty:

> "The Jews escaped slavery in Egypt because of three things. . . . Name, dress, and language. You two call each other by your goyishe names, Rachel instead of Ruchel; you speak a goyishe language; and now you're changing the way you dress. I will not have any of that in this house. This is a Chassidishe home."
>
> (*The Romance Reader*, 137)

Rachel is defiant about her lifestyle choices. She manages to convince her father that there is merit to the lifeguarding lessons; after all, she is being trained to save lives, a Jewish obligation, if needed. She also points out to her mother that she will earn money working as a lifeguard. The stockings are another story. Leah tells Rachel that she has gone too far by wearing nude sheer stockings and that she should have worn a color like navy. Their father purchases seamed stockings from a Satmar shop in Williamsburg and demands that his daughters wear them. Rachel begins wearing them over her sheer stockings when she leaves the house in the morning and takes them off when she gets to school.

That summer, Rachel and Leah get jobs lifeguarding for religious women's swim hours at a hotel, and Rachel fantasizes about her boss, Mr. Gartner. She thinks he might be a nonreligious Jew. She finds him more attractive then the hasidic men she knows. In addition to getting a chance to fantasize about older men, she likes the feeling of independence she gets from working.

After graduating from high school, Rachel gets a job teaching English at a Satmar girls' school. She likes the fact that there are less-religious Jews working there. Her family begins to buzz with talk of matchmaking. Rachel has hoped to put this off for a while, but her family has heard of a good match for her brother David. Rachel, as the eldest, needs to be married first. She begins to lose her opposition to marriage, seeing it as a way out of her parents' home. "I don't care who I marry. Once married, I at least won't have to worry about it. Married, I'll do and wear what I want. I'll be who I am" (204). This theme can be seen also in Tova Mirvis's *The Outside World*. A dissatisfied young haredi woman, Tzippy Goldman, becomes fixated on marriage as a way to get out of her house, away from her mother.

Once her best friend Elke becomes engaged, Rachel begins to wish for the things that come along with being married: having one's own apartment, new appliances, and no parents to check on the color or thickness of one's stockings. "I'm beginning to want things of my own. I want to live on my own. Married is the only way I can be on my own" (209). Notably absent from these fantasies, however, is any mention of a husband.

The *shadchan* (matchmaker) proposes Israel Mittelman as a candidate for marriage. While not overly impressed by him, Rachel is tired of fighting with her parents, and he seems nice. Rachel knows that her parents believe she will change when she's married. "As if sex with a man is supposed to make you better, softer, more religious" (219). She starts thinking about this when the subject of hair covering is raised. Israel's mother wears a wig, or *shaitel*, with a small hat and Rachel's mother wears a kerchief over her shaved head. Rachel will reluctantly opt for the more modern option of a wig.

According to Orthodox feminist Blu Greenberg's now classic *How to Run a Jewish Household*, there are three reasons Jewish women cover their heads:

> One is that it is a sign of dignity; the other, that exposed hair is a sign of licentiousness. Each of these associations reflects the

difference in rabbinic understanding of the Biblical law of the unfaithful wife. A married woman, charged with infidelity, was required to undergo an ordeal of bitter waters, during which the priest uncovered the woman's head. From this law, and from other sources, it was commonly understood that the proper Jewish women of the past went about with their hair covered, most likely with shawls or head veils.[37]

The third and most common reason is that married women should make themselves less attractive to men other than their husbands, and one's natural hair is particularly sensual. According to Greenberg, the tradition of wearing wigs began in the sixteenth century, with the explanation that a wig is less attractive than one's natural hair. Many rabbis opposed this practice, and it is still controversial today. The main point of contemporary contention is that today wigs often look *more* attractive than one's natural hair. In Naomi Ragen's *Sotah* this question is posed by a nonobservant Jewish woman to a haredi woman: " 'So tell me something. How can you put on that flashy, Barbie Doll wig and think you're being modest? Why, your own hair—and mine, for that matter—is much less attractive. Don't you think that it's a bit ridiculous?' "[38] From an outsider's perspective—and from some insiders—this wig wearing can be seen as confusing and, in its worst light, hypocritical. The right-wing practice among some hasidim of shaving one's head and wearing a headscarf (like Rachel's mother does in *The Romance Reader*) is a rebuke to the "modern" wearing of wigs.[39] Regardless, the covering of a woman's hair is considered essential to her *tznius*, modesty.

Rachel is displeased by all of these headcovering options. "I plan not to change one bit. I don't even want to wear a wig. I think if all women refused to shave and cover their heads, the rabbis would have to rethink the laws, change them. But I don't know anyone who agrees with me" (*The Romance Reader*, 219). Her best friend, Elke, who once rebelliously broke her fast with Rachel years ago on Yom Kippur, is excited about getting married, about being a nice hasidic wife, about wearing the wig that signifies a married woman. Unlike Danny Saunders, who has a friend with whom he can share his pain, Rachel feels alone within a world of women who are supposed to share the same desires, not harbor any doubts.

I think it's easier for Elke because she doesn't think about love in novels. She hates reading. She doesn't know any tall, dark men in boots. She thinks only about the Chassidic way, real life. For the first time, I see a reason not to read. (221)

The widespread fear of secular education is not unfounded; some studies have shown a correlation between levels of education and intermarriage.[40]

Rachel tries looking forward to her marriage, looking at the bright side: "Maybe living with Israel will be everything I want. I won't have to tell anyone where I'm going. I'll be free to read when I want, to stop reading when I'm ready. I'll wear anything, almost anything" (*The Romance Reader*, 229). Her father won't be able to inspect her stockings, or her bookshelf. Only she will decide if her lifestyle is kosher enough.

But Rachel's fantasies extend beyond her freedom as a newly married woman.

I stay in bed thinking about myself as a divorced woman. That makes me happy. If I can get divorced, getting married isn't so bad. I chant silently: I am engaged to be married and divorced. I am engaged to be married and divorced. . . . Someone should warn Israel. (232)

Her wedding will be in a gym, but she doesn't care. She doesn't believe that she should have a beautiful wedding, because she doesn't believe that her marriage will be beautiful. "A beautiful wedding is a lie. It shouldn't be beautiful like in a book. Novels are lies, lies upon lies" (236). Secular books have led her to expectations that will not be realized in her hasidic world. Rachel cannot reconcile the life of her mind and the life that she lives.

But she goes through with the wedding, going through the motions and wishing it would be over soon. "Israel puts the ring on my finger, and I don't like the way he proclaims the words that bind me to him as his wife. . . . I don't want to be bound to him by any law. But I remain silent; nothing is expected of me at this ceremony" (246–47). In an Orthodox Jewish wedding, only the groom speaks. Her expected silence highlights her removal from the experience.

Rachel has fantasized about sex. She has thought about what it would be like to be with a man, and she hopes that the wedding night will be good. She doesn't really believe that it will change anything, but she hopes it might. The night is a disappointment. Israel fails to perform, and they are both embarrassed. The next day her mother arrives with a razor to shave her head. At first she refuses, and then defiantly does it herself. She will wear the wig, but not without resentment.

Nothing is what she expected. While she believed that marriage would end her parents' control over her choices, she soon discovers that Israel is consulting with them on every issue. Israel asks her to cover the wig with a kerchief. He demands more modesty than she will give. She tells him that she wants to buy a radio. He says no and then wavers, suggesting that perhaps if they get a radio she will wear a kerchief. They decide to wait on a decision, and maybe they will get the radio when they visit his grandmother the following week. While Israel is at the synagogue, Rachel enjoys puttering around her new apartment, drinking coffee, and reading. She realizes that she is free to read whenever and whatever she wants and that wearing the kerchief is perhaps a fair trade.

The physical nature of their relationship remains at an impasse. After a few more clumsy attempts, the marriage remains unconsummated. Rachel goes back and forth as to whether she should stay in the marriage. "I can't decide what to do. To stay or to go. It's this wig. It makes me crazy. I can't think in this dead, hot wig. My head is burning" (282). On Friday morning, while they are preparing to visit his grandmother in Borough Park, Israel tells her that she should wear seamed stockings if they buy a radio. She realizes that her father is influencing Israel to make these demands on her and is furious. They get on a bus together and are separated there by the *mehitza*. "For once I'm happy with the curtain. I thank God for the curtain. I don't want to see any men. I want to live in a world with no men: with no fathers, no husbands; a world free of men" (286). Rachel gets off the bus at their stop, but when Israel does not, she realizes that he has fallen asleep and she is alone. Like Deborah in *Acts of Faith*, Rachel grabs the opportunity and walks away from her marriage. She checks into a hotel, eats non-kosher food, and thinks about her next move. The novel ends with her temporarily staying with her family, a divorced daughter.

There are striking similarities between Potok's *The Chosen* and Abraham's *The Romance Reader*, and the first comparisons can be made with the public personae of the authors. Both Chaim Potok and Pearl Abraham were raised in the hasidic world and chose to leave it behind for a wider world of writing; both have been interviewed frequently regarding this journey. Potok was ordained at the Conservative Jewish Theological Seminary and received a Ph.D. in philosophy from the University of Pennsylvania. His novels primarily attempt to reconcile religious belief with secular practice. His biography can be understood through his statement that "no one can work with the novel and remain inside any fundamentalist sect."[41] Abraham—another literary apostate—graduated from Hunter College and received an M.F.A. from New York University. While neither *The Chosen* nor *The Romance Reader* is strictly autobiographical, both reveal much about the earlier lives of their authors.

In these novels, Danny Saunders and Rachel Benjamin are both the eldest children of hasidic rabbis. They both make forbidden trips to the public library to read forbidden books. Their futures are predetermined: Danny will inherit the position of Rebbe and tzaddik from his father, and Rachel will marry and become a good hasidic wife and mother. And both Danny and Rachel do not want the life they have and yearn for another.

While they know that something is missing, Danny and Rachel try to convince themselves that if they give in to their communities' demands, if he becomes the rebbe and she becomes a wife, they will be free to do as they wish. Danny rationalizes his decision to Reuven (and to himself): "Once I'm a rabbi my people won't care what I read. I'll be sort of like a God to them. They won't ask any questions" (*The Chosen*, 81). Similarly, Rachel muses: "As long as I can read anything I want to, who cares about the kerchief? I went through the bookshelves and pulled out five books. They're in a pile on the table in the living room, and looking at the stack, five more books, I think I can stay awhile" (*The Romance Reader*, 272). Perhaps she can exchange some physical freedom for the freedom of her mind.

Rachel's forbidden books are romances, books that describe a world outside of the hasidic community.[42] Danny's books are mainly psychology books; he reads Freud (in German) and other works involving the mind. While Danny gathers the courage to tell his father of his decision at the time of his *smicha* (ordination), Rachel sees no alternatives to her impending marriage. Feeling worn down and defeated, she admits, "I thought there'd be more things a person could do, more choices. But there's nothing else" (*The Romance Reader*, 221). Rather than fight what she perceives as inevitable, she allows the marriage to happen, knowing that it will not stick.

Neither *The Romance Reader* nor *Acts of Faith* condemn the haredi world as dangerous or abusive, but they both explicitly critique the culture for its repression of women. In a 1992 interview, Potok described both the positives and negatives of living among the hasidim.

> It was essentially a fundamentalist atmosphere, which by definition is both joyous and oppressive simultaneously. . . . Joyous in the sense of knowing you belong to some cohesive community that will care for you; in whose celebrations you can participate fully; and who will help you mourn if you need a support group in time of personal tragedy. And repressive because it sets boundaries, and if you step outside the boundaries, the whole community lets you know.[43]

Significant is his mention of the "celebrations [in which] you can participate fully." *The Romance Reader* and *Acts of Faith* reflect the sadness of some young women who believe that they *cannot* participate fully in religious life.

Satirical examples of women who believe that their limited participation is nonetheless meaningful can be found in Tova Reich's *Master of the Return* (1988), a mocking portrait of fanaticism among penitent Jews who stand at the fringes of haredi society. These penitents are Jews who have had spiritually polluting earlier lives through excessive experiences with hard drugs and sex. In a moment of

female bonding through hashish on the holiday of Purim, one penitent, Bruriah Leah, muses:

> "Isn't it something, though? . . . No outsider can understand the
> absolute beauty of the Jewish woman's position. To the outsider, it
> looks like we're downtrodden and oppressed, like we're low, lower
> than low. We eat the leftovers. We're barred from the study halls.
> We're regarded as inferior and unclean. We're excused or simply
> forbidden from performing many of the rituals and mitzvot, from
> studying the more complicated and interesting texts. We get no
> help at all in the house."[44]

In this passage, it is hard to see how Potok's description of haredi
life as "joyous and oppressive simultaneously" is anything other than
oppressive for these women. But as Bruriah considers this long list of
prohibitions, she sighs, "That's how it looks from the outside. . . . But
we know the truth, don't we?"[45] Reich's tone and the broader context
of the novel suggest that Bruriah and her cohort are victims of false
consciousness, accepting the limits on education, the confines of marital purity laws, and the physical laws of separation between men and
women as means to a better life. The truth that Deborah and Rachel
come to know is that the prescribed boundaries of their communities
cannot hold them. They find their escape in books, and it is through
education that they—and many other Jewish women—come to redeem
their lives, and come as well to set the stage for change within contemporary Judaism.

BARRED FROM THE STUDY HALLS

The desire of Jewish women for education is certainly not new or
unique to the past two decades. Anzia Yezierska's *Bread Givers* and
Isaac Bashevis Singer's "Yentl the Yeshiva Boy" are but two examples of
early-twentieth-century literature that feature women longing for scholarly experience and achievement. The growing acceptance of Jewish
women's *Jewish* education is new, however, and owes much to the feminist movement and growing opportunities for women. Sylvia Barack
Fishman points out that the increase in women's Jewish education

also owes much to the unacknowledged "ubiquitousness of the Bat Mitzvah."[46] The need to prepare for such ceremonies has done as much as anything else to close the gender gap in Jewish education. Not surprisingly, the issue of education is found front and center in these narratives.[47] Neither Rav Luria nor Rav Benjamin sees extended education for girls as important. Deborah's father is surprised when she tells him that she might want to go to college, putting off marriage for a while. Segal and Abraham do not depict the rabbis as monsters but as relics from a patriarchal age. In the hasidic worlds of both *Acts of Faith* and *The Romance Reader*, women's education is seen as a privilege rather than a necessity or a right, one that can be taken away in the face of disobedience. Rachel's father threatens her for reading library books and claims that he will take her out of school if it happens again. Deborah is taken out of school when she goes to stay with the Schiffmans in Jerusalem. Segal makes much of the "abridged Code of Laws" (the Kitzur Shulchan Aruch) that women are supposed to learn in school. While this condensed Code of Laws is used by most haredim—regardless of gender—as a simpler guide for daily living, Segal's frequent mention underscores that this abridgement signifies the reduced involvement that women have in Jewish public life.

Women have abandoned Judaism over the past century because of this exclusivist attitude. In Anne Roiphe's *Lovingkindness* (1986), the secular protagonist, Annie Johnson, reminisces about her grandfather, a Bratslaver hasid. As a child, she had been attracted to his stories. He told her that they were not for her, a girl. As an adult, Annie rejects organized Judaism, seeing it as an institution that devalues women. Sylvia Barack Fishman quotes one feminist on the response of haredi men to women who demand equal access:

> "They are afraid of women taking things into their own hands. They are afraid of women having knowledge. They are afraid of being dispossessed in the synagogue. . . . [T]he Orthodox synagogue [is] the last remaining exclusive men's club in the world . . . It's their last fortress. It is very much a man's world. They are totally free to make the laws, make the codes of behavior, and dictate what is going to happen and how."[48]

The runaway success of Anita Diamant's *The Red Tent*, a retelling of the biblical story of Dina, is a reflection of the hunger for women's readings of the Bible, as well as for the need women have to see themselves reflected in tradition.[49] A haredi response to this hunger is the relatively new encouragement of women's learning. There is Jewish education across the board for Orthodox girls from Bais Rochel to Bais Yaakov to the coeducational Modern Orthodox Ramaz and Maimonides. Even the late Lubavitcher rebbe, Menachem Schneerson, encouraged the study of the Talmud for women (although that is not emphasized in Lubavitcher women's yeshivas).[50] It is, however, important that this education not remotely hint at a relationship to feminism.

There is also the increased understanding that without offering women an outlet in which to study, they will leave the community and attend secular institutions that will grant them degrees. According to Sylvia Barack Fishman, the "education of girls [within Orthodoxy] is widely viewed as a necessity for the preservation of a traditional Jewish way of life."[51] Education is meant to be a means to becoming a good wife and mother, not toward personal career achievements.

In *The Romance Reader*, Rachel's father is particularly concerned with her reading "goyishe books." He recognizes that these books lead to an engagement with the outside world. At one point Rachel is reading a novel in her new apartment and thinks, "There are questions the characters in this novel ask that I've never heard asked. Is there a God? Would a God allow so much suffering? The two boys each want what the other has" (270).[52] And Rachel wants the freedom to ask questions as well as the freedom to disagree with the answers. While she does not frame her frustration in explicitly feminist terms, it is clear that she sees a greater freedom enjoyed by boys and men.

Chaim Potok addresses the relationship between Orthodoxy and feminism in a 1986 interview:

> Orthodox Judaism [and feminism cannot be reconciled]. What they're going to end up doing is finding all sorts of ways to accommodate the women, but never on equal terms. They'll put window or glass in front of the *mehitzah*. They'll make the *mehitzah* on

the same level without anything in front of it. They'll give the women their own minyan; they'll let them dance with the Torah by themselves on *Simchat Torah*, though most Orthodox Jews will not even do those things. All kinds of things will happen, but there can never possibly be equal status among men and women in Orthodox Judaism.[53]

Potok's predictions were perceptive. In the past two decades, all of these projections have come to pass in Orthodoxy, including his belief that there will never be "equal status among men and women." This concern over the disparity between men and women in the Orthodox world is a primary factor in tensions between Orthodox and non-Orthodox Jews today.

We're Regarded as Inferior and Unclean

While Jewish education for women may be becoming more widespread among the Orthodox, Orthodoxy still comes under attack for continuing to affirm both the spiritual and physical differences of women.

The more Deborah learned, the more she became resentful. Not only because she was regarded as inferior, but because the sophistry of the teachers tried to convince the girls that this was not really the case—even while explaining that a woman who gives birth to a boy must wait forty days before she becomes "pure" again, whereas one who gives birth to a girl must wait eighty days. (Segal, *Acts of Faith*, 13)

Within Orthodox Judaism, family purity laws form a controversial practice. These are the laws that dictate ritual sexual separation between husbands and wives during the period of the woman's menstrual cycle and for five days afterward (culminating in a purifying ritual bath, the *mikvah*). In some circles, these couples will not even touch the same objects for fear of breaking with tradition.

This practice has gone through various changes in both articulation and purpose over the past centuries. A menstruating woman was often described as a poisonous, polluting, disgusting creature. It was sometimes said that a look from her could change wine to vinegar (and worse). In more recent times (and more recent literature), this practice has been articulated more as a way to keep a marriage alive and exciting. The practice has even gone from being called *hilkhot niddah* (which specifically refers to the menstruating woman) to *taharat hamishpacha* (family purity laws). This change in name signifies the reinterpretation of this shared experience of marital separation.[54]

In addition to changing names and changing views, those prescribing these practices are changing as well. In the past, most of the literature on *taharat hamishpacha* was written by men. Demonstrating a shift in demand, three recent popular manuals for *taharat hamishpacha* are written by women.[55] These authors, Tehillah Abramov, Tamar Frankiel, and a spokesperson for a Lubavitch women's organization revise the understanding of these laws. The cycle of separation, of hiddenness, is seen as imitating God's cycle from the world (sometimes God stands back). Another change is the promotion of the idea that the menstruating woman is not the pollutant; it is the man and the outside world which can be dangerous to *her* power during this period. Regardless of the way *taharat hamishpacha* is articulated, the separation is still based on the cycle of the menstruating woman. While *mikvah* itself is experiencing a renaissance among progressive Jews, the laws of *niddah* are not.

In *Acts of Faith*, as Deborah's sister was preparing for her wedding, Deborah's mother allowed her to remain in the room when she explained the family purity laws. "Deborah could not restrain her feelings of resentment at the notion that some day she, too, would be considered 'unclean' in her husband's eyes. For half a month she would be impure, besmirched, *untouchable*" (47). This sense of untouchability, coupled with the exclusion of women from many aspects of religious life, can lead to outrage on behalf of women who demand gender equity in all other areas of life.

Allegra Goodman's *Total Immersion* has a scene in which this tension is specifically addressed. An alternative Jewish congregation in Hawaii is debating the place of women in the service.

Alan: "I grew up in a Conservative congregation, and gender wasn't an issue for us. I think I would be uncomfortable if—"

"Uncomfortable!" Pat's voice rises. "How do you think women feel,
thrust into the audience? Always the echo in responsive readings.
I want to lead. The Torah reading is the heart of the service.
The *aliyah* is the heart of the reading. And that's just where I'm
excluded. For three years I've sat here patiently. I'm not a new
member. I've shown my commitment. Now I want this group to
give a little back to me. Let's face it. What we've got here is a
boy's club. This is my holy book too, and I want a piece of the
action. I want to sing. I want to mourn. It's a crime to shut me out.
You are negating me. You are denying me and relegating me to
second class because you think that I'm impure."[56]

Significantly, Alan claims that "gender wasn't an issue" because the
gender that is the issue is not his. Pat responds with fury, appealing
to Alan's normally liberal politics. How can he, in good conscience,
relegate her citizenship to "second class"? Narratives such as these
reflect the frustration felt in a congregation where some members favor
change and others favor continuity.

To the Outsider, It Looks Like We're Downtrodden and Oppressed

While the minyan may not count women and purity laws may limit
women, there is no better reminder of the difference and othering of
women than the physical barrier of the *mehitza*, which is addressed
in these narratives. Referred to as a "symbolic division in space" by
an Orthodox man in Zuckerman's study, the *mehitza* is also a physical
division.[57] It is the spiritual equivalent of a glass ceiling. In congregations where it exists, women cannot be rabbis or cantors. In some communities, *mehitzas* exist on buses as well. A woman in the study thus
expresses her views on the *mehitza*:

The purpose of the *mehitzah* is to divide people. To exclude a
group of people. And that's what it does . . . it's apartheid. It's the
back of the bus. You know, women don't count in the *minyan*. And
your voice is despicable, and you're not a full human being.[58]

The sense that women don't count as full people is at the core of the criticism leveled at Orthodox Judaism, and ultra-Orthodoxy in particular.

In Reich's *Master of the Return*, the men are described as near-mad, obsessed with following the strictest letter of the law. While highlighting the relationships among the separate spheres of women and men, Reich describes harsh dismissals of women. A striking example occurs when Ivriya, a widow, wishes to speak at her husband's funeral. The men present, after a long debate, determine that this would be permissible if she crossed over a stream and they could not see or hear her, resulting in an extreme sort of *mehitza*. Reich's representation of this debate echoes Isaac Bashevis Singer's foolish elders of Chelm, and her satirical tone indicates her bitterness toward the stupidity of the men who interpret the Law. While her women seem to be strong and intelligent characters, they choose to submit to these men. Painted as victims of false consciousness, they allow the men to discriminate against them. And as women who were not raised haredi, they should know better. Ivriya's mother, Dr. Frieda Mendelssohn, an outsider, thinks her daughter and community are completely crazy.

Another mother of a newly religious daughter is featured in Roiphe's *Lovingkindness*. The protagonist, Annie, observes a haredi rabbi and his wife—the leaders of her daughter's yeshiva, and considers the separation between men and women.

> Mrs. Cohen was a woman of valor. She was a carrier of the law, a maintainer of the body and the frame of the family. Rabbi Cohen was the mind. He was the one who made the decisions. He was the one who had the authority. His was the obligation to study and to learn. His was the reward and hers was the work. My skin crawled. Mrs. Cohen accepted the separation before God and she hadn't grasped that separation never results in equality but always serves to sweep power to one side or another.[59]

These issues of power and equality are intrinsic to every page of these narratives. Those who are encouraged to learn are better. Those who are able to pray aloud are heard. Those who are rewarded are men.

The fury that this exclusion sparks is somewhat tempered by a grudging respect for the traditional lifestyle that has allowed Judaism to survive. But this attitude is changing. In *Lovingkindness*, a friend of Annie's protests the haredi treatment of women:

> "Don't let them hide behind tradition," said my friend. "There is nothing sacred about cruelty to half the people on this globe. We don't have to respect every tradition: cannibalism, slavery, clitorectomies, facial scarring, burning of witches, wives to the funeral pyre, flagellation, hairshirts, binding of feet, worshipping of ancestors, infanticide and on with the list. I have no great respect for tradition."[60]

This long list of traditions that are now condemned by most of the West demonstrates that things don't change without someone rising up to challenge tradition. While Chaim Potok's *The Chosen* demonstrates a critique of the hasidic world over the matters of Talmudic interpretation and their anti-Zionist stance, it also reveals a nostalgia for that world. It has become somewhat of a meaningless cliché to criticize Potok for his sentimentality, but his narrative does imply that we, as readers or as Jews, have something to learn from the haredi world. They—the Reb Saunderses of the world—are defenders of the faith, the ones who keep the eternal flame eternally lit.

Twenty years later, new voices have emerged to critique the haredi world. This time those voices are angrier. They speak out against the polite protection of nostalgic narratives. These new narratives centralize the position of haredi women, those women who yearn to be full members of their communities. Written by non-haredi Jews, or former haredim, these stories critique the exclusive patriarchal structure of the haredi community. As Rachel Biale has observed, "Women's communal roles, women's spirituality, gender relations, sexuality, and feminist theology are among the most vital issues for discussion in contemporary Jewish life."[61] These themes in *Acts of Faith*, *The Romance Reader*, and similar narratives address the position of Jewish women in religious life and reflect the values of contemporary Judaism's reformist movements. The following chapter also examines narratives that centralize dissatisfied women in the haredi world, but these narratives fall into a different variety. Unlike the empowerment tales of Deborah and Rachel, which demonstrate a certain ambivalence regarding the transformation of tradition—an ambivalence shared with Danny Saunders in *The Chosen*—these next narratives highlight the abuses of women by ineffectual, perverse men who hide their deviance behind religious piety.

3

THE NEW JEWISH GOTHIC

A hundred years ago in a shtetl near Pinske, a young girl ran off into the woods. Her father wanted her to marry a scholar from the Pinsker yeshiva, but for some reason—maybe she was a little crazy, who knows?—she didn't want to. Anyway, she ran away. . . . They sat shiva in Pinske for the girl who had disappeared and everyone went on with their business. Until one day, just as suddenly as she had disappeared, the girl came back into town. . . . She was pregnant. In Pinske they said she got lost in the snow and was saved by a demon who made her his wife. That spring she gave birth to a baby girl. They called her Yitta. Our whole family is descended from Baba Yitta. If you don't watch out, you're going to end up just like her. . . . God didn't want her. . . . She wanders the earth like Cain, alone forever. —A Price Above Rubies

So begins Boaz Yakin's 1998 film, *A Price Above Rubies*. In what is later discovered to be a flashback, Yossi—a hasidic boy—is telling this story to his younger sister, Sonia. The meaning of this apocryphal tale is clear: don't rock the boat, listen to your parents, and marry a scholar. Conform, or this could happen to you.

Even at this young age, the boy is instructing his sister on how to behave, advocating conformity and submission for her future choices. This compliance would ensure her success within the haredi movement. The most pressing and visible difference between the haredim and other Jewish groups is the former's strictly defined gender roles, which outsiders often see as gender inequality. Contemporary anti-haredi works often choose to single out and critique women's status and prescribed roles in the community. The role of haredi men also falls under harsh scrutiny, particularly in a manner that presents yeshiva students as falling short of American standards of masculinity. By criticizing haredi gender constructions, these contemporary narratives fall into a recognizable literary pattern. When marginal groups come into conflict with a dominant culture, in this case the ultra-Orthodox with mainstream American Jews, certain tropes emerge, often ones that perpetuate existing stereotypes.

Using the examples of Boaz Yakin's film *A Price Above Rubies* (1998) and Naomi Ragen's novel *Sotah* (1993), in this chapter I will profile the archetypes of ultra-Orthodox men and women that are so prolific within contemporary popular culture. Mirroring cultural stereotypes and indicative of an increasing hostility toward the haredim from the Jewish American mainstream, these characters permeate Jewish literature, film, and even popular television dramas. These gothic-style captivity narratives featuring haredi men as villains and haredi women as victims in mysteries, romances, and crime dramas are supplemented by sensationalized press coverage of criminal court cases involving the haredim. These narratives both reflect and fuel contemporary hostility toward the haredim.

A Price Above Rubies and *Sotah* both follow the formula of gothic captivity narratives, a style characterized by a sense of forced isolation, impending violence, and the macabre. Gothic fiction, a literary genre developed in the eighteenth century, frequently targeted religion—most frequently Roman Catholicism—as a source of terror, as in Matthew Gregory Lewis's *The Monk* (1796). According to Susan J. Palmer, the genre of the "gothic myth," which includes "complaints of broken dreams, hardship, exploitation, and dystopian abuses," tends to inform "apostates' tales circulated in news reports and anticult literature."[1] The two narratives examined in this chapter, which feature women born into the haredi community, contain parallels to such apostate literature and propaganda. Both protagonists awaken to their imprisonment, recognizing the repression and oppression inherent in their status as haredi women.[2]

Unlike the female protagonists discussed in the previous chapter, who challenged orthodoxy from a religious perspective, these women willingly conformed and married. However, marriage fails to serve as fulfillment; if anything, it brings to light preexisting problems. The nature of the women's captivity is specific to being female, indicating the weight that gender holds among anti-haredi writers. These narratives feature young, married women who find themselves in unsatisfying marriages, choose paths deemed deviant by haredi society, and are consequently punished for their behavior. Ultimately, these women find safety and fulfillment outside of the haredi community. These tales reflect the anxiety and resentment inspired by a variety of inequities among Orthodox Jewish men and women, specifically the increasingly visible plight of *agunot*, literally "anchored women," unable to obtain Jewish divorces and therefore contractually bound to their husbands.

While these narratives chronicle the liberation of women, the obstacles and salvation are personified by different male types. It is therefore worth looking at the male characters alongside the female protagonists to see how both are depicted. How are masculine roles defined? Who are the superior men in these narratives? Who are the good guys? Who are the villains? Familiar anti-Semitic imagery has resurfaced in these tales, many of which construct a weak, feminized Jewish male who is portrayed as a sexual deviant. In these narratives, women tend to reject the idealized haredi male type and find happiness with a man who falls more into traditional nineteenth- and twentieth-century American ideals of the man as breadwinner.

"Yeshiva Boys" and "Women of Valor"

Much attention in masculinity studies has been paid to cultural images of Jewish men as feminized nebbishes.[3] By feminized, I refer to "a set of performances that are read as nonmale within a given historical culture."[4] These images reflect the perception that Jewish men may be less than *real* (i.e., gentile) men, and in some cases this effeminacy is interpreted as homosexuality.[5] Jewish men are often seen as softer than their gentile counterparts. We can observe these perceptions in contemporary popular culture. The most common places one finds the secular nebbish guy are on television sitcoms and dramas (e.g., Paul Buchman on *Mad About You*, Ross Geller on *Friends*, Jerry Seinfeld on

Seinfeld, Joel Fleishman on *Northern Exposure*). These television nebbishes are the direct descendents of Woody Allen, the classic Hollywood nebbish. These are not macho guys by contemporary American
standards. They are sensitive and funny, but not "manly." The nebbish
is not Richard Gere in *An Officer and a Gentleman*, he is not Bruce
Willis in *Die Hard*, and he most certainly is not Matt Damon in the
Jason Bourne trilogy. And while the wider culture rarely recognizes
Jewish men as particularly manly, this assessment is magnified by non-
Orthodox Jewish observers of the haredi world, projecting their own
anxieties and insecurities onto the ultra-Orthodox. The haredim are,
as Noah Efron remarks, "the overly *Jewy* Jews."[6] The haredi model of
masculinity is viewed as feminized. The ideal man is one who never
works with his hands, or exercises, or pays attention to maintaining his
body. An ideal haredi man is a scholar.

Boaz Yakin's *A Price Above Rubies* features Renee Zellwegger as
Sonia Horowitz, a young hasidic woman in New York. Recently married with a newborn child, she and her husband have just moved
to a new community to be closer to his family and to the rebbe, the
spiritual leader of their community. Her husband Mendel, played by
Glenn Fitzgerald, is a brilliant and pious scholar. In the opening scene
depicting Sonia as a child, her brother Yossi is reprimanding her for
saying that she loved him more than anyone because one should not
love anyone more than God. This sets the stage for Sonia's ongoing struggle with her feelings of alienation from the hasidic world.
She wants to name her baby after her brother, who died a tragic and
early death. Mendel, however, insists that the baby be named after the
rebbe. Her disappointment over this disregard for her wishes comes
up several times in the film. When the time comes for her son's circumcision, she demonstrates her discomfort within the community
by initially refusing to hand the baby over to anyone. She protests
that they are going to "sacrifice" her baby.[7] While many new parents
may be filled with anxiety over the experience of circumcising their
sons, her friends and family view her reaction as extreme. This scene
also offers an attempt at levity with Mendel, the child's father, growing increasingly nervous and ultimately fainting at the sight of the

ritual. This neurotic episode also serves to highlight his weakness from the beginning.

Sonia's interactions with others are fraught with anxiety. In one scene, Sonia is having sexual relations with Mendel and he pulls away from her when she responds to him, calling her indecent. For Mendel, God is everywhere and sees everything, and Sonia does not understand why it is indecent to enjoy sex with her husband. Mendel loves his wife, but his first allegiance—like that of her late brother Yossi—is to God and Torah. Both sexually and emotionally, he cannot satisfy his wife. Later, surrounded by people in her new home, Sonia has a panic attack while trying to breastfeed her baby, a traditional maternal responsibility. Another panic attack occurs when she is a guest for Shabbat dinner. While being soothed by Mendel's sister Rachel, Sonia reaches out and kisses her longingly. Rachel is horrified and arranges for Sonia to receive counseling. The problem is not just with her marriage, for Sonia cannot find any satisfying intimacy in her community.

This film is typical of other anti-haredi tales, featuring a beautiful, willful woman who slowly discovers herself oppressed or repressed by male figures and the communal norms, usually in the form of a father, a husband, and religious leaders.[8] The general atmosphere, as well as the social structure of the haredi community is depicted as oppressive, with other women reinforcing the rigid nature of these closed communities. These women may be mothers, sisters, in-laws, or friends who support the male authority and exert social pressure in order to maintain the status quo. In this case Rachel, the sister-in-law, exerts her influence in order to keep Sonia in line. Sonia explains that she is suffocating, but the counseling session—and the Orthodox male therapist—does not help her.

Sender Horowitz, Mendel's brother, enters the picture. The stereotype of the haredi villain, Sender is not a religious man, although he comes dressed in one's trappings. He is worldly, brash, and assertive. In one scene, he reaches out and takes Sonia's hand while his wife and his brother are in the next room (in haredi society, a man may only touch his wife). He asks her why, given her demonstrated talents, she never entered her father's jewelry business. She answers that her parents didn't want her associating with "unsavory" people. "They wanted me to marry a great scholar and live a decent, spiritual Jewish life." Sonia took the tale of Baba Yitta seriously. She listened to her parents. She married a scholar. But her conformity failed to bring happiness. Appealing to her emotional and creative frustration, Sender offers her a job working in his neighborhood jewelry store. His character is typical of the "devious haredi" archetype, a man who presents himself as religious in order to mask his inner perversions. This character can appear as the husband in these narratives or, as in this case, as a manipulative lover. The 1999 Israeli film *Kadosh*—a film with similar character types and motifs to *A Price Above Rubies*—has a character, also the brother-in-law, who fits this archetype. In the scene of his wedding night, this zealously religious man practically rapes his wife and, in a later scene, beats her. However, *Kadosh* treats this man's religiosity as a form of mania rather than as pretension. Likewise, Sender seduces Sonia in a disturbing scene that reads more like rape than seduction, but Sonia is so desperate for contact that she accepts it willingly. Sender seduces Sonia with sex, with unapologetic physical contact, but primarily with the promise of a world outside of Borough Park.

Sonia's new employment is not particularly radical, as haredi women often work outside the home. If the family can afford it, the husband does not work, which allows him to give full attention to scholarship. This traditional balance of labor partially grew out of anti-Semitic laws that hindered the professions of Jewish men. As Jewish women were seen as safer to the gentile populace, they were freer to join the work force.[9] Subsequently, scholarship among Jewish men became prized in lieu of professional work. As I discussed in the previous chapter, such scholarship among Jewish women does not receive the same level of acclaim. By no means are all haredi men scholars, nor do all aspire to scholarship. This lifestyle is reserved for those who demonstrate aptitude and for those who can afford it. An ideal marriage match is the daughter of a wealthy man to a scholar. If the husband's in-laws cannot afford to support him in study, the wife will often work to support him. When the daughters are old enough, sometimes they, too, will support him.

This tradition came to an end in America with nineteenth- and twentieth-century Jewish immigration, although remnants of this worldview could be seen in the autobiographical literature of the first generation, which reflects the rejection of such Old World traditions for what was often framed as "modernity" in the New World.[10] In the case of Anzia Yezierska's novel *Bread Givers* (1925), the father took advantage of his wife and daughters as they toiled to support him, as he claimed devout religiosity and yet did not contribute to the family's material well-being. This balance of labor was obviously at odds with late-nineteenth- and early-twentieth-century American standards, where upper- and middle-class white women were expected not to work. According to nineteenth-century modes of masculinity, "if a man was without business, he was less than a man."[11] Upon immigration, many Jewish women did attempt to fit in with contemporary standards. Sylvia Barack Fishman points out that "the readiness of American-Jewish women to terminate labor force participation was in itself an accommodation to non-Jewish behavior patterns."[12] Those who retained the old balance of labor were acting against acculturation.

The emphasis in Judaism on "learning"[13] led to a spin on what Americans consider the breadwinner ideology. The haredi community, which grew after WWII, sees these unemployed scholars as the ideal men among the haredim. This perspective is in direct contrast to the values of mainstream American society. Haredi social status is not measured by financial success, and it is the yeshiva scholar who receives status and honor. This ability to learn indefinitely is referred to as "conspicuous leisure."[14] A scholar must devote as much time as possible to the study of tradition and texts. This can be seen in *A Price Above Rubies*; Mendel works as a teacher in a boy's religious academy in order to support his family and his learning.[15]

The yeshiva scholar therefore relegates wage work to women because he has a higher calling, and haredi women help their husbands achieve this calling by working outside the house. Working, however, does not ensure equality for women in the community, although it does give them a measure of independence.[16] They are relegated to occupations determined to be "women's work," such as running shops or serving as teachers and secretaries. The significance here lies not in the kind of work they do but in the very fact of their working. Women are valued for contributing to the family income, but their work is not as valuable as scholarship. This inequality and the criticism it provokes are reflected in these narratives.

The haredi woman's role in the home remains consistent with our traditional concepts of femininity and domesticity. As Jeanne Boydston points out, "Conceptions of gender ... shape our perception of what constitutes work, of who is working, and of the value of this labor."[17] The haredi woman, through her domestic work (and possibly outside work) demonstrates *mesirat nefesh*, religious sacrifice and dedication.[18] Just because a man is not a traditional breadwinner does not mean that he should clean the house. While haredi men may oversee certain kitchen duties and may frequently shop for groceries, this activity might reflect more of a concern over proper kashrut than progressive politics. Many haredi women work the "double day." For a haredi woman, working to support her husband's learning is a badge of honor. While Mendel does not mind Sonia working at first—her income allows him to focus more on learning—he begins to complain about feeling neglected, about being served microwave dinners. The fact that the haredim break acceptable divisions of labor and challenge gender roles is reflected in much anti-haredi rhetoric, specifically in these narratives. These disparities underscore their difference and Otherness.

Sonia enjoys the freedom that comes with being Sender's business associate and lover. She gets to go into Manhattan in order to buy jewelry for his store, and she gets to have sex without any religious pretense. After a particularly unromantic sexual encounter on the jewelry store desk with Sender, she tells him that men are ugly and that he is the ugliest of men. But he is aggressive and sexual, whereas her husband is gentle and undemanding and asexual. While Sonia obviously loathes Sender, Mendel's delicate ways are also completely unfulfilling. The neglected wives in *Kadosh* and *A Price Above Rubies* respond to their loneliness by activities that are not seen as *real* sex: masturbation (*Kadosh*) and lesbianism (*A Price Above Rubies*). The message here is that the weaknesses of the haredi male, which include sexual inadequacy, result in a frustrated wife. For Sonia, Mendel is less than a man. He is unfulfilling as both a sexual partner and a companion. In Sender, she at least has a business partner.

That is, of course, until she meets Ramon Garcia on one of her trips to Manhattan. Ramon is a Puerto Rican jewelry-store clerk who makes his own jewelry and sculpture pieces in his free time. At first, she is drawn to his work and decides to represent him. While he is also in the jewelry business, he is different because his work is the *production* of jewelry and art. He works with his hands to produce beautiful things. Ramon is also a provider who cares for his mother living with him. Sender disapproves of this friendship and spreads a rumor (which is perpetuated by Rachel) that Sonia is having an affair with Ramon. This rumor spreads quickly and she comes home one night to find her apartment empty. She goes to Rachel's place and is informed that her baby will be staying there and that she will need to divorce Mendel.

In many ways, Ramon is the most complex character. He holds a job as a submissive clerk in a jewelry store to pay the bills, but he is a producer of art—a creative mind who works with his hands. He also is an overtly sexualized vision of the nonwhite "other." He has a couple of shirtless scenes, an obvious contrast to the modestly clad haredi clan and to the nonmuscular haredi men.[19] Ramon is the ultimate outsider to the haredim—a manly, dexterous Christian. This choice in *A Price Above Rubies* exaggerates the typical outsider status often found in these tales. Usually the outsider is a non-Orthodox Jew or someone who has rejected the community and left. By making Sonia's love interest a macho, Catholic Puerto Rican, Yakin expresses how seriously Sonia is rejecting Borough Park and all that comes with it. In the end, Sonia finds comfort, love, and passion with Ramon outside of the community. She and Mendel inevitably part amicably, agreeing it was not meant to be. In this film, Mendel is a good man but inadequate; the truly oppressive character is the hypocritical Sender, as well as the societal values and norms that confine Sonia.

Naomi Ragen's *Sotah* predates *A Price Above Rubies* by five years.[20] Ragen has written three novels and a play that feature haredi women as protagonists. Her success in this genre led one critic to remark, "Naomi

Ragen, an author in the Judith Krantz vein, has turned the lives of Chasidic women into pot-boilers."[21] The first half of *Sotah* takes place in Jerusalem, the second half in New York. Ragen's heroine is Dina Reich, a beautiful, naïve, haredi woman. Born into a poor family, she cannot be choosy about whom she marries. She first hopes to marry Abraham, a scholar, but when his parents find out Dina's financial situation, they put an end to the budding romance. Devastated, Dina gets introduced to other men by a *shadchan*, a matchmaker. She ultimately chooses—to everyone's surprise—Judah Gutman, a quiet, gentle man. He is a carpenter by trade, as well as an artisan; like Ramon Garcia, he works with his hands. He is also physically large, and much is made in the narrative of his contrast with Dina's delicate and tiny stature. Gutman is considered a good match for Dina because he is self-employed and well off; however, in this community, he is definitely considered a step down in status from that of a scholar. She grows to love him, and they have a baby. Unlike the frustrated wives in *Kadosh* and *A Price Above Rubies*, Dina is sexually satisfied by her husband. But unlike the men in those films, Judah does not fit the ultra-Orthodox ideal of masculinity. He is not a scholar, nor does he have a yeshiva-hall pallor. He is handsome, rugged, and strong, yet Dina cannot seem to shake her disdain for his occupation.

Her neighbor, Noach Saltzman, who represents the softer, non-rugged type of man she wishes she had married, manipulates and seduces her. Like Sender Horowitz, he merely plays at being pious. His religiosity does not prevent him from coldly plotting his seduction of Dina (and others). She plans to go away with him one weekend, but the "Morals Patrol"—a vigilante group of haredim who have taken it upon themselves to police the moral behavior of the community— follows them. When she returns, she is told by their leader, Reb Kurzman, that she must leave Judah and her child. Leaving a letter for Judah, she is shipped off to New York City to live with a secular Jewish family as a housekeeper. She develops a close relationship with the secular family, and they assist her in experiencing some of what the outside world has to offer. Dina returns home from New York just hours before the rabbinical court is to meet about her impending divorce. She explains that she did not sin with Noach; she changed her mind at the last minute because she realized her love for Judah. Judah, as a good man, takes her back and agrees to move with her away from the community, to a place where they can remain observant Jews but still enjoy the pleasures of a modern, tolerant society. This ending promotes the ideals of Modern Orthodoxy, believing that one can be an observant Jew and live alongside and within the greater culture.

YESHIVA SCHOLARS AND JEWISH CARPENTERS: MANLINESS IN THE HAREDI WORLD

Both narratives tell a story that begins in repression and ends in freedom. In both, repression is represented by one male type and freedom is signified by another. Dina originally found the yeshiva scholar attractive. Much like Mendel Horowitz in *A Price Above Rubies*, he embodied the ideal haredi type. When she met Judah, the carpenter, her first thoughts were, "He had no beard, and he was so big! Yet handsome, too, and manly."[22] Manly is not often a term used to describe yeshiva scholars. In *Acts of Faith*, Eric Segal described such Torah students as "characterized by cadaverous pallor and stoop shouldered frailty":[23] slight, delicate, pale maybe, but never manly.

Despite her physical attraction to him, Judah's physical labor disappoints Dina.

> She remembered the first time she'd seen him in his workshop: the dusty pants, the stained, greasy apron, the head peppered with sawdust and wood shavings. The appalling thought: This is my husband. A small, secret swell of shame had washed up from her bowels. —(Ragen, *Sotah*, 264)

At this moment she sees Judah as she imagines the rest of her community sees him. The character of Dina, as Naomi Ragen writes her, has few original thoughts and is very concerned about other people's opinions.

She later expresses guilt over being able to study after her marriage. Women are permitted, and even encouraged to learn in haredi communities. However, most do not pursue formal studies after marriage because they must work to help support their families while their husbands learn. Dina's guilt is associated with being able to afford the luxury of studying full-time, since her husband was not in *kollel*.[24] Ironically, female scholarship is not seen as conspicuous leisure. Freedom to study may indicate one of two things: a lack of children or a husband who works. Either way, female study is a sign of a lower social standing. "Only at this time did she fully realize how far her own status had fallen as the wife of Judah Gutman, full-time, successful, self-supporting carpenter" (220). She also found fault with Judah's quiet ways, wishing for the talkative, argumentative ways of yeshiva scholars.

Contrast these views of Judah with Dina's first close encounter with the neighbor Noach Saltzman:

> He held open the car door to the front seat for her. He was very tall and slim, and his black overcoat was a fine, pure wool, the kind she had seen on wealthy *kollel* men and yeshiva boys from England. As she brushed past him, she smelled the musky scent of something very male and very clean. The hands on the door handle were impeccable in their unblemished whiteness, unsullied by any physical labor. They were the hands of a scholar, she told herself. —(263)

Her husband, with his earthy, rugged character (scented with wood shavings) was "manly," but Noach's delicate nature was "very male and very clean." This latter scent is far more attractive to Dina at first than her husband's. Noach—despite appearances—is no scholar, although he feigns a sort of piety in order to manipulate Dina. He works in jewelry, but unlike the artist Ramon in *Rubies*, he is on the business end of things (just like that other bad man, Sender Horowitz). In the end, however, she does find happiness with Judah, as well as a respect for his capacity as a producer of goods and as a provider for his family.

This haredi social system is enforced by the society's emphasis on the importance of modesty and virtue, which provides tight restrictions on social conduct. One way that virtue is preserved is through fear of gossip and slander. If the fear of losing face is not enough to keep one within the bounds of agreed-upon morality, others may choose to punish the sinner. In *Sotah*, the slander comes from the Morals Patrol, led by a Reb Kurzman. Ragen describes this group as an extremist offshoot of the moderate, legalistic *mishmeret hatzinius*, "Modesty Protectors" (170). The Morals Patrol would go so far as to physically attack those who engage in illicit sex and do not adhere to *taharat mishpacha* (family purity laws).

These Modesty Protectors and Morals Patrols are not necessarily fictional. A subject in Hella Winston's sociological study *Unchosen* describes a fear of such a group: "She had long heard rumors that there were some men in the community who were designated to enforce the rules, sometimes beating up boys who got out of line."[25] A 2007 *New York Times* article described harassment suffered by Toby Greenberg, a Satmar woman living in Kiryas Joel—a self-sufficient hasidic village of 20,000 people in Orange County, New York. Greenberg claimed to suffer threatening phone calls and vandalism after "her decision to deviate slightly from the culture of modesty that defines and reinforces this Orthodox Jewish enclave of bewigged women in long-sleeved shirts and ankle-length skirts and bearded men in black hats and long black coats." Greenberg's statement to the police asserted that "she was singled out because she chose to wear denim skirts, long, natural-looking wigs made of human hair, and stockings without a visible seam." According to journalist Dan Levin, when someone steps out of line, "the 'vaad hatznius,' the rabbinically appointed modesty committee that enforces the village's rules of behavior and appearance, intervenes." David Ekstein, a member of the *vaad hatznius*, insists that the committee is both necessary and respected:

> "If we find they have a TV or a married woman won't wear a wig, we will invite them to speak with us and try to convince them it's unacceptable, or next year we will not accept their children into the school system. . . . There has to be some kind of watchdog. . . . But do we have any real power? We're not a government."

Despite the committee's views on propriety, Ekstein maintains that the *vaad hatznius* is not responsible for the harassment and finds it unacceptable. According to Levin, Greenberg's complaints of persecution are only the latest in three decades of such grievances from residents of Kiryas Joel who dare to walk too closely to the community's clearly defined line. And while the *vaad hatznius* denies allegations of involvement, members of the community suggest that she brought these inconveniences upon herself: " 'They see her on the street and have asked her nicely to stop wearing tight-fitted clothing, but she wouldn't listen.' "[26] Perhaps more dangerous than the Morals Patrol are the wagging tongues of such neighbors. In Hella Winston's *Unchosen*, one of her subjects revealed that he was "more afraid of spies and tattletales in his own community than he could ever imagine being of God, if there even was a God."[27] Similarly, in *A Price Above Rubies*, Sonia is the victim of malicious gossip. In her case, these rumors are perpetuated by men. Traditionally, gossip has been used as a woman's weapon, again showing the feminized nature of the haredi man. Kathleen Brown's study of gender in the American colonial period dealt extensively with the issue of women's using gossip as a means of grasping autonomy. "Women's gossip acted as a form of social control that competed with formal legal institutions and perpetuated gender-specific standards for reputation."[28] While women used gossip against men, the more likely victims were other women. In this case, the destructive rumor comes from Sender, Sonia's spurned lover.

In order to protect the honor of their families, Dina and Sonia are silenced and exiled. The concept of a family's honor being easily and irrevocably tarnished by gossip and rumor has great power in dictating one's behavior in conservative communities. Bertram Wyatt-Brown writes in *Southern Honor* about the uses of honor in the Old South: "[Honor] . . . provided a means to restrict human choices, to point a way out of the chaos. . . . It established signposts of appropriate conduct."[29] These signposts are also present in the haredi world.

Both women choose silence over protesting the false rumors spread about them, knowing that their dissent would only bring more attention to their situations. Not only are they sent away from their husbands and children, but they are also shunned by their parents. When Sonia is forced out of her home, Sender gives her the option of staying in "an apartment that he keeps in Manhattan for business," which she rejects. Sonia knows only too well that he wants to keep her as his mistress, cut off from the support of family and friends. In an analogous turn of events, Noach follows Dina to New York and offers her the same arrangement in *Sotah*. Both women find their lives threatened and forever changed because of the degree of control gossip has on such a closed community.

THE NEW JEWISH GOTHIC

In order to analyze these narratives, we must see them as representative of a larger pool of fictions. In a 1989 *New York Times* review of another Ragen novel (*Jephte's Daughter*), the reviewer remarked:

> In the process of telling this story, Ms. Ragen creates a new type of romance novel—Jewish Gothic—because the man Batsheva has married is indeed a sadistic monster who proceeds to abuse his bride in the name of God and whose mother gleefully razors Batsheva's magnificent hair into a black matted stubble that's easily hidden under the requisite wig and scarf.[30]

These narratives embrace characteristics common to gothic stories and captivity narratives.[31] Imaginings of closed communities disguised as exposés are quite common when the community itself is reluctant to provide information, often for fear of persecution. These "true" exposés have plagued Catholics, Mormons, and Muslims in their attempts to blend in with greater American society. The haredi community, with its distinctive dress and strict religious observance, is an urban curiosity. While the haredim live in closed communities with their own language, these communities are located in cities, so their members' differences are obvious to all who surround them. The foreign air of this group recalls an earlier place and age, often inspiring conflicting emotions.

Inevitably, the most popular concerns in controversial literature have to do with sex and the treatment of women; often the captivity tales describe fantastic visions of harems, veils, and polygamous marriages.[32] In the Western imagination, the harem is often conceived of as a place where scantily clad women are held hostage and exploited sexually by their master. In addition, it is often seen as a woman's sphere where illicit lesbian activity takes place. In reality, the harem was a woman's sphere where men who were not kin were forbidden to enter.

The harem and the convent share an element of distrust of outsiders: both are woman-only spheres under the control of men. The harem suggests attitudes toward sexuality and female identity that differ from prevailing Western ideas and therefore both disturbed and intrigued outside observers. A xenophobic tool, these tales feature a victim "like us" and a villain who is "not like us."

An example of this demonization of those in the Muslim world is the 1991 runaway success of *Not Without My Daughter*. Based on Betty Mahmood's memoir of being held captive by her husband, a Muslim doctor who, on a vacation to Iran, suddenly embraces a fundamentalist brand of Islam and refuses to allow his family's return to America. Thomas Grant writes on the contemporary captivity narrative: "The captives appeared to be ordinary Americans going about their business while their captors were the new 'heathens,' namely Arabs, whose strange dress, inexplicable behavior and unfathomable beliefs made them suitable Enemies."[33] While *Not Without My Daughter* features Iranian Muslims—not Arabs—as the heathens, a similar xenophobia is employed. Novels, "true stories," TV movies, and major motion pictures all serve to capitalize on the public's fears, prejudices, and hatreds, and these anti-haredi tales are no exception.

While appearing as a new genre of romance, a sort of haredi gothic tale featuring beautiful young women held against their will, these titillating "peep shows" fit into a variety of narrative that is already a source of fascination for Americans. Grant continues:

> Female "bondage" films have, of course, been a staple of the porn market, but increasingly they turn up on suburban mall cinemas, MTV and even family-hour TV, featuring vulnerable women, at the mercy of sinister predators, usually Black (or at least dark-skinned and swarthy). . . . [T]hey celebrate male power and female powerlessness.[34]

While the predator archetype in the Jewish stories is usually not black (although he is "black hat"), he is depicted as somehow foreign, alien to acceptable manners of masculinity. I write "usually" because Naomi Ragen's *The Sacrifice of Tamar* (1994) features the rape of her married protagonist by a black intruder. She inevitably becomes pregnant, hides the possibility that her child may not be her husband's (because her son appears white), but is ultimately found out when her grandchild is born dark-skinned.

The racial element of captivity has been a constant throughout the history of this captivity genre. The historian Joy S. Kasson describes a body of nineteenth-century artwork that featured white (often Greek) Christian women captured by Turks and sold into slavery or prostitution. At this time Turkey was considered a sensual, amoral place, filled with these fantastic harems. Kasson pays attention to the look of the captive's white skin next to the captor's dark, swarthy complexions, playing into the viewer's racial fears.[35]

This method of contrasting skin color is still used as a way of playing upon fears and prejudices. In a review of *Kadosh*, David Biale accuses the director of casting all the male roles with Sephardic or Mizrahi actors (from North Africa or Arab lands, notably considered "black" in Israel) and the female roles with Ashkenazi actors (from Europe). The contrast between the dark villains and the white heroines in 1999 is admittedly rather suspect.[36] Much of this concern over the position of women in these communities by outsiders is really a critique of the men in the communities.[37] These narratives describe haredi men as either weak and useless, devious and dangerous, or a combination of these characteristics. In *Sotah*, Noach is not the main target of Ragen's scorn. He is manipulative, but the real threat to Dina and her family is Rabbi Kurzman and his cronies in the Morals Patrol. It is Kurzman who threatens to expose Dina's secret, makes arrangements for her to leave for America without a word to her family, and ultimately convinces Judah of her guilt and unworthiness.

The sinister nature of the men pulling these strings further situates these tales in the gothic captivity plot.[38] These narratives "can be distinguished by the presence of houses in which people are locked in and locked out. They are concerned with violence done to familial bonds that is frequently directed against women."[39] Features of gothic fiction can include "ghosts, family secrets, mysterious crimes, sexual violence, confused wandering or desperate fleeing through dark streets. . . . Together these features create a nightmarish atmosphere, intense emotional involvement."[40] The narratives examined in this chapter exhibit many of these characteristics. Both Dina and Sonia find themselves locked out of their homes after a perceived transgression. Sonia is plagued by the ghosts of both Yossi, the dead boy who reprimands her for transgressing halakha, and a woman we come to recognize as Baba Yitta, the spawn of a demon. Dina is exiled from her husband and her country. Both are unable to return to the homes of their parents. And both find themselves prisoners of past transgressions and family secrets, forced to wander in confusion until their conflicts are resolved.

Another threatening element in these narratives is the refusal to release children. While this occurs in both *Sotah* and *A Price Above Rubies*, in both cases the children play no real part in the narrative. In fact, we almost forget that these women have babies, despite the fact that a haredi woman is valued for her ability to have children. The sense that the children are not viable subjects makes their captivity more distressing in the narrative. The withholding of children indicates the danger that the haredim pose for that beloved institution—the family. In *Sotah*, Dina and her husband reconcile and, together with their child, leave the haredim. In *A Price Above Rubies*, Sonia leaves alone, and her son remains with Mendel. She relinquishes custody surprisingly easily at the end of the film. The baby is in some ways more Mendel's son than hers, having been named for the rebbe against her wishes.

A threat to the family unit is a familiar trope in this type of literature, and the anti-haredi narratives exploit this fear.[41] The representation of the haredim as sinister villains who are responsible for breaking up the family is a rebuke to the claim of traditional practitioners of religion that they are responsible for maintaining family values. Of all the narratives analyzed in this book, the ones described in this chapter most resemble nineteenth-century anti-Catholic tales. The imagined limitless authority and power that Protestants saw Catholic priests exerting over their followers is similar to what non-haredim see the haredi society exercising over the members of their communities. Much of this concern relates to perceived haredi power over bodies. *A Price Above*

Rubies, *Kadosh*, and *Sotah* address sexual behavior (both marital and extramarital) and the influence of religious authority on that behavior. The Morals Patrol and the meddling hasidic community both serve as a wedge between husbands and wives, much like the menacing priest. Regardless of the cultural context, these narratives possess parallel plotlines and character types. In Naomi Ragen's books, the Morals Patrol is depicted as an institutionalized, sinister force, committing acts of blackmail and violence. Admittedly, no one physically holds these women hostage, but the pressures to remain in the community are great. Perhaps the real fear reflected in these narratives is not that haredim exist in powerful numbers but that they will enforce their way of life on others. In Israel, rumors of haredi plans to round up secular Jews and place them in concentration camps abound.[42]

While the menacing nature of these haredim is worthy of note, another significant element is the almost total absence of autonomous haredi women in these narratives. Almost all the negative imagery in anti-haredi works describing haredim refers to the men, never to the women. These narratives centralize the haredi woman as a victim (who overcomes victimhood by ultimately choosing not to be haredi). This view of haredim is true of nonfiction as well. Most—if not all—anti-haredi imagery detailed in Noah Efron's *Real Jews* refers to men, often using descriptive phrases such as "drowning in a sea of black."[43] If the threatening images are all male, where are the haredi women? In fact, the only women he describes in his book are secular women who are harassed by haredi men over immodest dress.

This perspective is pervasive in these narratives. Women rarely appear to be the threatening party. In *A Price Above Rubies*, Julianna Marguiles (Sender and Mendel's sister Rachel) probably comes closest. However, most haredi women are depicted as sympathetic characters. If they are painted as victimizers, it is usually because they are bowing to a man's wishes. An example of this hard but conflicted character is the mother in *Kadosh* who inevitably bows to rabbinic authority and presides over the ritual bath of her son-in-law's soon-to-be second wife. But she is simultaneously seen as victimized, begging the rabbi in futility.

HAREDIM IN HANDCUFFS

Haredim have also found their way into the crime and mystery genres as convenient suspects. In both Ayelet Waldman's *The Big Nap* (2001) and Harry Kemelman's *One Fine Day the Rabbi Bought a Cross* (1987), the haredi community is seen as suspicious, as if they are hiding something. *The Big Nap* concerns a missing haredi girl who happened to be the protagonist's babysitter; suspicion falls upon her father. Kemelman's novel examines a missing boy who joined a religious yeshiva and is mixed up in a murder case. In both cases, the original suspects turn out to be innocent, but the suspicion thrown upon them allows ample time for Waldman and Kemelman's less orthodox protagonists to describe what they don't like about the haredim.

"Parts," a 2005 episode of *Law and Order: Special Victims Unit* featured a young hasidic man who attacked and accidentally killed his girlfriend for being impure. He is shown as neurotic and obsessive-compulsive, and his religious fervor is seen as fuel for his mental illness. While he actually killed the woman, the true villains are depicted as the ones trafficking in body parts on the black market, those who profit from the murder. Even if the haredim are seen as "the bad guys," they are never "the worst guys."

A film that depicts haredim in a threatening light is *The Body* (2001) directed by Jonas McCord and based on a novel by late American-born Israeli author Richard Ben Sapir. The film stars Antonio Banderas as a priest who goes to Jerusalem for the purpose of identifying—or disproving the identity of—remains that may or may not be the body of Jesus. Of course, if they belong to Jesus, Christianity will be in tremendous danger. This investigation produces a subplot involving what is essentially a "gang" of hasidic Jews, who seem to exist in order to look sinister. They are involved in some intrigue over the archaeological dig. The haredim are seen as holding history captive. The secular Israeli character of Sharon Golban (played by Olivia Williams) gets to vent about their treatment of women. Darren Aronofsky's critically acclaimed *Pi* (1998) also featured a threatening group of hasidim, eager to exploit a young man's gifts. In all of these cases, the malevolent haredim are men.

Sidney Lumet's 1992 thriller *A Stranger Among Us*, a hasidic version of *Witness*, seems to be an exception to this pattern. In this "fish out of water" tale, a decidedly non-Jewish cop (Melanie Griffith) goes undercover to solve a murder in a hasidic community in Brooklyn. Her secular Jewish partner warns her that these people are crazy, that they have sex through a hole in a sheet, and are "a freaking embarrassment." However, the hasidim here are seen as a merry bunch; sepia-tinted scenes depict warm Shabbat dinners with a joyful soundtrack. It is Griffith—and her secular Jewish partner—who could learn a few things from this community. Despite the warmth in *A Stranger Among Us*, the movie follows the formula of the previously mentioned narratives; the killer is not hasidic—merely playacting at piety.

A 2007 best-seller by Pulitzer Prize–winning author Michael Chabon, *The Yiddish Policeman's Union* is detective fiction that goes well beyond these other narratives in its exploration—and judgment—of the black hat world. *The Yiddish Policemen's Union* is an alternative historical novel, set in Sitka, Alaska, in late 2007. According to the narrative, the Israelis lost the 1948 Arab-Israeli War, and the modern State of Israel as we know it never came to exist. Instead, the U.S. temporarily allotted a territory in Alaska for the displaced Jews of Europe. Sitka has therefore emerged as a religio-culturally Jewish space, with Yiddish as the lingua franca of the territory. Chabon's novel opens on the eve of Reversion, when the territory will be returned to Alaskan control. Rumors, anxieties, and messianic fervor abound, and it is in this imagined time and place that Chabon sets his 1940s-style noir murder mystery.

Typical of the hard-boiled, Spillane-style crime novel, the story opens in a fleabag hotel with the discovery of a dead body. Meyer Landsman, the down-on-his-luck, alcoholic protagonist, is a detective who happens to live upstairs from the deceased. Upon investigation, the detective discovers that the murder victim was both a chess player and heroin addict (who tied off with tefillin while shooting up). Landsman considers this unorthodox finding and muses, " 'Now that I think about it, he had the look. Like maybe he used to be black hat. They take on a kind of a—I don't know. They look shorn.' "[44] This hunch leads the inquiry in a new direction, and, even in this made-up Jewish world, the reader learns that fear and distrust of the ultra-Orthodox looms large.

Landsman and his partner, Berko Shemets, travel to Verbov Island, populated by the insular Verbover hasidim and dominated by their cruel and powerful leader, the tenth Verbover Rebbe. Landsman feels disapproving and hostile eyes upon him from every angle. "He goes clean-shaven and does not tremble before God. He is not a Verbover Jew and therefore is not really a Jew at all. And if he is not a Jew, then he is nothing." Despite this fictional world of Sitka, his feelings echo those of many contemporary American Jews, readily admitting that "the truth is, black-hat Jews make Landsman angry, and they always have. He finds that it is a pleasurable anger, rich with layers of envy, condescension, resentment, and pity" (103). And it is with palpable pleasure that Chabon describes the black hats of Sitka.

While Chabon makes reference to real hasidic groups such as the Lubavitchers and the Bobovers, the Verbovers are a fictitious community with a dark past and even darker present.

> They started out, back in the Ukraine, black hats like all the other black hats, scorning and keeping their distance from the trash and hoo-hah of the secular world, inside their imaginary ghetto wall of ritual and faith. Then the entire sect was burned in the fires of the Destruction, down to a hard, dense core of something blacker than any hat.

Like many of the displaced Jews of Europe, the ninth Verbover Rebbe, along with eleven disciples and one daughter, came to Alaska and began to rebuild.

> [H]ere he found a way to remake the old-style black-hat detachment. He carried its logic to its logical end, the way evil geniuses do in cheap novels. He built a criminal empire that profited on the meaningless tohubohu beyond the theoretical walls, on beings so flawed, corrupted, and hopeless of redemption that only cosmic courtesy led the Verbovers to even consider them human at all. —(99)

Not only are these hasidim seen as insular and superior—the expected critiques of the haredim—but the Verbovers are actually a "criminal empire." Not merely hypocritical or a bit shady, they are criminal master-minds in the pulp tradition of Lex Luther and other comic supervillains.

And it is in this empire that Landsman sojourns in order to solve the murder of the chess-playing heroin addict, believed to be Mendel Shpilman, the son of the tenth Verbover Rebbe. Upon further investigation, Landsman and Shemets learn that Mendel was considered a spiritually gifted and sensitive young man, one who was widely believed to be the *Tzaddik Ha-Dor*, the "man with the potential to be Messiah [that] is born into every generation" (141). If that is not enough, the detectives learn that Mendel left the Verbovers because he was gay and the Verbovers could not possibly accept such a *tzaddik*. The marriage of the rebbe and his wife also falls under scrutiny as a partnership far from equal.

The rest of the novel delves into a conspiracy led by a group of militant Orthodox Jews dedicated to reclaiming the Temple Mount in Jerusalem and an American evangelical cabal preparing the world for the Second Coming of Jesus. With this plot, Chabon moves beyond his condemnation of haredi patriarchal and homophobic attitudes and reflects a progressive Jewish unease over the current odd alliances made by pro-Israel evangelicals and some right-wing Jews. Chabon's novel offers no safe harbor for his hasidim, no joyous Shabbat dinners, not even lip service to the virtues of mysticism or learning. Only Mendel and his mother receive sympathetic treatment, but this falls under the exemption of women and queers as "not quite" Jews. Mendel could have saved the world; he was the real thing, a *tzaddik*. It's a shame that the haredim were too narrow-minded to let him.

Chabon's narrative pointedly suggests a deliberate perversion of religion. Common among these narratives is one pious haredim who seems reasonable, in contrast to the hoards of religious fanatics who have gotten it wrong. *A Price Above Rubies* shows Mendel (despite his cluelessness) in a sympathetic light. In *Sotah*, Ragen is careful not to directly demonize Dina's first love, Abraham (the scholar). His family (standing in as the culpable haredi community) was to blame, but he is seen as weak and gutless for not standing up to them. Judah Gutman, Dina's husband, ultimately does stand up to the community.

Both Judah and Mendel Horowitz are good men, but both are weak and refuse to see problems with their wives. It is outside influence that forces them to act. This situation is true in *Kadosh* as well; the community's rabbi forces his son to leave his wife when she does not bear children. These stories do not purport to be completely antireligious because there is always at least one pure religious figure. The message is that everyone else has perverted the religion.

In the case of these anti-haredi writings, since the critics of the community are also Jews, there seems to be a blurring of insider/outsider identity. While not actually members of the communities they expose, there is a sense of ownership on the part of these critics, especially since some of the critics are Orthodox (e.g., Naomi Ragen). Contemporary "insider peeks" into the haredi lifestyle are influential in both informing and inflaming the Jewish culture war. Fictional narratives such as *A Price Above Rubies* or *Sotah* incite conversation and give viewers the sense that they know enough to be experts on the ultra-Orthodox community, that they know the "true" story. In the case of *Kadosh*, screened at many American film festivals, the subtitled film's Hebrew gave an additional aura of authenticity to American viewers. Of course, this community would be much more likely to be speaking Yiddish than Hebrew. Nonetheless, there is a sense of safety among non-haredi Jews: these writers feel confident critiquing a society that non-Jews would be unable to criticize without running the risk of being labeled anti-Semitic.

In Israel, where fear and distrust of the haredim runs rampant, this type of literature is quite common, often taking the shape of titillating exposés.[45] In addition to these themes in popular fiction, the emergence of a new theme within Israeli science fiction features a secular family trapped in a futuristic haredi-controlled state, which clearly reflects anxiety about the growing power of haredim in politics.[46] But what about anxiety in the United States? Why the panic? There is little likelihood that ultra-Orthodox Jews will ever have any tangible political power here given their small numbers.[47] Where their influence is felt is in the claim they have as bearers of tradition, defenders of the faith. The haredim see themselves, and are often seen by others, as passing on the same tradition that Moses received on Mount Sinai. Of course, no religious tradition lasts several thousands of years without serious changes, so this perception of authenticity is debatable.

Ironically, the appeal of the ultra-Orthodox is also the cause of the hostility that is so visible in these anti-haredi narratives. The haredim, by virtue of their "authentic" clothing and cocooned lifestyle, condemn non-haredi Jews to illegitimacy. What separates them is also what comes under attack from more liberal Jews. In *A Price Above Rubies*, Sender says to Sonia, "It is the quality of our sins that sets us apart." And what sets the haredim apart the most is their understanding of gender roles and the place of women.

The "Anchored Woman"

A 2004 *Law and Order* episode, "All in the Family," featured an Orthodox Jewish woman (played by Mercedes Ruehl) pushed to murder since her husband refused to give her a Jewish divorce, known as a *get*. While the trial prosecuted the woman, the nature of the crime ultimately painted the Orthodox man as the villain. *Law and Order*, famous for its "ripped from the headlines" plots, often reflects some public awareness. If it is on *L&O*, it has likely been in the news. The mid- to late 1990s saw much public outcry in the Jewish press regarding the issue of the *agunah*, literally an anchored woman. According to Jewish law, a man must give his wife a *get* in order for a divorce to be binding. If a woman remarries without the *get*, it will not be a legitimate marriage.[48] Progeny from that marriage are seen as *mamzerim*, bastards born in an adulterous relationship.[49] This designation prohibits the children's marriage to other Jews. Men may also be anchored if a woman refuses to produce a *get*, but this is far less frequent. Contemporary women's rights groups have pointed out the use of the *get* by abusive husbands for extortion purposes. Such men often punish their wives by pressuring them to remain in bad marriages, demanding large sums of money or insisting upon sole custody rights to children.

Faye Kellerman's *Sanctuary* (1995) features the married Orthodox detectives Pete Decker and Rina Lazarus and their investigation of the disappearances of Rina's childhood friend Honey and her children. The family had been visiting from a "Leibbener" hasidic village in New York, one presumably modeled after the Satmar village of Kiryas Joel. Honey comes to Rina, complaining of her diamond-dealer husband's increasingly odd, fanatical behavior. What Rina does not know is that Honey left town so that the community could place pressure onto the husband to produce a *get*. After Honey's disappearance, Rina and Peter get word that her husband has been murdered. Suspicion falls upon Honey. The couple pursues the case, finding that the death of Gershon Klein, Honey's husband, was the accidental result of a community exorcism designed to force him to release his wife from the marriage.

Women who are affected by the law of the *get* are mainly in the Orthodox movement, and even then primarily those within haredi communities. The Conservative movement has long suggested signing a prenuptial agreement called the Lieberman clause that automatically grants a Jewish divorce in the event of a civil one. The Jewish Orthodox Feminist Alliance has similar protection for those who choose to adopt it. The Reform movement has come under attack by some because it does away with the need for a *get* altogether.

Articles regarding this issue peppered the Jewish press in the 1990s, particularly local Jewish newspapers and national magazines such as *Tikkun* and *The Forward*. One particular case that embarrassed the Orthodox community dealt with child betrothal—the promising of an eleven-year-old girl to a man. This man's identity was kept a secret by the girl's father in a bitter custody case with his wife. Because the father refused to release the name of the future bridegroom there was no way to reverse the process—and therefore no hope for the girl to ever marry someone else.[50] While child betrothal is a rare and unacceptable occurrence, the affair brought to light a variety of Jewish divorce dramas. Not surprisingly, as a women's issue, the forum that featured the most publicity over the *agunah* issue was *Lilith*, a progressive, feminist magazine.[51] The politicized articles in *Lilith* called for action on the part of the Jewish community to provide more support for women in these situations. Other papers focused on the sensationalistic aspects of some of these cases.

Most religious movements have instituted gender differences and have asserted power over the expression of sexuality in some way. Most often—but not always—these restrictions or controls are placed on women. Some theories of gender attribute this relationship to biology; because women bear children, they will always be oppressed.[52] In the case of the *agunot*, men have a *halakhic* power over women, a power that sanctions restrictions on women's bodies and lives. The inherent inequity in the issue of Jewish divorce lends itself easily to embellishment and the captivity themes seen in this chapter's narratives. In *Rubies* and *Sotah*, a *get* is offered readily to Sonia and Dina, but their children are kept behind, demonstrating that women's importance lies primarily in their ability to produce babies for the community. Wives are replaceable, but not children.

If You Don't Watch Out, You'll End Up Just Like Her

Sonia disregarded her brother's warning about Baba Yitta, and her standing in the community was changed forever. Regardless of whether these fictional accounts accurately reflect the communities described, their subjective and prejudicial interpretation is what is important. *Sotah* and *A Price Above Rubies* both purport to offer a peek inside a traditional community. The bias of the authors is evident and therefore useful in our attempt to look at the gender construction of the narratives. The feminized Jewish male is ultimately portrayed as an unattractive, unfulfilling character, while the rugged, individualistic, independent provider is the hero. In one scene the hunky Ramon says to Sonia, "Walls got to be broke down so you can see what they've been hiding inside all along." By breaking down the walls of Yakin's (and others') imaginings of haredi life, we can begin to see the reflection of non-Orthodox anxieties about gender and religious authority implicit in these archetypes. While these works depict the suffering, oppression, and repression of women, their true aim is to claim the soul of contemporary Jewry. By rescuing the woman from captivity, the soul of the community itself is rescued. The underlying message is that *we* (the representers) are enlightened. *We* (those of us doing the exposing) are the *real* Jews. These works reflect the ongoing culture war over who represents the authentic spirit of today's Judaism. It is what these representations of the haredim tell us about the author, rather than what they disclose about the actual subject, that is significant.

Defector or apostate literature can provide "smoking gun" evidence against a group.[53] These apostates claim a certain credibility which often is fabricated, or at the very least, exaggerated. Writers profess membership in order to authenticate their authority. Naomi Ragen is such a writer; her biography demonstrates her early fascination with the ultra-Orthodox and her later disillusionment with them. The credibility given to her novels comes from the public knowledge that she "once lived among them." While this may be true, she was not raised in the community, and she also chose to leave. She writes:

> It's true that all of my books are based in some way on fact—I never wrote about something completely imagined. It was based on people I know, or something I read about in the newspaper. But what you can do with autobiographical material is to get as close to possible to some kind of truth that is impossible when you try to put yourself in another person's shoes.[54]

It's possible that her books are more rooted in reality than even she indicates. Plagiarism charges were leveled against Ragen in 2007 by a haredi woman who claimed that elements of *Sotah* were taken from her published diary.[55] This is the second such charge against Ragen; the first came from the Israeli novelist Michal Tal, who claimed that Ragen's *The Ghost of Hannah Mendes* was plagiarized from Tal's *The Lion and the Cross*. Ragen denies both charges.

Ragen further denies that she is biased against the haredim despite the abuse within the ultra-Orthodox world highlighted in her novels.

> I think that my books are very sympathetic to the ultra-Orthodox community. The bad things I say about them are all true, but I don't present an unbalanced picture. . . . The books that I wrote [after my experience in the community] that show both sides of that world came from perhaps a sense of surprise that those early positive experiences of that world were not the only side of that

community, that it had a darker side as well . . . and it's important
to show both sides as a writer.[56]

Ragen has written and spoken publicly about her disappointment with
the increasing rigidity of the Israeli haredi world. In January 2007,
Ragen joined a group of women in filing suit against the Israeli Egged
bus company. Since 1977, there have been voluntarily segregated public
bus lines that service haredi neighborhoods (these bus lines are called
mehadrin). In recent years, complaints of harassment of women who
refuse to comply have increased. In the fall of 2007, news was made of
the physical assault of a religious woman on an Egged bus by a group of
haredi men because she refused to move to the back of the bus.[57]

For writers and directors such as Naomi Ragen and Boaz Yakin, their
work is a form of activism. By passively reading or viewing these narratives of Jewish women in danger, we as readers are actively involved
in a means of judgment and salvation. Ragen and Yakin present black
and white worlds, ones with obvious villains, devoid of any ambivalence.[58] *Sotah* and *A Price Above Rubies* employ the trope of hypocritical haredim who cloak their deviance in religious robes. In a way, these
narratives serve as a means of reverse proselytism, a defense created
in order to counteract the religious outreach of Orthodox groups like
Chabad and Or Sameach.[59] Employing the same sorts of motifs found
in anti-cult literature—specifically the gothic myth—these stories
exploit societal fears. By describing a world dangerous for and abusive
to women, as well as perpetuating these archetypes (and stereotypes)
of ultra-Orthodox men and women, narratives such as *Sotah* and *A
Price Above Rubies* serve the same purpose as nineteenth-century anti-
Catholic tales and any other propagandistic narratives written in times
of cultural contestation. They even serve the same purpose as Yossi's
tale of Baba Yitta. They serve as a warning.

4

MUGGERS *in* BLACK COATS

In hushed phone conversations this past week, they had compared
whose children returned from Israel the greater strangers. Everyone
was afflicted with this new malady, this fierce, fervent virus. And
they, the parents, couldn't figure out how to treat it. —Tova Mirvis,
The Outside World

THE VIRUS

America has long been touted as a land of great opportunity,
a place where class can be transcended and anything can be
achieved. Given these convictions, parents want to present America
as an exciting array of possibilities: their children can have anything,
be anything, as long as that "anything" conforms to certain middle-
class, professional aspirations. But some kids have surveyed the buffet
laid out for them and concluded that it's not to their liking, and their
parents don't know how to react. This chapter addresses the literary
evidence of American Jewish anxiety over the growing visibility of the
haredim, particularly within their own families. Parental fears regarding the captivity of their children by ultra-Orthodox groups mirror the
greater anxiety over the nature of American Judaism as a whole being
held captive by these bearers of authentic Jewish tradition. Despite sta-
tistics that show that Orthodoxy's numbers have declined in America,
Orthodoxy in its current incarnation is a confident, fervent entity, one
made more visible by its ranks of newly Orthodox Jews.

The concern over what this chapter's epigraph describes as a "virus,"
the embrace of a rigid, traditional lifestyle, manifests itself in narratives
that often feature motifs of brainwashing and kidnapping. By drawing
primarily upon two novels, written two decades apart, I will examine

these themes, which are predicated upon two communal fears: the fear that haredim will seduce, kidnap, or brainwash nonobservant Jewish children, forcing them to follow orthodox doctrine; and the fear that this converted generation of haredim will be the next dominant wave of American Jewry. According to this anxious logic, these converts will serve as the converters of American Judaism as a whole to a faith more orthodox than their parents intended. Additionally, this haredization would effectively undo efforts Jews have made toward becoming comfortable within the American mainstream.

The first novel, Anne Roiphe's *Lovingkindness* (1987), shows the growing rift between secular and Orthodox Judaism, and the second, Tova Mirvis's *The Outside World* (2004) shows the emergent schism within orthodoxy itself. Both are about parents whose children reject the American Jewish lifestyle in which they were raised; both are primarily set in New York yet feature Israel as the seductive and threatening location of their children's conversion; and both accentuate an American Jewish fear of takeover by an ultra-Orthodox lifestyle yet display an ambivalence toward an outright rejection of ultra-Orthodoxy.

Lovingkindness is one of the first Jewish American novels to engage intellectually with Israel and the ultra-Orthodox. Demonstrating the ambiguity and ambivalence that many liberal Jews feel about both Israel and the haredim, *Lovingkindness* features a mother and daughter, Annie and Andrea Johnson. Annie is a professional woman, an intellectual, and a feminist, and Andrea is the result of a sad marriage with a non-Jewish poet who died while Annie was pregnant. Annie, while Jewish, embraces her identity as a liberal one. Her parents were not religious; in fact, they found the remnants of the religiosity her grandfather brought from Europe somewhat embarrassing. Andrea, her daughter, has been a troubled child who experimented with drugs, had countless abortions, and had even more failed relationships. She was supposed to be the successful child of the feminist era. Instead, she is fragile, sad, and aimless. Told mainly in epistolary form, *Lovingkindness* is the story of Andrea's joining a religious women's yeshiva in Israel and her mother's struggle to accept that her once free Andrea would choose a rigid structure in which to live her life over the choices Annie gave her. Upon hearing of her daughter's new lifestyle, Annie muses:

> I was always waiting for some definitive end-of-the-line call. We've found your daughter in a ravine outside of Las Vegas with her throat cut, we've found your daughter dead of an overdose in a pickup truck with a Hell's Angel, we've found your daughter naked hallucinating on the L.A. freeway. I had anticipated a lot of phone calls. I had not thought of the Yeshiva Rachel.[1]

As Blanche d'Alpuget writes in her favorable review of the book: " 'Lovingkindness' is an argument between Lucifer and God—or, for those as squeamish about religion as Annie is, between Reason and Faith. And it is the argument of a secular Jew for her soul."[2] The title of the work itself echoes an ancient debate over religious observance: "I desire acts of lovingkindness, not sacrifice; Obedience to God and not burnt offerings" (Hosea 6:6). *Lovingkindness* marks the beginning of a literary argument for the soul of American Jewry, one that insists that the spirit of the Jewish people is not to be found behind yeshiva walls but engaged lovingly in the world.

This argument is not only between liberalism and traditional societal formations. While much of this cultural tension has taken place between the liberal branches of Judaism (such as Reform and Conservative Judaism) and ultra-Orthodoxy, Modern Orthodoxy has felt the strong pull to the right as well, leaving many Jews who identify as observant feeling left out in the cold. Even the term "Modern Orthodox"—once a point of pride—has fallen out of vogue and is seen in a pejorative light. This shift to the right among much of the leadership has led to Yeshiva University president Rabbi Norman Lamm adopting the more acceptable title "Centrist Orthodoxy."[3]

The Outside World features two families: the Goldmans, who reside in an ultra-Orthodox neighborhood in Brooklyn, and the Millers, who are part of a modern Centrist Orthodox community in northern New Jersey.[4] Tzippy Goldman finds herself rebelling against what she sees as the strictures of her lifestyle, and Bryan Miller simultaneously rejects what he sees as the leniency and hypocrisy of his parents' religious practice. Tzippy leaves to study in a women's yeshiva in Jerusalem in order to escape the pressure of countless failed *shiduch* dates (match dates set up by a third party). Bryan has attended a year in yeshiva before starting at Columbia. As is common in the world of the yeshiva, he begs his parents to stay for another year. He then returns home after his second year to announce that his parents' house is not kosher enough and that he will not be attending Columbia at all.

Such an announcement comes as a blow to parents who felt that they were observant Jews who had given their children the best possible balance of both worlds. Mirvis writes:

> In Laurelwood, they thought they had successfully combined tradition with modernity. They lived their lives on the seam of this compromise. Like Orthodox Jews anywhere in the world, they spent Saturday at shul, praying to God. Like suburbanites in any other neighborhood in New Jersey, they woke up on Sunday and loaded their kids into minivans. They went to Little League games and stopped for pizza on the way home. Here, they didn't have to choose. They belonged to state-of-the-art health clubs. They ate kosher sushi. They had no problem with interdenominational dialogue or R-rated movies. They didn't feel the need for the added strictures of separate seating at weddings. They believed it was necessary and valuable to be involved in the secular world. They managed to find space for the modern, and possibly problematic, concepts of pluralism and multiplicity of interpretation.[5]

These Orthodox Jews are living the original dream of Modern Orthodoxy. They—like the haredim—are Torah-true Jews, keepers of the commandments, but unlike the haredim they have created an America where they can be engaged with all that modernity has to offer. But this way of life becomes increasingly unacceptable for some of Laurelwood's children, who see this lifestyle as compromising, hypocritical, and even transgressive. Haym Soloveitchik writes of this growing phenomenon: "A new generation has emerged which finds the past ways of its parents and grandparents too unthinking, too ignorant, and yes, if truth be told, simply too lax and accommodative."[6] This attitude reflects the haredi derision for Modern Orthodox Jews as merely "rule followers"[7] or worse, as "fakers" with "no feeling, no heart."[8]

Bryan and Tzippy find each other on parallel journeys to and from tradition. While Tzippy's parents experience their own struggles, it is Joel and Naomi Miller who prove most introspective and ambivalent over their son's transformation. Bryan's new religious commitment forces them to explore their own religious convictions and identity. In both *Lovingkindness* and *The Outside World*, American Jewish parents confront their personal distaste for and embarrassment by the religious right. Rather than admit that their children are rejecting their liberal lifestyles for a purposely restrictive one, these parents imagine scenarios that include mind control and captivity to explain their children's behavior. Part of what is remarkable about Mirvis's tale is how unremarkable a story it is among families formerly known as Modern Orthodox. *The Outside World* indicates that it is not only secularists who are afraid that the ultra-Orthodox are stealing their kids. Even if your kitchen is kosher, it might not be kosher enough for your own children.

I Have Changed My Name

In *Lovingkindness* and *The Outside World*, respectively, Andrea and Bryan announce to their parents that they are now going by different names. Both announcements are received heatedly and serve to reinforce the parents' beliefs that their children have been brainwashed. For whatever reason, we tend to believe that names say something about people, and so parents choose names with meanings they hope will grow to be part of their child's identity, especially when they name them after someone loved or respected. For a child to reject his or her name is to reject the first gift given by a parent.

Despite the hurt inherent in this choice, changing names has a long tradition among the Jewish people. In biblical literature, the first to do so were Abraham and Sarah (originally Abram and Sarai), and two generations later Jacob became known as Israel after wrestling with the angel. In the Bible, name changing occurs when one's life is touched by God and subsequently altered. There are Jews who still change their names in this way, sometimes after an illness or to indicate a new relationship with Judaism. In Philip Roth's *The Counterlife*, Henry changes his name to Hanoch when he abandons his family, moves to Israel, and joins a right-wing religious community in the West Bank. Tova Reich's novels *Master of the Return* and *The Jewish War* feature large casts of characters, all secular Americans who have embraced ultra-Orthodoxy and changed their names (i.e. Jerry Goldberg becomes Yehudi HaGoel). Allegra Goodman's 2005 short story "Long-Distance Client" features a man, Mel, whose wife becomes increasingly involved with a local proselytizing Bialystocker hasidic group. To his dismay, Mel's wife tells him that she wants to be called by her Hebrew name, Basha, instead of Barbara. " 'I'm not a barbarian,' " she insists.[9] Ironically, American Jews often changed their names in the past in order to acculturate, to sound *less* Jewish. Shortening names, doing away with the tell-tale Stein or Berg, was a way to become more American. What Bryan and Andrea are doing, along with Henry, Jerry, Barbara, and a new generation of Jews, reverses that sort of acculturation.

Annie Johnson receives the news of Andrea's new name through the mail. Having accepted a collect phone call from Israel and feeling that her daughter sounded much changed, she wrote to Andrea at the yeshiva, questioning the new direction in which she seemed to be heading. She subsequently received the following letter from Andrea:

> Dear Mother,
>
> Please call me Sarai, I have changed my name to one in keeping with my new life. I will not answer or read any letters addressed to Andrea. I honor you, of course.
>
> Love, Sarai
>
> (Roiphe, *Lovingkindness*, 15–16)

Paradoxically for Annie, the sentence "I honor you"—which Andrea also used in her phone call—gives her chills. This young woman is not the daughter she knew. Sadly, Annie believes that the respectful tone with which Andrea has addressed her is a sign of trouble. It is almost as if she would find it preferable that someone found Andrea dead "in a ravine outside of Las Vegas." This new person, this "Sarai," is troubling.

In the upcoming weeks, she begins corresponding both with Rabbi Cohen and her daughter, trying to reconcile this image of Sarai with the Andrea she knew. Not having seen her daughter since her transformation, Annie seems frantic to prove that she still exists. Annie sees her daughter's choice of the Yeshiva Rachel as a result of "programming" and "blatant manipulation" (83).

Not surprisingly, the choice of the name Sarai is significant. According to a letter from Rabbi Cohen at the Yeshiva Rachel, this name was chosen for Andrea because the biblical Sarai (later known as Sarah) was the mother of the Jewish people. And, he adds, Andrea was in much need of mothering when she arrived at the yeshiva. Annie Johnson takes this news personally.

> Andrea had been the name I had selected sometime in the fourth month of pregnancy. . . . Andrea was a name to imagine with, not like Sarah, which reminded of barren old ladies whose desires were granted too late to bring real satisfaction, a bitter old lady who banished her rival and the child of her rival. Sarah was the name of the matriarch whose namesakes darted through the landscapes of the Ukraine gasping for air. I wanted my daughter to have a name that wouldn't hint at limit or confinement. (16)

For Annie, biblical names are limiting. Like those Jews who changed their names to better acculturate, Annie gave her daughter a name that in her perception offered no limits, only possibilities.

Leora, the protagonist of Dara Horn's novel *In The Image* (2002), invokes the biblical book of Ezekiel and imagines a "valley" of such discarded names: "Perhaps there was a place somewhere where all the unused names were gathered, a giant dried-out desert valley where the names, shriveled and lifeless, lay at the bottom." Her boyfriend, Jason, had embraced hasidic Judaism and accordingly changed his name. "Leorah knew that Yehudah was a dried-out name, one that Jason had found at the bottom of that valley and that he wanted to speak back to life."[10] With Andrea's new name, she is likewise speaking back to life an earlier time and place, one that Annie has no interest in visiting.

But it is this time and place that Rabbi Cohen offers Andrea/Sarai. It is a place that Annie's parents rejected and one that she has no first- or even second-hand knowledge of. Joseph Soloveitchik, founder of Boston's Modern Orthodox Maimonides School, explained that the child should see his parent as a teacher but also that "the teacher of the child is [as] his parent."[11] In the absence of parental religious authority, the teachers become invaluable. Not only does Rabbi Cohen imply in his letter that Annie has been a bad mother, but he has also taken from Andrea the name with which her mother spent so much time dreaming and replaced it with the name of a woman whose story Annie finds deeply troubling. In a way, with this name change Cohen has actually taken Andrea from her; he is as her parent.

Bryan's name change is different. He does not reject a given name by his parents, yet he manages to leave them feeling rejected. He merely announces that he wants to be known as Baruch, his Hebrew name. In "Long-Distance Client," Barbara—now Basha—invites her rabbi to her home. While at the house, the rabbi calls Basha's husband, Mel, by the name Mordechai:

> "Who's Mordechai?" Mel asked, bewildered. Then he realized that the Rabbi had called him by his Hebrew name. A searing flame swept up his left side. Barbara must have told the Rabbi. He felt utterly exposed. Betrayed. His Hebrew name was like his parents' living room, a place no one entered except for weddings and funerals. His Hebrew name was his mother's white sofa; it was her silver tea set on the sideboard, garish and grandiose, mummified in plastic wrap, never tarnished and never used.[12]

Among Jews in the diaspora, common practice is to give two names, one an official name that is recognizable in the land in which they live, and a second unofficial name that is called a Hebrew name. This name is often biblical, although more and more Jews are giving their children nonbiblical Israeli names as well. This Hebrew name is usually only used in Jewish rituals such as a bar or bat mitzvah or marriage ceremony. In an interesting reversal, Allegra Goodman's 1999 novel *Kaaterskill Falls*, about an ultra-Orthodox community that summers in upstate New York, features protagonist Elizabeth Schulman who officially names all of her daughters after English literary heroines, sadly knowing that they will never go by these names, only by the Yiddish versions of their Hebrew names.[13]

In *The Outside World*, Bryan/Baruch's parents, Naomi and Joel, react to his choice to be known as Baruch much as Mel responds to the rabbi's easy use of Mordechai.

> He wanted to use his Hebrew name, Baruch, which they had given him in memory of Joel's grandfather. But they had never intended it for use in the outside world. Because Baruch carried with it the dreaded *ch*, the modern-day shibboleth. As in Chana and Chaviva and Yechiel. Chaim, Nechama, Zacharyah, and Achiezer. Not a *Ch* as in Charlie, not a *Sh* as in Shirley, but a guttural sound that came from the back of those throats that had been trained to utter it from birth. —(Mirvis, *The Outside World*, 27)

This choice of name is not a rejection of his parents; after all, *they* had given him his name. It is a reclaiming of something his parents had not wanted for him. By no means are the Millers ashamed of being Jewish; they sent their kids to Orthodox day schools (which were meant to prep their students for the Ivy League). They also sent Bryan to yeshiva in Israel, since all his classmates did the same. But they wanted their son, Bryan Miller, to be both proud of his heritage and successful in something secular. They were not prepared to have a son, Baruch Miller, who studied Jewish texts in yeshiva indefinitely.

For secular Israelis, those haredim who spend a large portion of their lives in yeshiva are shirking responsibility, not to mention being an economic drain on the country. For Americans, it means to be locked away somewhere foreign (much like a convent). Either way, this counter-acculturation is a defiant rejection of all that the Millers have built in Laurelwood. Baruch perceives that this name puts him more in step with the black hat world he embraces. Additionally, his parents' objections only serve to fuel his strong belief in the hypocrisy of their chosen lifestyles.

JEWS AND THE ANTI-CULT MOVEMENT

The zeal with which the *ba'al teshuvah* approaches his new life-style is not unlike any other conversion, where the new convert might tend to overdo religious obligations in order to prove his allegiance.[14] This commitment to following even the finest points of doctrine can be jarring to those around them. Baruch's parents watch and wonder:

> They thought his fervor was the result of his age, the kind of certitude only a nineteen-year-old could muster. They had seen their friends' children pass through this stage of fervent religiosity. They had heard stories about children who came home from Israel and carted off all the dishes in the house to be dunked in the local mikvah. If they could, these children would kidnap their parents and dunk them too. They rattled off every commandment their parents overlooked, eager to let them know why they and all their friends were hypocrites. And these were the more pliant children. Others refused to set foot back on American soil. The only way they would leave Israel was kicking and screaming.
>
> (Mirvis, *The Outside World*, 27)

Within the haredi world, religious leaders hold great influence with *ba'alei teshuvah*, and almost every decision can be prefaced with, "The rabbi (or rebbe) says." This literal adherence can be interpreted by others as a form of mind control, particularly when the behavior seems out of character for the newly religious person. For many American Jews, haredi communities began to be seen in the same (negative) light as various new religious movements that gained popularity with elite counterculture youth. Particularly in detective fiction—such as Harry Kemelman's and Faye Kellerman's work, discussed in the previous chapter—yeshivas (specifically Israeli yeshivas) are seen as repositories for wayward American youth. This disapproving feeling is not restricted to parents of *ba'alei teshuvah*. While non-Jews tend to be curious about the movement, other Jews feel threatened and somewhat hostile.[15]

In his study of *ba'alei teshuvah*, M. Herbert Danzger writes:

While the mass media focused on the cultists, the Jesus freaks, the followers of Moon, and the Children of God, the Jewish media focused on the ba'alei t'shuva. It became clear that the newly Orthodox were not simply "people already committed but lacking background"; they were trying out and testing a new commitment. Media attention to these newly Orthodox therefore reframed the phenomenon and for the first time questions began to be raised as how to deal with people who choose to become Orthodox.[16]

It should be noted that *ba'alei teshuva* exist outside of the Orthodox world. Both Reform and Conservative families may see a similar zealous recommitment to Judaism (albeit a more progressive strain) from their children after Jewish summer camp or Israel teen-tour experiences. While comparable family dynamics may exist, attention is more focused on those children who choose to be Orthodox because of what is seen as an extreme conversion.

"Brainwashing" as an explanation for why people convert was one response to this phenomenon of mainstream youth who join alternative movements. The late 1970s and early 1980s saw a rampant fear of cult activity in America, expressed mainly in the media. While there had been mistrust of "different" or "new" religious movements in the past, the events at Jonestown magnified the alleged danger of such groups. Members of Jim Jones's religious organization, the People's Temple, settled a commune in Guyana, called Jonestown. In 1978, Jones initiated a mass suicide where 913 people died, including himself, most by drinking poisoned Kool-Aid. This event propelled the cult scare into a national emergency. Anti-cult literature and after-school specials were geared toward both parents and children.[17] Deprogrammers became popular, as they were deemed necessary to undo the brainwashing that converts to these so-called cults had experienced. While deprogrammers and anti-cult activists were not new, they received much more sympathy and a new level of credibility with the public after Jonestown.[18]

The majority of sociologists and scholars of religion dismiss brainwashing as a factor in conversions to new religious movements. Brainwashing "rests on an assumption that the beliefs and/or behavior of certain individuals are the result of their having had their freedom removed."[19] The sociologist David Bromley has stated that "brainwashing" versus conversion "is a case of competing political narratives," narratives connected with agency.[20] Conversion is an active pursuit on the part of the convert, while brainwashing connotes a passive behavior. The idea of brainwashing also serves to perpetuate a stigma toward religious nonconformists. Regardless of whether or not brainwashing actually exists, many parents who claim to have lost children to overzealous religiosity believe that their children have been "brainwashed" or even kidnapped.

The dangers of separatist new religious movements appeared to be proven again during the 1993 ATF siege in Waco, Texas, which led to the deaths of seventy-six Branch Davidians, members of an apocalyptic Christian sect. Four years later, a highly publicized mass suicide in San Diego of thirty-nine members of the religious movement Heaven's Gate demonstrated again the possible outcomes of such nonconformist religious beliefs. Each disturbing episode—as thrashed out in the media—suggested the coercive tactics of and possible brainwashing by charismatic leaders of the movements. These events, in addition to heightening discomfort with such unorthodox movements, provided a vocabulary for discussing unpopular religious movements. For the purposes of the narratives analyzed here, brainwashing functions as a rhetorical trope, an effective metaphor that demonstrates a communal anxiety.

Tova Reich's 1995 novel *The Jewish War*, about a group of American *ba'alei teshuvah* who move to the contested region of Hebron, features numerous allusions to Jonestown, as well as to Masada (a famous historical case of zealous Jewish mass suicide). The title of the novel references narrative of the same name by the first-century Jewish historian Josephus, a contested work that describes the events at Masada. Reich describes the "cult"-like attributes of these extremist groups in a manner that evokes both Jonestown and Waco but does not claim that these folks were unfairly recruited. Reich's "fanatics" are there because they are believers. She gives them the autonomy that "brainwashing" removes. However, the male leaders' treatment of their own children (and their own women) is seen as deplorable. Toward the end of *The Jewish War*, the leaders of the commune allow their children to entertain themselves by playing "Holocaust" as well as calling for the followers to "Choose Death" in a recreation of Masada or Jim Jones's White Night. Her story, as one might imagine, does not end well.

In Reich's earlier work *Master of the Return*, children are *literally* carried away by the ultra-Orthodox. While the parents in *Lovingkindness* and *The Outside World* display an ambivalence about the "loss" of their children, in *Master of the Return*, the kidnapping is real, the captors—ultra-Orthodox Jews—are seen as crazed fanatics. Noah Efron's *Real Jews* quotes an Israeli on the "anxiety about ultra-Orthodox snatching children . . . my neighbors are completely terrified of it."[21] In Roth's *The Counterlife*, the protagonist, Nathan Zuckerman, sees his grown brother, Henry (now Hanoch), to have been kidnapped by religious zealots in Israel. In addition, Henry's wife fears that her "suburban husband who turned himself into a born again Jew" will take her children to the foreign world he has embraced. She goes on to say that Henry's conversion is "like having a child become a Moonie," likening the ultra-Orthodox to a group popularly considered to be a "cult."[22] This fear of the active *taking* of children, not of their recruitment, raises a question: How are children—or in reality in most of these cases, young adults—taken? Is it the physical removal of these kids from their parents, the mental and emotional distance, or a combination of the two that is the danger? In *Lovingkindness*, the geographical distance between Annie and Sarai at the beginning of the novel allows for the imagining of a physical kidnapping, whereas Baruch Miller stands in his parents' kitchen and yet in their view he might as well be halfway around the world and in another civilization. Annie of *Lovingkindness* remarks, "I'm not sure what to do. I feel like someone has handed me a ransom note and I don't have the money to redeem even the cold body" (Roiphe, *Lovingkindness*, 114). It is language like this that implies that their children—as they once knew them—are now dead.

Lovingkindness and *The Outside World* demonstrate a Jewish discomfort with overt religiosity both from a secular feminist perspective and from a liberal, Modern Orthodox perspective. Both narratives imagine manipulative captors who keep the children from fulfilling their potential. Both narratives point to the fears of parents who imagine their children being held captive, possibly to be sacrificed—like Isaac in the Akedah—for a holy war in which they do not believe. And both narratives describe the way these children are captivated by the haredi life.

The kidnapping theme prevalent in these novels, as well as in others of this time period, is thick with descriptive imagery specifically identifying the captors as haredim—men in black hats and coats. Stories of religious folk kidnapping innocents and forcing faith on them are not new. Like earlier captivity narratives featuring Indians, Catholics, and Mormons as villainous captors, these narratives demonstrate anxiety over an alien culture encroaching on the dominant one. This visible increase in anxiety corresponds with the growing concern regarding the shift to the right of American Judaism—specifically within Orthodoxy—and it manifests itself in tales of manipulative rabbis in seductive locales who prey on the mistakes and inadequacies of parents. In *Lovingkindness*, Annie writes to Rabbi Cohen: "You have my daughter captive. I believe that in time I will give her a full life in which she will not need to cower under the tent of nomads who could not convince their God to let them stay unmolested in or out of the Promised Land" (82). Annie sees this devout, legalistic form of Judaism as both foreign and threatening.

While these fictional accounts of parental anxiety over the possible kidnapping and brainwashing of their children by men in black hats and coats may seem irrational, the media was telling the public otherwise. Like earlier fears about the International Society for Krishna Consciousness or the Unification Church (popularly known as Hare Krishnas and the "Moonies"), there were stories of "abductions" and "forced" conversions that could be found in both the Jewish and mainstream press. Stories such as these helped raise the anxiety levels among Jewish parents.

If You Don't Want Your Child to Be Religious, I Have the Right to Take Him Away from You

The early 1990s saw a widely publicized and contested instance of kidnapping. The case was followed closely in the Jewish press, but it also garnered much attention in the mainstream press. A LexisNexis search produced more than two hundred articles, including thirteen full-length articles in the *New York Times* following the growing melodrama. In 1992, thirteen-year-old Shai Fhima's mother and stepfather (non-religious Jews) approached Rabbi Helbrans from the hasidic yeshiva Lev Tahor (Pure Heart) in New York and asked him to tutor their son for his bar mitzvah. Shai was drawn to the hasidic lifestyle and wanted to spend more time at the yeshiva. His parents forbade him, and one day he disappeared in the company of a hasidic friend. His parents insisted that he had been kidnapped by Rabbi Helbrans, who would not produce the boy.

Shai resurfaced almost two years later during Helbrans's trial, claiming that he had left his home to escape abuse and because his mother "was not religious."[23] At that time, Shai asked that an Orthodox rabbi from Rockland County—Arye Zaks—be appointed as guardian. Complicating the case was the petition for custody by his father, Michael Reuven, who resided in Arad, Israel. While his parents and legal representatives attempted to figure out the best custodial situation for Shai, negotiations that included his continuing religious education, Shai was living temporarily with a religious family. Several months later, Shai disappeared again.

Rabbi Helbrans was ultimately charged with kidnapping. Despite Shai's earlier testimony that he had not been kidnapped, the jury found Rabbi Helbrans guilty and sentenced him to twenty-five years in prison (he was released after serving two years). In the months leading up to and during the trial, a flurry of articles brought attention to the ongoing case. Headlines such as "Kidnapped or Converted?" "Mother Tells of Pressures on Jewish Son by a Rabbi," and "The Rabbi and the Runaway" served to influence public opinion.[24]

Hana Fhima was repeatedly quoted, saying "I believe the rabbi brain-washed him."[25] Ms. Fhima also reported that the rabbi had said to her, "If you don't want your child to be religious, I have the right to take him away from you."[26] The police were quoted claiming that the case "is just one of a series of reported abductions linked to the rabbi and his yeshiva."[27]

The Jewish press speculated greatly on the way this case affected the Jewish community. The underlying tone of this coverage was one of warning. In Boston's *Jewish Advocate*, Jonathan Mark explored the current culture war in "Kidnapping Trial in NY: A Battle over Jewish Souls." Mark quoted Professor Samuel Heilman, a sociologist well-known for his work on the ultra-Orthodox, as saying, "this happens in Israel a lot . . . because they are fighting over souls." Mark added that this battle is over both the individual and national soul:

> With Helbrans under arrest, and his tactics now disowned by the Satmar and haredi communities, many observers explained that while the haredim may be winning recent skirmishes within the Orthodox domain, they may be in retreat and losing the ultimate battle for the Jewish soul: After all, they say, the major question is not only why that community cannot produce the missing Shai Fhima, but how they could produce someone such as Rabbi Shlomo Helbrans in the first place.[28]

Reporting for the Jewish Telegraphic Agency, Debra Nussbaum Cohen observed that this case brought up the complicated feelings many Jewish families have over *ba'alei teshuva*.

> The fervently Orthodox community has a mystique about it which non-religious Jews find alluring at times, said observers.
>
> 'It is a world which clearly tells you what is right and what is wrong, and at a time of confusion tells you what to do,' said Esther Perel, a psychologist in New York, who is not fervently Orthodox but who has clients who are, including some who are newly religious.
>
> 'It has the allure of unconditional acceptance for people who often do not feel at home in their own home or integrated into their own family,' said Perel. This is especially true, she said, when there is an emotionally turbulent home environment.

According to Perel, cases of a child being kidnapped from a secular family and brought to a fervently Orthodox community 'are not uncommon story.'[29]

Given his young age, Shai Fhima was certainly no ordinary *ba'al teshuvah*. Nussbaum Cohen's article demonstrates the appeal of the haredi lifestyle but warns that beneath the charm, these folks are dangerous. Additionally, her report gives the impression that these kidnappings of secular youths happen *all* the time.

In the *New York Jewish Week*, Michael Lesher argued that "the setting of Rabbi Helbrans' Story—with its charismatic clergyman and its youth turned fundamentalist—was quintessentially American. But that's exactly why American Jews ought to give Rabbi Helbrans' story more thought: In these days of instability and religious revival, something like it could easily happen again." Within his cautionary tale, he explained the two perspectives on the case.

First there is the right-wing Orthodox view. In this parable, Shai is the religiously orphaned child afloat in the shipwreck of assimilated American Judaism. Rabbi Helbrans is the hero who tried to save him; the American courts (which condemned him) are engines of the sort of anti-Semitism, a repression of Jewish tradition under the bulldozer of secularism.

The contrary view, held by most non-Orthodox Jews who have written about the case, casts it as a contest between the rights of parents and the rights of missionaries. This may sound like a political story, but it in fact touches on many a parents' personal nightmare: a stranger, deranged by dogma, persuading an impressionable child that his parents are sinners.

Rabbi Helbrans here is a predatory ideologue; Shai is his dupe. And Hana Fhima is a double victim—of religious slander and of the worst of thefts.[30]

While irreconcilable stories are regular features of custody disputes, the Fhima case was no conventional case. Both sides were trying to "save" the boy, with one party concerned about Shai's soul and the other concerned about his life.

Public fascination with these sorts of custody cases allow for a close look at communal values and fears. In January 2008, an episode of *Law and Order: Special Victims Unit* featured a strikingly similar plot to the Fhima/Helbrans case from fifteen years earlier. Entitled "Unorthodox," the episode begins with a child rape victim, David. While interviewing the boy's mother, Rachel, the detectives learn that the parents are estranged; Rachel describes her ex-husband Avi as having become "a zealot" who "got caught up with some crazy stuff . . . religion." After interviewing the father—whose beard and side curls are amazingly long for one who just embraced religion—suspicion falls upon the boy's bar mitzvah tutor. The detectives visit the yeshiva and receive little help from the rebbe and his cohort. Detective Munch (the Jewish cop) knowingly explains to Detective Stabler that the hasidim harbor a "suspicion of secular authorities: they close ranks around the accused." Stabler compares the situation to scandals in the Catholic Church, where pedophile priests were moved instead of dismissed, calling it a "cover-up." It turns out that the tutor is no pedophile, and suddenly the news comes in that David has been kidnapped.

Rachel fears that the boy's father is taking him to Israel after the cops discover that Avi has forged her signature on a passport application, but his car has been spotted driving upstate. It turns out that they're going to a hasidic village named Kehilat Moshe (a carbon copy of the Satmar village Kiryas Joel, complete with Web site). Rachel spitefully relays that they have their own ambulance corps, police, and schools, and Munch (again knowingly) explains that they have the youngest median age in the state because every family has an average of six children. This information is useful because we now know that Kehilat Moshe is an easy place to hide a kid. Detective Fin says that the place "sounds like a cult," but Munch replies, "No, it's more like the Amish."

Munch and Stabler embark on a road trip to Kehilat Moshe and Rachel voice-overs:

> They're encouraged to procreate. . . . He wanted them to live a pure life away from the immoral influences of the outside world. They're extremely Orthodox, the women wear long skirts. They're separated from the men on the buses and in the shuls, many barely speak English, there are no cell phones, very few cars. They have no television, movies or magazines. They're totally sheltered.

After a skirmish with the Yiddish-speaking cops and a tumultuous yeshiva-hall scene, the detectives find the father who insists that he was following the rebbe who has taken the child. Munch and Stabler arrest the rebbe and return to the city. In an *L&O* twist, it turns out that David left willingly with the rebbe because the child is being abused by a classmate at his public school. The attorney of the rapist blames the media for putting too much sex on television. The case leads Munch to muse, "Maybe the Hasidim are on to something, unplugging their kids from modern life." In the end, the rebbe looks like a good guy, one who was looking out for the best interests of the child.

This episode, much like the crime stories discussed in the previous chapter, first lays suspicion on the haredim, allowing Rachel to describe the backwardness of the community before exonerating these men in beards and black coats. However, "Unorthodox" suggests fears of pedophilia, which tend to be rare in this anxious Jewish literature, perhaps reflecting more recent public concerns over Catholic priests molesting boys in their care. It is surprising that this is not a more popular feature of these sorts of stories, given the single-sex nature of yeshiva life. As in the Fhima case, the child goes willingly into this sheltered community in order to avoid unhappiness in the outside world. But in both cases, the rabbis act illegally, leaving anguished parents searching for their children—and for answers.

The fictional setting of the crime drama allows for a greater—if still ambivalent—endorsement of the comforts of religious life, given the stark contrast with a bitter divorce and physical abuse. While these factors were present in the Fhima case as well, media coverage was far clearer in its condemnation of Helbrans, as well as the community that helped hide Shai from his parents for so long. These different platforms—crime drama and crime coverage—offer different freedoms for intoning opinions.

In a follow-up to the case in 2001, a grown Shai Fhima attempted to set the public record straight, explaining that he had reconciled with his family five years earlier. While he is no longer hasidic, he is an observant, religious Jew. "They [my parents] feel I was brainwashed. I don't."[31] That same year, Elaine Grudin Denholtz published *The*

Zaddik: A Battle for a Boy's Soul, which described the case. Denholtz's account approached the case from Hana Fhima's perspective, including her allegations of brainwashing.

The book's jacket dramatically proclaims:

> If this book were not based on actual events, the plot of Elaine Grudin Denholtz's gripping suspense story might seem preposterous. But her tale is all the more shocking because it is true. . . . Denholtz creates a dramatic portrait of religious fanatics who arrogantly defy the law. . . . *The Zaddik* is more than a tale of kidnapping, the battle for a boy's soul, and a mother's anguish. It invites us to ask ourselves, Where does religious devotion end and evil begin?[32]

Tipping her hand as to where her sympathies lie, Denholtz freely admits that her perspective has been informed by "studies of cults, religious abductions, and law. . . . I talked with a number of therapists with a specialty in cults, deprogramming, and mind control and they helped me to understand how brainwashing works."[33] As discussed earlier in this chapter, scholars of religion, as well as anthropologists, psychologists, and sociologists have long been skeptical about the credibility of brainwashing arguments. However, an alternative, nonscholarly school of thought has also emerged, consisting primarily of journalists, community organizers, and religious leaders who insist that brainwashing remains a real danger to the nation's youth.[34]

Denholtz accepts these arguments and writes from a place of righteous outrage, at times going so far as to exaggerate the facts.

> Hana Fhima's story of scandalous political corruption and ultra-orthodox religious kidnappings rocked me to the core. Because until Hana blew the whistle, kidnappings by hasidic groups were largely ignored. Kids vanished. Their parents never saw them again. Nobody did a thing about it.[35]

Her indictment of the religious community continues:

> One question continued to plague me: Is there an international conspiracy in which small but highly dangerous religious cults kidnap secular boys and turn them into ultrareligious hasids? . . . Perhaps we will never know the answers fully about how brainwashing works, but we do know how Rabbi Helbrans stole Shai's soul.[36]

In line with turn-of-the-twenty-first-century conspiracy theories, her introduction would lead one to believe that American cities are a haven for ultra-Orthodox kidnapping gangs and that their actions are hidden by an elaborate cover-up.[37]

But even if Denholtz presents an alarmist version of events, the kidnapping of a minor is clearly a felony. And even if there is no "international conspiracy," the Fhima case was not the first such instance of religiously motivated kidnapping in Jewish memory. In 1957, a Russian refugee in Israel, Nachman Shtarkes, refused to hand over his seven-year-old grandson, Joseph. Shtarkes took and hid the boy—known as Yossele—from his parents because they were not Orthodox. What became known as the "Yossele affair"—thanks to international headlines asking "Where's Yossele?"—led to a very public trial. In 1962, Israeli intelligence agents found Yossele in New York and reconciled him with his parents.[38]

Highly publicized cases like the Yossele affair and the Fhima case create the impression that haredim may view themselves above the law. A recent financial scandal in the haredi community—coupled with the defense "that the misappropriations were justified because the money was used for religious and communal purposes"—led one Yeshiva University professor to comment, " 'What I seem to be seeing is [a] rather brazen quality of defiance in the Hasidic community that they have the right to trump whatever law is not consistent with their community's need.' "[39] Jewish critics of this behavior refer to the Talmudic mandate of *dina d'malchuta dina*—the law of the land is the law—and argue that this behavior is antithetical to Jewish law, no matter how "Jewish" the perpetrator.

Despite Shai Fhima's claims (both as a teenager and as an adult) that he was never kidnapped nor brainwashed, *The Zaddik* reflects only his mother's side of the case. Shai was not interviewed for this work. Whether he declined an interview or was not approached is not addressed, but it is clear from his public statements that his perspective would work against Denholtz's premise, which denies any active role to the convert and relies on the passive theory of brainwashing. *The Zaddik* is therefore an example of the type of media sensationalism that both informs and fuels the already existing anxiety over coercive haredi influence among many American Jews.

TREYF WIGS AND WATER: A FURTHER SHIFT TO THE RIGHT

The fictional narratives examined in this chapter demonstrate the discomfort of many American Jews with the overt religiosity and otherness of the ultra-Orthodox. Unlike most American Christians, many Jews do not believe in a personal, judging God, and many are uncomfortable with the concept of an afterlife. Moreover, most American Jews view their Jewishness as compatible with liberal, mainstream American culture. Sylvia Barack Fishman describes a fear of being "too Jewish."[40] This fear is aptly captured in a 2000 *New Yorker* cartoon depicting a man trying on a suit in a clothing store. He sports a big black hat, glasses, a beard, and a black suit in the haredi style. The caption is a question from his wife: "Too Jewish?" Similarly, in *The Outside World*, Joel Miller is struck by the way his son looks in his black hat.

> All he could see was Baruch's black hat. In his mind, it took different shapes. It flattened at the top, grew taller and became a top hat. It curved out at the sides, sloped in at the middle, and became a cowboy hat. It grew larger until it swallowed him entirely. — (Mirvis, *The Outside World*, 27)

Nowhere is there a better example of someone being "too Jewish" than the visibly identifiable ultra-Orthodox man with black coat and hat. The hat symbolizes otherness, wanting to stick out. And Joel sees the black hat itself as physically possessing his son.

A change in Baruch's behavior was immediately apparent when he returned from Israel, but the scope of his new observance became clear through a dispute about dish racks. Baruch placed them in the sink, and Naomi removed them. He placed them in the sink again, and Naomi silently removed them. This passive resistance went on for a while, and finally Baruch was forced to tell his mother that without the racks, the dishes would be rendered nonkosher by contact with the porous material of the sink. Naomi, who felt that her home was kosher enough, was forced to give in to her son—who would otherwise no longer eat in her home. She asks her husband, "What do you want me to tell him? We want you to be religious, just not this religious, to take it as seriously as we do, but no more, thank you?" (44).

Similarly awkward encounters between parents and newly religious children occur in other contemporary Jewish fiction. In Allegra Goodman's *The Family Markowitz* (1996), Ed Markowitz curiously observes his daughter's behavior at the family's Passover seder and muses:

> She has become very puritanical, his daughter, and it baffles him. They had raised the children in a liberal, rational, joyous way— raised them to enjoy the Jewish tradition, and Ed can't understand why Miriam would choose austerity and obscure ritualism. . . . How can a young girl be attracted to this kind of legalism?[41]

Ed is both puzzled and saddened by her rigidity. When he learns that her plans for a religious wedding include separate dancing for men and women (and therefore no father-daughter dance), he is outraged. This change in wedding style is indicative of the rightward shift in Modern Orthodoxy. Thirty years ago, such weddings would have mixed dancing, and Ed could have danced with his daughter *and* with his wife. For Ed, the omission of mixed dancing is both disappointing and embarrassing.

The family frictions depicted in the works of Goodman, Mirvis, and Roiphe aptly capture the tensions present when a child "returns to tradition." In Israel, these encounters within families are even more common. According to an interview in *Real Jews*:

> Nearly every family in this neighborhood has a close relative who became ultra-Orthodox, and it's a lousy situation. One day a kid comes home and won't eat with the family because they're not kosher enough, and tells them that they're not religious enough, and it makes the family resentful and angry.[42]

While the percentage of haredim among Israeli Jews is far greater than among American Jewry, there is still a sense among American Jews of a rising threat of right-wing Orthodoxy at the door.

The increasing rigidity of Orthodoxy is partially a tribute to the acceptance Orthodox Judaism has experienced in America. If one can easily adhere to Orthodoxy, it loses the element of effort, of difference. The desire to set Orthodoxy apart from Conservative Judaism, or even from the more liberal Orthodox, has led to more stringent interpretations of Jewish law. Recent public debates over the kosher-ness of New York City drinking water and wigs made in Indian Hindu temples have led some observers to critique the passion with which such matters are argued. But this fervor over what some see as minutiae—arguing over having dish racks, separate sinks, refrigerators, or even kitchens for the separation of milk and meat—is what others see as haredi distinctiveness. In any case, these arguments over details—both small and large—are what are dividing families.

The unlimited power outsiders see rabbis holding over their students has led to much criticism of right-wing yeshivas. Both *Lovingkindness* and *The Outside World* feature parents attempting, and generally failing, to understand why their children would find such a dictated lifestyle so attractive, wondering where they went wrong in bringing up their children. In the case of *Lovingkindness*, both the women's movement and secular humanism are examined. Annie Johnson (who married a non-Jew) recalls to her daughter the traditional, and somewhat mythical, practice of sitting shiva for a child who married a gentile.[43] "Today I am in mourning for you for having turned into the kind of Jew who might mourn if your child married out. . . . I feel a grief as great as if I were never going to see you again . . . as if I had lost you. Who are you?" (Roiphe, *Lovingkindness*, 58). Again, she exhibits the grief of someone who has lost a loved one through death. One has the sense that perhaps that death is preferable since her sadness is rivaled only by her distaste for Andrea's lifestyle.

While Annie sadly admits that her method of raising her daughter did not result in the creation of a happy, successful, confident woman, she writes in a letter to Rabbi Cohen:

> I admit all that without admitting that you and your friends at
> the Yeshiva Rachel are any more than muggers in black coats; in
> ancient language, with soothing words, with rules and promises,

you have bruised my daughter, brainwashed my daughter, so that she considers giving up what she had not yet given up, her mind, her independence, her knowledge of the multiple realities, the multiple choices, her willingness to be accountable to herself, for herself, under the sky, to be human without wailing to the clouds, to be human, and know that when we cry, we cry only in each other's arms or we cry alone. (81)

How did second-wave-feminist Annie Johnson (the alter ego of second-wave-feminist Anne Roiphe), with all her available choices, fail to pass on values to her daughter that made her feel safe? As a secular Jew and a feminist, Annie cannot easily accept that her daughter is resigning herself to a lifestyle where behavior and belief are interpreted and dictated by men. Her disappointment grows when she learns that Andrea is to be married to another *ba'al teshuvah*, a yeshiva student.

A marriage! A marriage to a pale-face fuzzy bearded boy with a long black coat and a round black hat and black shoes on his long skinny feet with ingrown toenails . . . a boy with shoulders rounded from studying the footnotes to the footnotes of forgotten decisions, a boy with glasses and unbrushed teeth and hair growing out of his ears, permanently rocking back and forth on his toes, afraid to make a decision for himself without consulting the rabbi or maybe five rabbis, a boy who would consider himself the superior of my daughter, a boy who would say each day, "Thank God I was not born a woman." (97)

At this point, Annie's thoughts recall the stereotypical yeshiva scholar described in my previous chapter. She imagines a feminized, nonsexual boy who neglects his body—not a legitimate partner for her daughter. As one who is sensitive to gender inequality, the idea of a boy thanking God that he was not born a woman makes her skin crawl.

She has never approved of Andrea's choices of men before; Annie saw them as taking advantage of her daughter, emotionally and sexually. Here is a boy who wants to marry Andrea, to have a life with her. The irony here is that prior to Andrea's arrival at the Yeshiva Rachel, Andrea was truly lost. She had rotting teeth, a drug problem, and no foreseeable goals. Annie's aversion to what she sees as a fundamentalist movement makes Annie loath to accept that her daughter is thriving in Israel, both spiritually and physically.

ISRAEL IN THE JEWISH AMERICAN IMAGINATION

As seen in the previous chapters, Israel functions as a site of both escape and exile in contemporary Jewish American literature. But this engagement with Israel is relatively new; Israel as a viable, physical, authentic center of Jewish life is a late-twentieth-century occurrence, usurping nostalgia for the shtetl. In response to the new Israel-centrism of American Jewry, a character in Philip Roth's *Operation Shylock* remarks: "Grandpa didn't come from Haifa. Grandpa came from Minsk."[44] It is actually Roth, with the chapter "Judea" in his 1986 novel *The Counterlife*, followed swiftly by Roiphe and *Lovingkindness* that ushered in an era of serious interest in Israeli settings. However, as much as American Jewish writers may demonstrate a preoccupation with Israel, this sixty-year-old nation-state is not usually a final destination. In her work on Jewish American literature, Tresa Grauer writes, "When Israel appears in the literature at all, it is not as the end of the journey for American Jews—not as the culmination or climax of the story—but as a temporary sojourn on the way back home."[45] This "just visiting" approach often reveals little about the day-to-day realities of Israel for "even when contemporary American Jewish novels take place almost *entirely* in Israel, they are still—and perhaps not surprisingly—very much about America, and American Jews."[46]

Both Annie Johnson and the Millers see their children's conversions to be the fault of seductive but misleading rabbis and the seductive location of Jerusalem—which exists in both narratives as a symbolic space. Jerusalem is the place where both Bryan and Andrea decide to embrace a right-wing Judaism. However, this Jerusalem is a specific Jerusalem, an Old City Jerusalem—one in keeping with romantic visions of "authentic" Judaism. The choice to set both narratives in Israel is meaningful. For the plot of Roiphe's *Lovingkindness*, a Chabad House in California or Brooklyn could have worked just as well. However, this chosen setting increases physical distance between the old life and the new one and has the authentic flavor of an old-time Judaism. For Mirvis, the setting mirrors the reality of the de rigueur experience of Orthodox kids' spending (at least) a year in an Israeli yeshiva.

In Naomi Sokoloff's review of *Lovingkindness*, she sees the choice of an Israeli yeshiva rather than an American one as significant. First, it provides an authenticity of milieu, featuring messed up American kids, and she notes that "the physical distance between New York and Jerusalem underscores the spiritual distance between mother and daughter." Similarly, the "walled city of conviction" represents the boundary between Andrea and Annie, between faith and reason.[47] For Roiphe's Annie Johnson, the world of the hasidim is an outmoded one, out of line with Enlightenment values. She sees the yeshiva as a cult that has kidnapped her daughter, and the walls that keep her daughter from her are high.

The theme of escape is central to both *Lovingkindness* and *The Outside World*, both to and from haredi communities and from the worldliness of secular, modern Judaism. For Bryan/Baruch, Israel is where he can live an "authentic" Jewish life, steeped in the teachings of his forefathers and his rabbis. For Tzippy Goldman (his fianceé), it is where she has the opportunity to be free of her stifling family. For Andrea/Sarai, it is where she feels peace from the outside world, a haven where she can rehabilitate herself. Sylvia Barack Fishman, in Allon Gal's collection *Envisioning Israel*, writes:

> As American Jews journey psychologically and physically to and from Israel, they wrestle with their own personal counterforces. Israel is the place where the American Jewish writers confront the counterlife; it has become the sacral center, if not the geographical center, of the American Jewish psyche.[48]

Israel has become a symbol of authentic Jewish life. But not everyone sees it as the answer to everything. In the left-wing Jewish magazine *Tikkun*, Anne Roiphe writes on the growing power of haredim in Israel:

> Fundamentalism, the oh-so-sweet certainty that your truth is the truth, that the word has been given and must not be changed,

that law and order will follow the revealed truth—this fundamentalism, the tranquilizer of ambivalence, the amputator of doubt is with us again.[49]

Annie—and through her, Roiphe—sees a threatening place where haredim are gaining control over politics, religious life, and the lives and bodies of women.

Until recently, American Jews tended to prefer their own idealized vision of Israel rather than the actual people, soil, and land that Israel encompasses. In his article "The Projection of America as It Ought to Be: Zion in the Mind's Eye of American Jews," Jonathan Sarna describes American Jewish projections from the eighteenth to the early twentieth century. His analysis approaches the establishment of the state of Israel. He writes, "The Israel of American Jews—the Zion that they imagined in their minds, dreamed about, and wrote about—was for centuries a mythical Zion, a Zion that reveals more about American Jewish ideals than about the realities of Eretz Israel."[50] This mythical Zion hardly disappeared with the creation of an actual nation-state. The great success of Leon Uris's novel *Exodus* (1958) and the subsequent film starring Paul Newman (1960) created an American image of Israel that lasted for decades. In recent years, Israeli tourism—particularly Birthright Israel, a program for college-age Jews—continues to cater to certain idealized projections of Israel.

Israel is not the only country that American Jews have idealized; Jews have had an unrealistic view of America as well. Sylvia Barack Fishman notes in her introduction to *Jewish Life and American Culture* that Jews have created a distinctively Jewish notion of what defines the true America. This America has no place for religious extremists or fanaticism.[51] Historically, Jews have seen being *less* religious as a way of being *more* American. However, America is an extraordinarily religious country, with an increasingly conservative Protestantism dominating much of its culture. Ironically, the secularism of Jewish culture is what makes them less *American*.

Despite the statistical religiosity of Americans, American Jews are nervous about the haredim. Perhaps this anxiety comes out of the embarrassment that some Jews feel when they see the Lubavitchers approaching passers-by with the questions, "Are you Jewish? Did you lay tefillin today?" The Lubavitchers themselves are aware of their discomfiting presence, with Chabad emissaries admitting that "most of the people screaming at you are Jews."[52] Perhaps these screaming American Jews are afraid (much like nineteenth-century acculturated Jews) that the *visibility* of these haredim bearing gifts of tefillin and candlesticks will enhance anti-Semitism and reflect negatively on them as well. Perhaps they see these Jews as posing an extreme alternative to the Jewish mainstream, which has spent the greater part of the past century trying to avoid the hyphenated persona of "Jewish-American." To choose to be haredi is to reject any national identity other than a Jewish one. They are first and foremost Jews living in America, not American Jews. The haredim threaten Jewish assertions of American-ness. They threaten to take over visible Jewish identity. That they threaten to take over their children is even worse. The haredim have invaded their homes.

They Could Be Anything They Wanted: Even Vice President

Both *Lovingkindness* and *The Outside World* reflect the parental concern that children will not fulfill their potential—at least not in the way that their parents measure potential. These "children" are the offspring of educated, wealthy folks. Would anyone care if Orthodoxy attracted people who seemed to have no other destiny or opportunities? Who would care if they decided to become mothers or housewives or scholars with little to no breadwinning potential? What would they be giving up? But children of middle-class acculturated and educated Jews are another matter. These American Jewish parents have high hopes for their children. They should be doctors, lawyers, M.B.A.'s, not yeshiva scholars or housewives in a household filled with kids. These parents express a sense of helplessness. How do they save or rescue their adult children?[53] Similar concerns over new religious movements emerged in the late 1970s and early 1980s, particularly over the Children of God and the Unification Church. These groups were seen as specifically targeting affluent, middle-class youth.

In *Lovingkindness* and *The Outside World*, Sarai and Baruch—unlike the thirteen-year-old Shai Fhima—are old enough to make their own choices, but this does not stop their parents from interfering with those decisions, not to mention being hurt by them. In *Lovingkindness*, Annie entertains the idea of allying herself with a set of parents (the Roses, Sarai's future in-laws) who, through extreme means, intend to kidnap their son, Michael, from the haredi community. In a letter addressed to Annie, Arnold Rose makes his intentions clear:

> My wife and I are convinced that this marriage, arranged by the people I consider the captors of my son, will be a further entanglement, will make escape so much more difficult and will aid the entire brainwashing process that my son is undergoing, which has changed him from an average American boy into a religious fanatic who has sworn an oath of citizenship to a nonexistent ancient Israel whose traditions seem (like the tentacles of an octopus) to have wrapped themselves firmly around his throat. Do you share my sentiments? Can we collaborate on a plan to redeem or reclaim our own flesh and blood from the zealots who have imprisoned them? (Roiphe, *Lovingkindness*, 110)

This arrangement is interesting, especially when compared to the marriages discussed in the previous chapters. In those cases, the *parents* pressured their children to get married. In *The Outside World* and *Lovingkindness*, the parents see marriage as a conspiracy. Believing their son to be captive and "imprisoned," the Roses hatch a plan to *re*-kidnap Michael. They attempt to enlist Annie, assuming that her virulent opposition to her daughter's new lifestyle and this arranged marriage matches their own. The Roses believe this plan to be in the best interests of their son, but in actuality it derives from their vision of how he should live his life. Arnold remarks, "I will allow him to find his own path as long as it is here in Cleveland and doesn't require the support of anyone's orthodoxy. I want Michael to be a free man" (141). He seems unaware that the freedom he supports is a dictated one as well. Michael will be free if he succumbs to his father's wishes; free if he moves home; free if he gives up his faith and his fiancée. These competing visions of freedom are at the crux of these parents' anxieties.

Similarly, in *The Outside* World Baruch's father threatens to cut him off financially if he insists on studying at the yeshiva rather than at Columbia.

> [Joel] was still trying to formulate why supporting his son in college *was* different from supporting him in yeshiva. They had the money, so he could easily help them out if he wanted to. But he wasn't going to pay for something he so strongly disagreed with. There wasn't one single path he wanted Baruch to follow. He wasn't looking to replicate himself, nor hoping to vicariously fulfill any lost fantasy. He wasn't of the generation that insisted on their sons becoming doctors or lawyers. He would have been happy with his son the professor, his son the architect, his son the aspiring artist. (Mirvis, *The Outside World*, 83)

Joel truly believes that he has his son's best interests at heart; he doesn't need him to be a doctor, just a free thinker. Of course, religious literalism does not fit into the category of "free thinking."

Annie too has dreams for her daughter:

> I had plans of my own for Andrea. They began when she was just learning the words for shoe and nose, table and dog. I thought I saw in her eyes the spark of intelligence, the speed of thought that would have made her a fine lawyer, a civil rights lawyer, who argued for justice, to uphold the Constitution, the amendments, who worked in dark places with poor clients to see that the country moved forward toward equal opportunity, a better life, a better land. (Roiphe, *Lovingkindness*, 78)

Annie imagines a daughter who will engage with the world in order to make it a better place, not one who chooses an insular community that, by design, disengages from the world. Both Sarai and Baruch are making autonomous, adult choices about their lives, careers, and marriage. From their perspectives, their parents want them to be like themselves, people they are not. Sarai and Baruch are freely choosing to give up the liberal ideals of their parents in exchange for conservative haredi commitments. These narratives reveal that their parents' liberal ideals only go so far; they have little tolerance for religious conservatism.

Both complain to their parents that they have unreasonable expectations for them. Baruch protests to Joel, "[E]very time I tell you what I want to do, every time I'm not exactly like you wish I was, you disapprove. You want me to be this person you have in your head. Well, it's not going to happen" (Mirvis, *The Outside World*, 160). Sarai describes a new yeshiva friend to Annie, "Hadassah went to Smith College but she dropped out because she didn't care about anything she was learning. Her parents wanted her to be a doctor" (Roiphe, *Lovingkindness*, 46). Again, we see parents asserting their own values. Baruch and Sarai reject not just their parents' religious beliefs but their lifestyles and ideals.

In *The Outside World,* Joel cannot understand why giving his son choices would lead to his refusing everything his father wanted for him.

> But what was the point of all this hard work if his son had no interest in what he wanted to give him? Baruch wanted to throw everything away at the age of twenty-one, close off his options before he even had a chance to explore them. Joel had worked hard to give his kids whatever they wanted: music lessons and trips to the museum, tickets for plays and concerts. Their kids were supposed to be the generation that knew no limits. They could be anything they wanted: even vice president, Naomi liked to say. Presented with an abundance of choices, Baruch was selecting the most restrictive of possibilities.
>
> (Mirvis, *The Outside World*, 84)

Assuming that Joel had any choice in the matter, allowing Baruch to go his own way would be to sacrifice Joel's own dreams for his son.

In addition to the themes of coercion, references to the Akedah (Genesis 22:1–19)—the biblical story of the binding and intended sacrifice of Isaac—appear frequently in contemporary narratives about haredim. Roiphe's novel is filled with these allusions. "In the flesh, in the here and now, when it was the vulnerable form of my daughter Andrea bound on the same altar as Isaac, I would have felt better had there been more rams in the thicket and less blood on the stone" (Roiphe, *Lovingkindness*, 244). Earlier, she writes: "Perhaps I really didn't accept this marriage but was only stalling for time, keeping in touch, not losing her to the bowels of the yeshiva, where they were sure to grind her into a kosher offering for the temple of their Lord" (238). Annie cannot determine whether leaving Andrea/Sarai at the yeshiva is the right thing to do; for Roiphe, her sacrifice is a symbolic one. Tova Reich's novels, unlike Roiphe's, depict the sacrifice and kidnapping of the haredi children by their own parents. The children are bred as soldiers in order to amass an army, a nation, and their sacrifice is expected. The sacrifice of Isaac is a prominent theme in both *Master of the Return* and *The Jewish War*. Kidnapping comes up in both works as well. In the first, we believe the child has been kidnapped by his father (and later attempted to be bound on the Temple Mount in re-creation of the sacrifice of Isaac), and the latter describes a mysterious kidnapping that is never solved. In Reich's work, the reenactment of the Akedah is a literal one.

To choose to be haredi is often to choose to be nonprofessional and noncompetitive and to live frugally, more like the working class than the middle class. And when kids choose to become haredi, they are deciding—for the most part—that they will be poor. And that *their* children will be poor (since secular education, as well as employment that may get in the way of religious observance is prohibited). Throughout *Lovingkindness*, there are allusions to a generation's scorn for its parents' upward mobility, as well as the parents themselves wondering what they could have done differently. Annie Johnson: "If I had married again and provided a stable two-parent home for Andrea, would she now be in a postdoctoral program in biochemistry at Yale?" (53). This preoccupation with her daughter's future continues. When she contemplates kidnapping Andrea with the Roses, she calls Andrea's childhood psychiatrist, Dr. Wolfert. She asks if medication will help. He asks if she's looking for a pill that will make Andrea a happy, accomplished grad student. Desperately, she says yes.

But Now I Am Right

While kidnapping is a recurring theme, it masks the reality that the haredi lifestyle is usually freely chosen. The fear that the younger generation is choosing a rigid, legalistic form of Judaism after being offered an abundance of choices, plagues mainstream Jews in America today. Annie responds to a letter from the Roses (her future in-laws):

> It is hard to believe . . . that our children have been brainwashed. The yeshiva is in the middle of Jerusalem. The children are free to go and come. They see the secular normal life of the city around them. Rabbi Cohen has invited me to visit and to talk with Andrea. There is no element of coercion that I can detect. The truth, harder for us to accept, is that our children are at this moment satisfied to stay in a place that asks voluntary restraint in so many areas of life. (114)

She reluctantly admits that "[My daughter] is willingly shrinking herself to fit into someone else's box." This underlying truth is what is most painful, not that a mysterious man in black is holding their children hostage but that this lifestyle has been chosen by those who have other (and what many would see as better) choices. It is with this admission that the poignancy of these narratives emerges.

Sarai writes to her mother:

> Dear Mother,
>
>   . . . Sometimes I think of you left in New York with all the voices talking at once and wish you would come here and see my yeshiva. I believe now that Gd is good, that when He created this earth He intended man to be good, He intended His creation to be good, and He intended me to play my part. Can you, will you try to understand? You must understand because you are my mother. Gd is a Gd of Lovingkindness. He is the Master of Life and Death. He is the Redeemer. He brings flowers to the field and sweetness to the fruit. Rabbi Cohen says I am a good student. This is the first time you've heard that. Are you surprised? Mrs. Cohen is teaching us about the Mikvah and the laws that married women follow. I am so amazed. I thought my body didn't matter to anyone but me. Mrs. Collins says that even the crevices, even the parts that get stained, can be cleansed and made good and serve their rightful purpose. When I learn more I will write you about it. I know that you think that purity laws are against women but that's because you don't understand. The truth is they bring us closer to Gd. You

never believe me. You never listened to me. You have such strong
opinions about everything. But now I am right. Love, Sarai (94)

Andrea never saw the world as good, never saw herself as a good student, and never saw herself as a woman whose body was sacred. Somehow Annie missed this, despite all good intentions. But much like
Deborah in *Acts of Faith* and Rachel in *The Romance Reader*, Annie
sees these purity laws as limiting, antiquated edicts that indict women
as pollutants. Ironically, these same laws, as explained to Sarai, suggest
that there is something good and potentially clean about her body. And
now Sarai's choices both challenge and indict Annie. These parents
see this lifestyle choice as the ultimate rebellion. In *The Outside World*
Joel muses, "Had Baruch come home with no yarmulke, he wouldn't
have elicited this strong a reaction. But their son was too smart for that.
He knew how to find their weakest spot and take aim" (82). In a fight
Baruch yells, "What about you? You hate anyone who's more religious
than you. You pretend it's about college and jobs and getting married
too young. But the truth is, you hate seeing me believe in something so
strongly, when you don't believe in anything" (160–61). The authors
have pointed to a sore spot in contemporary Jewish attitudes. A recent
survey of American Jews showed 83 percent of participants agreeing
with the statement "It bothers me when people try to tell me there's a
right way to be Jewish."[54] In the case of Annie Johnson and the Millers,
their children are informing their parents that there is a right way to be
Jewish. The fervor with which *ba'alei teshuvah* embrace their new lives
is itself sufficient to indict their parents for choosing a wrong path.
They may even imply that their parents have robbed them of something they see as their birthright.

Upon learning of Sarai's impending marriage, her mother worries:

And now I had two fears. The first was that Andrea would be married in Jerusalem to a boy she hardly knows in a language in which
she can barely request a dozen eggs, much less call out for help,
tell a friend a long story or report to a doctor the exact nature of
a particular pain. I was afraid that his marriage would seal her into
this place where I could not follow, where my grandchildren would
be strangers speaking a language in which I could not even ask

for a glass of water, following rules I believed the invention of the human mind, petty, bizarre and self-righteous.

(Roiphe, *Lovingkindness*, 155)

Annie expresses sadness not just for her child but for grandchildren not yet conceived. Not just our children, but what of the future? These are the same questions parents might ask if their child intermarried or abandoned Judaism altogether.

In the early twenty-first century, the *Jewish Daily Forward* newspaper revived its advice column "A Bintel Brief," begun by Abraham Cahan in 1906. Its new incarnation—"A Bintel Blog"—invites guest writers to answer letters. In January 2008, pop singer-songwriter Lisa Loeb replied to a parent's concern about his daughter's impending marriage.

My daughter, a beautiful, brilliant college graduate with a law degree and a good job is about to become engaged to a Chabadnik (who, by the way, has no job except for being what I call a lay "Jew for Moses" with Chabad).

It's obvious that if she marries this parasite, she will become a second-class citizen and a baby factory, and I'll never have any contact with my grandchildren, because, while we are proud Jews, we aren't kosher and obviously don't keep all the Shabbat commandments. (Don't tell me I'm wrong. I've had other friends whose kids have drunk the Orthodox Kool Aid — this is what happens.) How do I let her know my feelings? And don't tell me to keep quiet! Frankly, I'd rather she married a gentile than a borderline Hasidic Jew.—FATHER KNOWS BEST

Loeb responded: "It sounds like you're mostly concerned about the fact that he doesn't have a job. I'd stick to that as the issue, instead of bringing his religious practice into the mix."[55] The father's distress over "this parasite" who will force his daughter to become a "baby factory" and ultimately lead to a family estrangement echoes the anxieties in *Lovingkindness*. Additionally, "Father knows Best" equates Chabadniks with members of Jim Jones's Peoples Temple, referring to those who have "drunk the Orthodox Kool Aid."

Ultimately, these narratives describe a deep discomfort with and hostility toward the *ba'alei teshuvah* movement. *Lovingkindness* and

The Outside World depict children captivated by haredi culture, not captives of haredim. The children are both converts and converters of the faith. Unlike tales of people kidnapped and forced into utterly foreign faiths, this approach implies an ownership of, if not a theft of, Judaism. These authors are engaged with (or invested in) Judaism, so there is an agenda afoot: "Who stole Judaism?" or "Who owns Judaism?" These narratives of kidnapped children reflect a fear that religion itself has been kidnapped.

Lovingkindness ends in a compromise. In Blanche d'Alpuget's *New York Times* review, she writes:

> Such is the tension between Lucifer and God that until the last moments of "Lovingkindness" one does not know which side will prevail in Annie's soul. Ms. Roiphe brings to the drawing of her main character such a depth of insight that the denouement—the reverse of what I wanted to happen—lifted the book from its pages, exhilarated me with its elegance.[56]

Sarai remains with the yeshiva folk. Her mother decides that in order to do right by her daughter, she must respect her choice. She sacrifices her daughter to a world she doesn't believe in. The Akedah and the Greek myth of Demeter and Persephone become interchangeable as a woman mourns for her daughter. But while Demeter roams the earth in the cold months of winter waiting for Persephone to return, Annie Johnson contents herself with the knowledge that these shifts are cyclical and that one day, just as her parents rejected her grandparents' religiosity, the pendulum will swing back her way. She fantasizes:

> When my granddaughter is eighteen and restless with all she has been taught, I will invite her to visit me. Once she is here I will slowly introduce her to science and math and deductive reasoning and Chekhov and Dostoevsky, Locke and Susan B. Anthony, and when she is ready I will suggest that she become a doctor and stay here and go to college...She can change her name to Jane for Jane Austen or Charlotte for Charlotte Bronte, to Simone for Simone de Beauvoir, to Amelia for Amelia Earhart. There are so many names that would suit. (Roiphe, *Lovingkindness*, 278)

Roiphe's protagonist plans to wait for the coming of age of an unborn granddaughter, one who may wish to taste the worldly delights of New York and feminism. Maybe she will want to go to college. Maybe she will change her name from Chana to Charlotte. Maybe she will validate Annie's choices. This passage clearly demonstrates the opposition between mother and daughter over the issue of acculturation.

The fear that comes across in these narratives is not really that the haredim have kidnapped children but that the haredim have kidnapped Judaism in general, transforming it into an eighteenth-century form of Eastern European Judaism (with even more restrictions). Contemporary liberal Jewish discourse frequently bemoans the rightward shift of Judaism, and those on the right worry that an increasingly permissive generation will result in the eradication of Jewish life.

The Jewish people are not alone in their identity crisis. Histories of Jewish studies and American religion in general show that these patterns of adopting more conservative, less liberal interpretations of religious traditions are equally present in other American religious groups. Who is a Jew? Who is a Muslim? Who is a Christian? And can there be a possibility of pluralism even though the right rejects the left? These have all become increasingly urgent and controversial questions.

Lovingkindness and *The Outside World* are examples of an emerging literary genre that reflect not only the rifts within contemporary Jewish families but the fissures within American Jewry as a whole. While these narratives reflect the anxiety and ambivalence felt by many Jewish Americans whose lives are personally touched by the *ba'alei teshiva* movement, both *Lovingkindness* and *The Outside World* result in compromise. These parents must figure out a way to keep their children in their lives, to accept this shift to the religious right as part of a transition in a family history.

CONCLUSION

THEY ARE US *in* OTHER CLOTHES

An ultra-Orthodox rabbi is riding a train when he notices a woman angrily staring at him. He could tell that she was Jewish, albeit "modern." Eventually, she starts speaking to him quietly, "I don't know who you are Mister, but I just want you to know how embarrassed I get whenever I see Jews dressed like you from another century. You make the rest of us look ridiculous. If you have to dress like that, the least you could do is stay home." The rabbi is mortified, but when he recovers he explains to the woman that she has made a mistake. He is actually not Jewish; he is Amish. The woman immediately apologizes, exclaiming, "I have so much respect for you people, the way you keep your traditions!"[1]

This anecdote, recounted in the 1991 film *The Quarrel*, reflects a paradox in the way that many American Jews view the haredim. In principle, American Jews are vigilantly dedicated to cultural and religious tolerance. Not only do they tolerate the Other, they embrace the Other. They champion the underdog. They admire "exotic" religious groups. As the woman on the train put it, American Jews have "so much respect" for the way others keep their traditions. However, for many American Jews, this tolerance and love for the Other ends at home. The Amish are not equivalent to the ultra-Orthodox in much of the Jewish American imagination, even though from a distance, the Amish and the ultra-Orthodox man can be confused.[2] Unlike the potentially menacing black coats of the haredim, the similar black coats of the Amish are quaint. The traditional trappings of the Amish present no threat to mainstream American Jewry, because no gentiles will see an Amish man and think, "Why won't those Jews just try to fit in?" Jews are not threatened by the Amish because, very simply, the Amish are not Jews.

The 2004 Broadway revival of *Fiddler on the Roof* and Marc Chagall's unending popularity are testaments to the continuous enjoyment of the imagery of shtetl life. As singing and dancing villagers in a musical, haredim are acceptable, even beloved figures that represent Jewish continuity. As men in black hats, black coats, and long beards that ride the same subway, they are a source of anxiety and embarrassment for "modern" Jews. According to a certain anxious logic, the traditionally clad ultra-Orthodox man is the personification of Jewish distinctiveness, of a refusal to acclimate to the host environment. And this man in black is threatening to Jewish comfort in America.

The irony in imagining the haredim as representing authentic Judaism to the outside world is that this perception has long been perpetuated by Jews themselves, and not just by the ultra-Orthodox. By romanticizing tales of hasidic and shtetl life in both literary and musical form, by donating money to haredi yeshivas in order to pay homage to Jewish continuity, and by hiring haredi instructors to teach Jewish subjects in Modern Orthodox schools, mainstream Jews have—until recently—maintained the impression that the ultra-Orthodox are the "real" Jews. But, as Thomas Friedmann points out, "dangers lurk in the dissemination of the simplistic and unexamined question that deems only the Orthodox authentic Jews."[3] The most obvious and infuriating danger of regarding only ultra-Orthodoxy as authentic Judaism is the de facto delegitimization of all other forms of Judaism. Such attitudes, especially those demonstrated by the haredim themselves, have led to a radical polarizing of Jewish movements in America.

Out of this culture war, with Jewish liberal and traditionalist movements battling each other for the title of authentic Judaism, a new genre of film and cinema has emerged. These contemporary narratives dispute haredi rights to this title, highlighting the ways in which haredim have broken with the authentic spirit of Judaism as understood by liberal Jews. By examining cinematic and literary representations of the ultra-Orthodox from the last two decades, my study demonstrates the growing divide between haredi and non-haredi Jews in America. While the texts pursued in this book depict a perception that the haredi world is a place of suffering, oppression, and repression for many of its inhabitants, the underlying aim of these tales is to claim the soul of contemporary Jewry, to take the title of authenticity back.

DEMONIZING THE HAREDIM

The narratives analyzed in this study are painful ones. Pearl Abraham's *The Romance Reader* and Erich Segal's *Acts of Faith* demonstrate the repression some young people find within the haredi world and the pain their families feel when their children choose to abandon Orthodoxy. Abraham and Segal highlight the multiple ways that haredi women are excluded from public Jewish life, and they both try to validate egalitarian Jewish movements by expressing the hurt felt by some of those women. Advocating Jewish options that do not limit the participation of women, these narratives propose that the haredim are behind the times when it comes to women's roles.

Boaz Yakin's *A Price Above Rubies* and Naomi Ragen's *Sotah* employ different tactics in their critique of haredi life. Both works depict the alienation of women forced by harsh societal pressures to conform to a lifestyle or risk losing everything. Yakin and Ragen create a gothic image of the haredi world, illustrating a community that is physically, sexually, and emotionally abusive to women. Making use of stark stereotypes of ultra-Orthodox Jewish men, these narratives suggest that not only does haredi society devalue the religious participation of women, but it is a sadistic, hypocritical community and is to be feared.

While Abraham and Segal describe the perspectives of young people who reject the ultra-Orthodox lifestyle of their parents, Tova Mirvis's *The Outside World* and Anne Roiphe's *Lovingkindness* do the opposite. These novels explore the anguish felt by parents whose children reject their liberal Judaism in favor of the haredi world. The anxieties presented in these narratives parallel fears about the seduction of children by new religious movements. Both narratives demonstrate a deep ambivalence toward the allure of ultra-Orthodoxy and aversion to its severe limitations. *The Outside World* and *Lovingkindness* present characters that prize open-mindedness as a virtue, even as they illustrate the limitations of tolerance.

AUTHENTICITY AND AUTHORITY

This ambivalence recurs throughout this cultural family feud. The tug between nostalgia and hostility is a difficult one, and reversing the image of the haredim as the "real" Jews is not easy. A character in Mirvis's *The Outside World* asserts that "gefilte fish can be the next sushi. You want to know why? Because people are hungry for something authentic. They remember what they used to eat at their bubby and zaidy's house. They miss the past. Even if they never had it, they still miss it."[4] Liberal Jews may fear that if ultra-Orthodoxy is successfully packaged and marketed as "authentic" Judaism, a nostalgic consumer may buy it.

These narratives, all of which are highly critical of ultra-Orthodoxy, combat this marketing of authenticity in different ways. The Reform rabbi in Segal's *Acts of Faith* argues with haredi biblical interpretation in order to prove his point. Others, such as Roiphe's secular protagonist in *Lovingkindness*, protest that even if this religious behavior is the authentic practice of one's great-grandparents, tradition alone does not make it just. Annie Johnson demands of her neo-traditionalist daughter, "What is the point of going back two generations, sliding down the historical ladder, slamming doors of opportunity behind you, as if someone hadn't struggled hard and long to open those doors for you?"[5] For these Jews, the past holds little authority when it contradicts contemporary egalitarian values.

Ultimately, these liberal Jewish narratives present a discomfort with both the patriarchal Judaism of the past and the potential reactionary Judaism of the future. This Jewish culture war is growing increasingly bitter with each step that liberals and traditionalists take in opposite directions. As the battles result in deeper fissures and wounds, each side becomes more and more convinced that the other is responsible for the mess in which it finds itself. Post-Holocaust, post-1948, diaspora Jewry is in transition, and this is the story of Judaism trying to figure out what it is in today's world. While Orthodoxy is still a minority, its confidence has been bolstered by its increased comfort in America, and, ironically, it is this comfort that is so disquieting to non-Orthodox Jews, resulting in this prevalence of anxiety-laden narratives.

These anti-haredi narratives have not gone unnoticed by the ultra-Orthodox. A 2005 *New York Times Book Review* essay by Wendy Shalit—a returnee to tradition—raised the issue of this new abundance of ultra-Orthodox characters in Jewish literature, bemoaning their characterization as religious hypocrites.

> There will always be people who fail to live up to their ideals, and it would be pointless to pretend the strictly observant don't have failings. But before there can be hypocrisy, there must be real idealism; in fiction that lacks idealistic characters, even the hypocrite's place can't be properly understood.[6]

This is not the first time such a charge has been leveled at Jewish authors who write about Jews. Shalit's essay is reminiscent of an earlier *Times* piece regarding Philip Roth's 1959 *Goodbye Columbus*. A rabbi critiqued Roth's work, calling for a "balanced portrayal of Jews as we know them." Roth responded publicly, in print, that he believed that the rabbi was really worried over the question of "What will people think? Or, to be exact: What will the goyim think?"[7] Almost half a century later, American Jews are still battling out their anxieties about getting comfortable in America, both in print and on screen.

NOTES

INTRODUCTION: A FAMILY FEUD

1. Samuel G. Freedman, "Yeshivish at Yale," *New York Times*, May 24 1998.
2. Ibid.
3. *Hack v. President and Fellows of Yale College*, 16 F Supp 2d 183 (D. Conn. 1998), 237 F.3d 81 (2nd Cir. 2000).
4. James Davison Hunter, *Culture Wars: The Struggle to Define America* (New York: BasicBooks, 1991), 34.
5. Paula Hyman, "Where Do We Go from Here? Feminism and Changing Gender Expectations and Roles in Jewish Communal Life," in *Creating the Jewish Future*, ed. Michael Brown and Bernard Lightman (Walnut Creek, Calif.: AltaMira Press, 1999), 194.
6. It should be noted that in this work I will be referring primarily to Ashkenazi communities (the dominant Jewish group in the United States). Sephardi and Mizrahi Jews have had quite different approaches to modernity, both in the United States and Israel. For further studies on the Jewish response to modernity, please see Jacob Katz, *Emancipation and Assimilation: Studies in Modern Jewish History* (Farnborough, U.K.: Gregg, 1972); Jacob Katz, *Jewish Emancipation and Self-Emancipation* (Philadelphia: Jewish Publication Society, 1986); Michael A. Meyer, *Judaism Within Modernity: Essays on Jewish History and Religion* (Detroit: Wayne State University Press, 2001). For more on secularism and broader American religious life, please see Tracy Fessenden, *Culture and Redemption: Religion, the Secular, and American Literature* (Princeton, N.J.: Princeton University Press, 2006).
7. Samuel G. Freedman, *Jew Vs. Jew: The Struggle for the Soul of American Jewry* (New York: Simon & Schuster, 2000), 23.
8. Steven Martin Cohen, *Content or Continuity? Alternative Bases for Commitment* (New York: American Jewish Committee, 1990), 71.

9. William R. Hutchison, *Religious Pluralism in America: The Contentious History of a Founding Ideal* (New Haven, Conn.: Yale University Press, 2003), 57.

10. Similar narratives reflect anxiety about new religious movements "targeting" middle-class teenagers. A good overview is Marie Anne Pagliarini, "The Pure American Woman and the Wicked Catholic Priest: An Analysis of Anti-Catholic Literature in Antebellum America," *Religion and American Culture* 9, no. 1 (1999): 97–128.

11. Jenny Franchot, *Roads to Rome: The Antebellum Protestant Encounter with Catholicism* (Berkeley: University of California Press, 1994), examines the often-contradictory reactions of attraction and repulsion that Protestants had with regard to Roman Catholicism. Franchot argues that "anti-Catholicism operated as an imaginative category of discourse through which antebellum American writers of popular and elite fictional and historical texts indirectly voiced the tensions and limitations of mainstream Protestant culture" (xvii). Introducing popular anti-Catholic narratives, Franchot analyzes the perceived danger from the Catholic Church to Protestant familial domesticity, not unlike the threat that the haredim purportedly present to liberal Jews' sense of comfort in America.

12. Lillian Schlissel, Byrd Gibbens, and Elizabeth Hampsten, *Far from Home: Families of the Westward Journey* (New York: Schocken Books, 1989), xvii–xviii.

13. Dara Horn, *In the Image: A Novel* (New York: Norton, 2002), 47.

14. Robert Wuthnow, *The Struggle for America's Soul: Evangelicals, Liberals, and Secularism* (Grand Rapids, Mich.: W. B. Eerdmans, 1989), 178. Wuthnow specifically describes the bifurcation of one movement, the Presbyterian church, over moral issues.

15. Freedman, "Yeshivish at Yale." Yale has traditionally accommodated the needs of most Orthodox students, providing consideration for dietary restrictions and Sabbath observance.

16. Saul Nadata, "Yale's Jewish Students Keep Faith and Thrive," *New York Times*, September 14, 1997.

17. Tovia Smith and Bob Edwards, "Yale Religious Controversy," report on *Morning Edition*, NPR, September 24, 1997.

18. J. J. Goldberg, *Jerusalem Report*, October 30, 1997.

19. For more information on ultra-Orthodoxy, please see Murray Herbert Danzger, *Returning to Tradition: The Contemporary Revival of Orthodox Judaism* (New Haven, Conn.: Yale University Press, 1989); Sue Fishkoff, *The Rebbe's Army: Inside the World of Chabad-Lubavitch* (New York: Schocken Books, 2003); Samuel C. Heilman, *Defenders of the Faith: Inside Ultra-Orthodox Jewry* (Berkeley: University of California Press, 2000); Jack Wertheimer, *The Uses of Tradition: Jewish Continuity in the Modern Era* (Cambridge, Mass.: Harvard University Press, 1992).

20. Samuel Heilman, *Sliding to the Right: The Contest for the Future of American Jewish Orthodoxy* (Berkeley: University of California Press, 2006), 2.
21. "Ba'al Shem Tov": literally, Master of the Good Name. Ba'al Shem meant "healer" or "miracle worker" among Eastern European Jews.
22. Lis Harris, *Holy Days: The World of a Hasidic Family* (New York: Simon & Schuster, 1985), 49.
23. For more on hasidic Judaism, please see Janet S. Belcove-Shalin, *New World Hasidim: Ethnographic Studies of Hasidic Jews in America*, SUNY Series in Anthropology and Judaic Studies (Albany: State University of New York Press, 1995); I. Etkes and Tauber Institute for the Study of European Jewry, *The Besht: Magician, Mystic, and Leader* (Waltham, Mass.: Brandeis University Press/ Hanover. N.H.: University Press of New England, 2005); Jerome R. Mintz, *Hasidic People: A Place in the New World* (Cambridge, Mass.: Harvard University Press, 1992), Jerome R. Mintz, *Legends of the Hasidim: An Introduction to Hasidic Culture and Oral Tradition in the New World* (Northvale, N.J.: Jason Aronson, 1995), J. G. Weiss, Ada Rapoport-Albert, and Institute of Jewish Studies, *Hasidism Reappraised* (Portland, Ore.: Vallentine Mitchell, 1996).
24. Laurence D. Loeb, "Habad and Habban: '770's' Impact on a Yemenite Jewish Community in Israel," in *New World Hasidim: Ethnographic Studies of Hasidic Jews in America*, ed. Janet S. Belcove-Shalin (Albany: State University of New York Press, 1995), 69–85.
25. For a concise explanation of the tzaddikate, please see Solomon Poll, "The Charismatic Leader of the Hasidic Community: The Zaddiq, the Rebbe," in *New World Hasidim: Ethnographic Studies of Hasidic Jews in America*, ed. Janet S. Belcove-Shalin (Albany: SUNY Press, 1995), 257–75.
26. For more on the distinctions between these two groups, please see Samuel Heilman and Menachem Friedman, "Religious Fundamentalism and Religious Jews: The Case of the Haredim," in *Fundamentalisms Observed*, ed. Martin E. Marty and R. Scott Appleby (Chicago: Chicago University Press, 1991), 197–264.
27. *Yeshivot* (plural); yeshiva (singular).
28. Janet S. Belcove-Shalin, "Home in Exile: Hasidim in the New World," in *New World Hasidim: Ethnographic Studies of Hasidic Jews in America*, ed. Janet S. Belcove-Shalin (Albany: SUNY Press, 1995), 214.
29. Haym Soloveitchik, "Rupture and Reconstruction: The Transformation of Contemporary Orthodoxy," in *Jews in America: A Contemporary Reader*, ed. Roberta Rosenberg and Chaim I. Waxman (Hanover, N.H.: University Press of New England for Brandeis University Press, 1999), 345–47.
30. Blu Greenberg, *How to Run a Traditional Jewish Household* (New York: Simon and Schuster, 1983), 186.
31. Israel Herbert Levinthal, *Point of View: An Analysis of American Judaism* (London: Abelard-Schuman, 1958), 55.

32. While Reform, Reconstructionist, and Conservative Judaism are the most popular forms of liberal Judaism, they are also joined by small yet vibrant growing movements such as Jewish Renewal, Humanistic Judaism, and the Havurah movement.

33. For more information on American Jewish movements please see Jonathan D. Sarna, *American Judaism: A History* (New Haven, Conn.: Yale University Press, 2004); Jack Wertheimer, *A People Divided: Judaism in Contemporary America* (Waltham, Mass.: Brandeis University Press, 1997).

34. Jacob Neusner, *Judaism: An Introduction* (London: Penguin, 2002).

35. Heilman, *Sliding to the Right*, 3.

36. Ibid., 4.

37. Jenna Weissman Joselit, *New York's Jewish Jews: The Orthodox Community in the Interwar Years* (Bloomington: Indiana University Press, 1990), 150. In addition to Joselit's work, other sources on Modern Orthodoxy include Jeffrey S. Gurock, *American Jewish Orthodoxy in Historical Perspective* (Hoboken, N.J.: KTAV, 1996); Jeffrey S. Gurock, *From Fluidity to Rigidity: The Religious Worlds of Conservative and Orthodox Jews in Twentieth-Century America*, David W. Belin Lecture in American Jewish Affairs 7 (Ann Arbor: University of Michigan Jean and Samuel Frankel Center for Judaic Studies, 1998); Samuel C. Heilman and Steven Martin Cohen, *Cosmopolitans and Parochials: Modern Orthodox Jews in America* (Chicago: University of Chicago Press, 1989).

38. Please see: Jacob Katz, "Orthodoxy in Historical Perspective," *Studies in Contemporary Jewry* 2 (1986). Michael K. Silber, "The Emergence of Ultra-Orthodoxy: The Invention of a Tradition," in *The Uses of Tradition: Jewish Continuity in the Modern Era*, ed. Jack Wertheimer (Cambridge: Harvard University Press, 1992).

39. Soloveitchik, "Rupture and Reconstruction," 386. For his reference, please see Nancy Tatom Ammerman, *Bible Believers: Fundamentalists in the Modern World* (New Brunswick, N.J.: Rutgers University Press, 1987), 8.

40. Samuel C. Heilman, "Quiescent and Active Fundamentalisms: The Jewish Cases," in *Accounting for Fundamentalisms: The Dynamic Character of Movements*, ed. Martin E. Marty and R. Scott Appleby (Chicago: University of Chicago Press, 1994), 173.

41. Chaim Isaac Waxman, "The Haredization of American Orthodox Jewry," *Jerusalem Letter/ Viewpoints*, no. 376 (1998): 1–5.

42. Freedman, "Yeshivish at Yale."

43. Belcove-Shalin, "Home in Exile," 212–13. Boro Park is also spelled Borough Park.

44. For more on the Modern Orthodox Jewish day school, see the chapter "'The School of Yesterday and Tomorrow': The Modern Yeshiva," in Joselit, *New York's Jewish Jews*, 123–46.

45. Samuel C. Heilman, "How Did Fundamentalism Manage to Infiltrate Contemporary Orthodoxy?" paper presented at the Association for Jewish Studies, Boston, 2003. Comparisons could be made here to contemporary Islamic *madrasas*, where parents bring in religious teachers to fill in the holes of their knowledge. For more information on Orthodoxy's shift to the right, see Heilman, *Sliding to the Right*.

46. Hunter, *Culture Wars*, 15.

47. Jonathan Z. Smith, *Relating Religion: Essays in the Study of Religion* (Chicago: University of Chicago Press, 2004), 269.

48. Michel de Certeau, *The Practice of Everyday Life* (Berkeley: University of California Press, 1984), 87.

49. Angela McRobbie, "The Politics of Feminist Research," *Feminist Review* 12 (1982): 51.

50. David Weaver-Zercher, *The Amish in the American Imagination* (Baltimore, Md.: Johns Hopkins University Press, 2001), 5.

51. Marshall Sklare, "Intermarriage and the Jewish Future," *Commentary* (1964): 47.

52. Sylvia Barack Fishman, *A Breath of Life: Feminism in the American Jewish Community* (New York: Free Press, 1993); Sylvia Barack Fishman, *Follow My Footprints: Changing Images of Women in American Jewish Fiction* (Hanover: University Press of New England for Brandeis University Press, 1992); Sylvia Barack Fishman, *Jewish Life and American Culture* (Albany: State University of New York Press, 2000).

53. Examples include Rebecca Goldstein, *The Mind-Body Problem: A Novel* (New York: Random House, 1983); Allegra Goodman, *The Family Markowitz* (New York: Farrar Straus and Giroux, 1996); Allegra Goodman, *Kaaterskill Falls: A Novel* (New York: Dial Press, 1998); Allegra Goodman, *Paradise Park: A Novel* (New York: Dial Press, 2001); Allegra Goodman, *Total Immersion: Stories* (New York: Harper and Row, 1989); Horn, *In the Image: A Novel*.

54. Examples of this scholarship include Terryl Givens, *The Viper on the Hearth: Mormons, Myths, and the Construction of Heresy* (New York: Oxford University Press, 1997); Rebecca Reed and Maria Monk, *Veil of Fear: Nineteenth-Century Convent Tales*, intro. Nancy Lusignan Schultz (West Lafayette, Ind.: NotaBell Books, 1999); and, to a certain extent, Edward W. Said, *Culture and Imperialism* (New York: Knopf, 1993); Edward W. Said, *Orientalism* (New York: Pantheon Books, 1978).

55. In this project, the term "liberal" refers to a religious worldview, not necessarily a political one. For example, Naomi Ragen is an outspoken activist on religious women's issues, yet is notoriously conservative regarding Israeli politics.

56. In Israel's earlier days, the most common way to refer to Jews was either *dati* (religious) or *lo dati* (not religious).

57. Heilman, *Defenders of the Faith*, 12.

58. Jenna Joselit points out that the relatively common use of words such as *"frum"* or *"halakha"* (Jewish law) by American Jews is a sign of the influence that orthodoxy has had on contemporary American Judaism (*New York's Jewish Jews*, 149).

59. In Israel, head coverings among men connote specific meaning. For example, a knit *kippah* (yarmulke) designates a religious Zionist. A black satin kippah refers to a more traditional mitnagid or hasid. For more on this, please see Heilman, "Quiescent and Active Fundamentalisms," 175.

60. Freedman, "Yeshivish at Yale," 34.

61. Philologos, "A New Mixed Marriage?," *Forward*, May 28 2004.

62. Heilman, *Defenders of the Faith*, 12.

63. Thomas Friedmann, "Back to Orthodoxy: The New Ethic and Ethnics in American Jewish Literature," *Contemporary Jewry* 10, no. 1 (1989): 68.

1. Orthodoxy and Nostalgia in the American Jewish Imagination

1. Woody Allen and Marshall Brickman, *Annie Hall*, ed. Woody Allen, United Artists (1977). Keaton's character remarks of her grandmother: "She hates Jews. She thinks they just make money."

2. For an article that argues the authenticity of Reform Jews, please see Simeon Maslin, "Who Are the Authentic Jews?" *Reform Judaism* Summer (1996), http://reformjudaismmag.net/696sm.html.

3. For more information on contemporary American Jewish life, please see Steven Martin Cohen and Arnold M. Eisen, *The Jew Within: Self, Family, and Community in America* (Bloomington: Indiana University Press, 2000); Sylvia Barack Fishman, *Jewish Life and American Culture* (Albany: State University of New York Press, 2000); David Kaufman, *Shul with a Pool: The "Synagogue-Center" in American Jewish History* (Hanover, N.H.: University Press of New England, 1999); Jonathan D. Sarna, *American Judaism: A History* (New Haven, Conn.: Yale University Press, 2004).

4. Svetlana Boym, *The Future of Nostalgia* (New York: Basic Books, 2001), xviii–xiv.

5. Daphne Merkin, "Trouble in the Tribe: How Jewish Do American Jews Want to Be?" *New Yorker*, September 11, 2000, 52.

6. Boym, *The Future of Nostalgia*, xviii.

7. For more on contemporary attraction to conservative religious groups, see Nancy Tatom Ammerman, *Bible Believers: Fundamentalists in the Modern World* (New Brunswick, N.J.: Rutgers University Press, 1987); Brenda E. Brasher, *Godly Women: Fundamentalism and Female Power* (New Brunswick, N.J.: Rutgers Uni-

versity Press, 1998); Lynn Davidman, *Tradition in a Rootless World: Women Turn to Orthodox Judaism* (Berkeley: University of California Press, 1991); R. Marie Griffith, *God's Daughters: Evangelical Women and the Power of Submission* (Berkeley: University of California Press, 1997); Debra R. Kaufman, *Rachel's Daughters: Newly Orthodox Jewish Women* (New Brunswick, N.J.: Rutgers University Press, 1991); Susan J. Palmer, *Moon Sisters, Krishna Mothers, Rajneesh Lovers: Women's Roles in New Religions*, Women and Gender in North American Religions (Syracuse, N.Y.: Syracuse University Press, 1994).

8. Boym, *The Future of Nostalgia*, xv–xvi.

9. The best known haredi outreach community is the Lubavitch hasidic community, also known as Chabad. The Lubavitchers like to boast that anywhere in the world one can find both Coca-Cola and a Lubavitch emissary. See Sue Fishkoff, *The Rebbe's Army: Inside the World of Chabad-Lubavitch* (New York: Schocken Books, 2003).

10. Samuel G. Freedman, *Jew Vs. Jew: The Struggle for the Soul of American Jewry* (New York: Simon and Schuster, 2000). Freedman describes several fierce fights within Jewish neighborhoods in this work.

11. Henry Goldschmidt, *Race and Religion Among the Chosen Peoples of Crown Heights* (New Brunswick, N.J.: Rutgers University Press, 2006).

12. Samuel C. Heilman, foreword to *New World Hasidim: Ethnographic Studies of Hasidic Jews in America*, ed. Janet S. Belcove-Shalin (Albany: State University of New York Press, 1995), xi.

13. Susan J. Palmer, "Frontiers and Families: The Children of Island Pond," in *Children of New Religions*, ed. Susan J. Palmer and Charlotte Hardman (New Brunswick, N.J.: Rutgers University Press, 1999), 154.

14. Fishkoff, *The Rebbe's Army*, 5.

15. Lis Harris, *Holy Days: The World of a Hasidic Family* (New York: Simon and Schuster, 1985), 11.

16. Stephen G. Bloom, *Postville: A Clash of Cultures in Heartland America* (New York: Harcourt, 2000), 24.

17. Ibid., xiv.

18. For feminist critiques of Orthodoxy, please see Aviva Cantor, *Jewish Women/Jewish Men: The Legacy of Patriarchy in Jewish Life* (San Francisco: HarperSanFrancisco, 1995); Laura Levitt, *Jews and Feminism: The Ambivalent Search for Home* (New York: Routledge, 1997); Miriam Peskowitz and Laura Levitt, *Judaism Since Gender* (New York: Routledge, 1997); Tamar Ross, *Expanding the Palace of Torah: Orthodoxy and Feminism* (Lebanon, N.H.: University Press of New England for Brandeis University Press, 2004); Danya Ruttenberg, *Yentl's Revenge: The Next Wave of Jewish Feminism* (Seattle: Seal Press, 2001).

19. This tolerance is currently being tested with the Jewish Theological Seminary's 2006 decision to ordain homosexuals as Conservative rabbis.

20. Of all American women, Jewish women hold the highest rates of education (Fishman, *Jewish Life and American Culture*, 49).

21. Fishkoff, *The Rebbe's Army: Inside the World of Chabad-Lubavitch*, 167.

22. Anzia Yezierska, *Bread Givers: A Novel* (1925; New York: Persea Books, 1999), 138.

23. Ibid., 296.

24. Boym, *The Future of Nostalgia*, xv.

25. Hana Wirth-Nesher, "From Newark to Prague: Roth's Place in the American Jewish Literary Tradition," in *What Is Jewish Literature?* ed. Hana Wirth-Nesher (Philadelphia: Jewish Publication Society, 1994); Hana Wirth-Nesher and Michael P. Kramer, eds., *The Cambridge Companion to Jewish American Literature* (Cambridge: Cambridge University Press, 2003); Ruth R. Wisse, *The Modern Jewish Canon* (New York: The Free Press, 2000).

26. Philip Roth, "Eli the Fanatic," in *Goodbye, Columbus, and Five Short Stories* (Boston: Houghton Mifflin, 1959), 247–98.

27. Ibid., 261.

28. Ibid., 253.

29. Ibid., 262.

30. Thomas Friedmann, "Back to Orthodoxy: The New Ethic and Ethnics in American Jewish Literature," *Contemporary Jewry* 10, no. 1 (1989): 71.

31. Andrew Furman, *Israel Through the Jewish-American Imagination: A Survey of Jewish-American Literature on Israel, 1928–1995* (Albany: State University of New York Press, 1997); Nathan Glazer, *American Judaism* (Chicago: University of Chicago Press, 1957); Arthur Hertzberg, *The Jews in America: Four Centuries of an Uneasy Encounter: A History* (New York: Simon and Schuster, 1989).

32. Leon Uris, *Exodus* (Garden City, N.Y.: Doubleday, 1958); Leon Uris and Dalton Trumbo, *Exodus*, dir. Otto Preminger, MGM, 1960.

33. Chaim Isaac Waxman, "Israel in American Jewish Life," in *Jews in America: A Contemporary Reader*, ed. Roberta Rosenberg and Chaim I. Waxman (Hanover, N.H.: University Press of New England for Brandeis University Press, 1999), 217.

34. Susannah Heschel, "Imagining Judaism in America," in *The Cambridge Companion to Jewish American Literature*, ed. Hana Wirth-Nesher and Michael Kramer (Cambridge: Cambridge University Press, 2003), 43.

35. Irving Howe, introduction to *Jewish American Stories*, ed. Irving Howe (New York: Mentor, 1977), 1–17.

36. Marshall Sklare, "Intermarriage and Jewish Survival" in *Commentary* (March 1970) volume 49, no 3.

37. Friedmann, "Back to Orthodoxy," 70. *"Shiksa"* is a pejorative term used to describe a non-Jewish woman; it literally means "vermin." Examples of this literature and film include Allen, *Annie Hall*; Roth, *Goodbye, Columbus*; Arthur Laurentis, *The Way We Were*, dir. Sydney Pollack (Columbia Pictures, 1973).

38. There are notable exceptions of course. Cynthia Ozick's and Chaim Potok's work contained Orthodox themes and characters. Examples of Ozick's work include Ozick, *The Pagan Rabbi, and Other Stories* (Syracuse, N.Y.: Syracuse University Press, 1995); Ozick, *The Puttermesser Papers* (New York: Knopf, 1997). In addition to Chaim Potok, *The Chosen* (New York: Fawcett Crest, 1967), please see Potok, *Davita's Harp* (New York: Knopf, 1985); Potok, *My Name Is Asher Lev* (New York: Knopf, 1972); Potok, *The Promise* (New York: Knopf, 1969).

39. Marshall Sklare, *Conservative Judaism: An American Religious Movement*, new ed. (New York: Schocken Books, 1972), 266.

40. For some of Kahane's works, as well as criticism, please see S. Daniel Breslauer, *Meir Kahane, Ideologue, Hero, Thinker: An Expositin and Evaluation* (Lewiston, N.Y.: E. Mellen Press, 1986); Robert I. Friedman, *The False Prophet: Rabbi Meir Kahane—from FBI Informant to Knesset Member* (Brooklyn: Lawrence Hill Books, 1990); Meir Kahane, *Israel: Revolution or Referendum* (Secaucus, N.J.: Barricade Books, 1990); Meir Kahane, *Listen World, Listen Jew*, 3rd ed. (Jerusalem: Institute for the Publication of the Writings of Rabbi Meir Kahane, 1995); Meir Kahane, *The Story of the Jewish Defense League* (Radnor, Penn.: Chilton, 1975); Meir Kahane, *Why Be Jewish? Intermarriage, Assimilation, and Alienation* (Miami Beach, Fla.: Copy Service, 1977); Raphaël Mergui and Philippe Simonnot, *Israel's Ayatollahs: Meir Kahane and the Far Right in Israel* (London: Saqi Books, 1987).

41. Heschel, "Imagining Judaism in America," 45.

42. "*Ba'al teshuvah*": literally, "master of repentance."

43. This revival of Orthodox Judaism has many parallels to fundamentalist Christianity in America, hailed in the 1920s as "essentially the extreme and agonized defense of a dying way of life" (George Marsden, *Fundamentalism and American Culture* [Oxford: Oxford University Press, 1982], 4).

44. Haym Soloveitchik, "Rupture and Reconstruction: The Transformation of Contemporary Orthodoxy," in *Jews in America: A Contemporary Reader*, ed. Roberta Rosenberg and Chaim I. Waxman (Hanover, N.H.: University Press of New England for Brandeis University Press, 1999), 358 n. 21.

45. Azriela Jaffe, *What Do You Mean, You Can't Eat in My Home? A Guide to How Newly Observant Jews and Their Less-Observant Relatives Can Still Get Along* (New York: Schocken Books, 2005); Margery Isis Schwartz, *What's Up with the Hard Core Jewish People? An Irreverent yet Informative Approach to Judaism and Religious Devotion from a Reform Jewish Mother's Perspective* ([Bangor, Maine]: Booklocker.com, 2006). Similar guides have been written claiming to assist those whose friends and family had joined new religious movements. For an example, please see Eileen Barker, *New Religious Movements: A Practical Introduction* (London: H.M.S.O., 1989).

46. Allegra Goodman, "Long-Distance Client," *New Yorker*, July 11 2005, http://www.newyorker.com/archive/2005/07/11/050711fi_fiction?currentPage=all.

47. Donna Rifkind, "Defenders of the Faith," *Weekly Standard*, December 18, 1995, 41.
48. Allegra Goodman, *Kaaterskill Falls: A Novel* (New York: Dial Press, 1998); Eileen Pollack, *Paradise, New York: A Novel* (Philadelphia: Temple University Press, 1998).
49. Anne Richardson Roiphe, *Lovingkindness: A Novel* (New York: Summit Books, 1987), 26–27.
50. Irving Howe, "Immigrant Chic," *New York*, May 12, 1986, 76.
51. Philip Roth, *The Counterlife* (New York: Farrar Straus Giroux, 1986), 155.
52. For more on the culture war in Israel, please see Noah J. Efron, *Real Jews: Secular Versus Ultra-Orthodox and the Struggle for Jewish Identity in Israel* (New York: Basic Books, 2003); Aviezer Ravitzky, "Religious and Secular Jews in Israel: A Culture War?" in *Creating the Jewish Future*, ed. Michael and Bernard Lightman Brown (Walnut Creek, Calif.: AltaMira Press, 1990), 80–100.
53. For more on these nation-specific tensions, please see Janet O'Dea Aviad, *Return to Judaism: Religious Renewal in Israel* (Chicago: University of Chicago Press, 1983); David Biale, "Israeli Secularists' Revenge," *Tikkun* (July 2000); Noah J. Efron, "Men in Black: The Politics of Jewish Identity in Israel," *Tikkun* (September–October 2003); Efron, "A Political Fantasy for Our Time," *Midstream* 48, no. 2 (2002); Efron, "Trembling with Fear: How Secular Israelis See the Ultra-Orthodox, and Why," *Tikkun* 6 (1991): 15–22, 88–90; Aviezer Ravitzky, *Messianism, Zionism, and Jewish Religious Radicalism* (Chicago: University of Chicago Press, 1996); Ravitzky, "Religious and Secular Jews"; Chaim Isaac Waxman, *Israel as a Religious Reality* (Northvale, N.J.: Jason Aronson, 1994).
54. Efron, "Men in Black," 26.
55. Efron, "Trembling with Fear," 21.
56. Ibid.
57. Ibid.
58. Erik Schechter and Amotz Asa-El, "The Anglo Difference: Contributions of English-Speaking Jews to Israel," *Jerusalem Post*, October 2, 2003.
59. Efron, "Trembling with Fear," 19.
60. Ibid., 16.
61. "*Halakha*": Jewish law.
62. Jack Wertheimer, "Religious Movements in Collision: A Jewish Culture War?" in *Jews in America: A Contemporary Reader*, ed. Roberta Rosenberg and Chaim I. Waxman (Hanover, N.H.: University Press of New England for Brandeis University Press, 1999), 382.
63. Ibid., 388.
64. Jack Wertheimer, *A People Divided: Judaism in Contemporary America* (Waltham, Mass.: Brandeis University Press, 1997) 177.
65. Wertheimer, "Religious Movements," 382–88.

2. Rebbes' Daughters: The New *Chosen*

1. Sylvia Barack Fishman, "Negotiating Egalitarianism and Judaism: American Jewish Feminisms and Their Implications for Jewish Life," in *Jews in America: A Contemporary Reader*, ed. Roberta Rosenberg and Chaim I. Waxman (Hanover, N.H.: Brandeis University Press, 1999), 165.

2. For more on the Reform movement's claims to authentic practice, please see Samuel G. Freedman, "The Battle Over Reform Judaism," Salon.com, May 1, 1999, http://www.salon.com/news/feature/1999/05/01/jews/, accessed June 11, 2005; Simeon Maslin, "Who Are the Authentic Jews?" *Reform Judaism* (Summer 1996), http://reformjudaismmag.net/696sm.html. Also see Leonard J. Fein, *Reform Is a Verb* (New York: Union of American Hebrew Congregations, 1972).

3. Phil Zuckerman, *Strife in the Sanctuary: Religious Schism in a Jewish Community* (Walnut Creek, Calif.: AltaMira Press, 1999).

4. For examples of coming-of-age narratives in other strict religious contexts, please see Barbara Kingsolver, *The Poisonwood Bible* (London: Faber and Faber, 2000); Mary McCarthy, *Memories of a Catholic Girlhood* (New York: Harcourt Brace, 1957); Loida Maritza Perez, *Geographies of Home* (New York: Viking, 1999); Anna Quindlen, *Object Lessons* (New York: Fawcett Columbine, 1997); Jeanette Winterson, *Oranges Are Not the Only Fruit* (London: Pandora Press, 1985).

5. Sheldon Grebstein, "The Phenomenon of the Really Jewish Best Seller: Potok's the Chosen," *Studies in American Jewish Literature* 1, no. 1 (1975): 23–31.

6. Chaim Potok, *The Chosen* (New York: Fawcett Crest, 1967), 267.

7. Potok did write one novel that focused on the experience of a young woman struggling with Jewish tradition. Notably this work was published in 1985, the same year that the Conservative movement ordained its first female rabbi. Please see Chaim Potok, *Davita's Harp*, 1st ed. (New York: Knopf, 1985).

8. "*Shabbes goy*": Literally, "Sabbath gentile." Since observant Jews are restricted from activities such as turning on and off lights on Friday night, some religious communities employ non-Jews to take care of some of these things for them. For more on this tradition, please see "The *Shabbes Goy*," in Alan Dundes, *The Shabbat Elevator and Other Sabbath Subterfuges: An Unorthodox Essay on Circumventing Custom and Jewish Character* (Lanham, Md.: Rowman and Littlefield, 2002).

9. Erich Segal, *Acts of Faith* (New York: Bantam Books, 1992), 27.

10. Variations on the spelling of this school will be seen throughout this study (i.e., Beth Yakov, Beis Yaakov, etc.), as these spellings are transliterations of the Hebrew words meaning House of Jacob.

11. Fishman, "Negotiating Egalitarianism," 176.

12. Haim Shapiro and Andy Court, "Police Rout Worshippers with Tear Gas. Extremists Attack Women Holding Fast of Esther Prayer at Wall," *Jerusalem Post*, March 21, 1989.

13. Sylvia Barack Fishman, *A Breath of Life: Feminism in the American Jewish Community* (New York: Free Press, 1993), 171.

14. "Whose Western Wall?" *Jerusalem Post*, March 22, 1989.

15. Samuel G. Freedman, *Jew Vs. Jew: The Struggle for the Soul of American Jewry* (New York: Simon and Schuster, 2000), 22.

16. This quotation came from Rabbi Meir Yehuda Getz, the rabbi in charge of the site. See "Uproar at Wailing Wall," *Herald*, December 2, 1988.

17. Fishman, *A Breath of Life*, 171.

18. For in-depth coverage of the experiences of women praying at the Wall, please see Brenda E. Brasher, "Women of the Wall: Claiming Sacred Ground at Judaism's Holy Site," review of Chesler and Haut, *Women of the Wall*, *Nashim* (Fall 2003): 241; Phyllis Chesler and Rivka Haut, *Women of the Wall: Claiming Sacred Ground at Judaism's Holy Site* (Woodstock, Vt.: Jewish Lights, 2003).

19. Joseph Telushkin, *Jewish Literacy: The Most Important Things to Know About the Jewish Religion, Its People, and Its History* (New York: HarperCollins, 2001), 708.

20. *bima*: literally "elevated place." The *bima* is the platform in the synagogue from which the Torah is read.

21. Alice Shalvi, "Alice Shalvi," in *Half the Kingdom: Seven Jewish Feminists*, ed. Francine Zuckerman (Montreal: Vehicule Press, 1992), 36.

22. Deborah's mother asks, "What kind of a rabbi calls himself 'Steve'? He can't be one of ours" (Segal, *Acts of Faith*, 261).

23. Hillel Halkin, "In Orthodoxy, Ritual Trumps Morality," *Jerusalem Post*, May 27, 2005.

24. Susannah Heschel, *On Being a Jewish Feminist: A Reader* (New York: Schocken Books, 1983), xix. Wisse's concerns have echoes today with growing worries about the feminization of American Judaism in all but the Orthodox ranks.

25. Pamela Susan Nadell, *Women Who Would Be Rabbis: A History of Women's Ordination, 1889–1985* (Boston: Beacon Press, 1998). There are several women who have obtained *smicha* (ordination) from Orthodox rabbis, but these ordinations find no recognition within the movement and are in fact met with more hostility than a woman with same level of education who does not claim the title of rabbi.

26. Segal's novel does more than push for changes in Judaism. In the subplot featuring Timothy Hogan, Tim becomes involved with a movement that supports married priests.

27. Pearl Abraham, *The Romance Reader* (New York: Riverhead Books, 1995), 16.

28. Zuckerman, *Strife in the Sanctuary*, 184.

29. For the seminal work on the multiple functions of romance novels, please see Janice A. Radway, *Reading the Romance: Women, Patriarchy, and Popular Literature* (Chapel Hill: University of North Carolina Press, 1991).

30. Ruth Bienstock Anolik, "Appropriating the Golem, Possessing the Dybbuk: Female Retellings of Jewish Tales," *Modern Language Studies* 31, no. 2 (2001): 48.

31. Tova Mirvis, *The Outside World* (New York: Alfred A. Knopf, 2004), 61.

32. Please see the conclusion to this volume.

33. Samuel C. Heilman, *Defenders of the Faith: Inside Ultra-Orthodox Jewry* (Berkeley: University of California Press, 2000), 309.

34. Hella Winston, *Unchosen: The Hidden Lives of Hasidic Rebels* (Boston: Beacon Press, 2005), 31.

35. Bais Rochel: literally, "House of Rachel" (another example of the varieties of transliteration).

36. Abraham, *The Romance Reader*, 137.

37. Blu Greenberg, *How to Run a Traditional Jewish Household* (New York: Simon and Schuster, 1983), 187.

38. Naomi Ragen, *Sotah* (New York: HarperCollins, 1993), 373.

39. For more historical and halakhic information on Jewish women and hair covering, please see Leila Leah Bronner, "From Veil to Wig: Jewish Women's Hair Covering," *Judaism: A Quarterly Journal of Jewish Life and Thought* 42, no. 4 (1993): 465–78.

40. The same data has been interpreted differently by others however. Historically, intermarriage was seen as an aid in upward mobility, and those who sought higher education as a way out of their neighborhoods were more likely to marry "out." Particularly high rates of intermarriage were seen among college professors. However, with the high rates of education among today's American Jews, some studies have shown that more education leads to higher Jewish involvement. See Sylvia Barack Fishman, *Jewish Life and American Culture* (Albany: State University of New York Press, 2000), 46. Also see Sylvia Barack Fishman, *Double or Nothing? Jewish Families and Mixed Marriage* (Hanover, N.H.: University Press of New England, 2004).

41. Margalit Fox, "Chaim Potok, 73, Dies; Novelist Illumined the World of Hasidic Judaism," *New York Times*, July 24 2002.

42. For an in-depth analysis of evangelical Christian romance novels (and their readers), please see Lynn S. Neal, *Romancing God: Evangelical Women and Inspirational Fiction* (Chapel Hill: University of North Carolina Press, 2006). Like Rachel, many of these women see the novels as escape.

43. Quoted in Fox, "Chaim Potok, 73," 17.

44. Tova Reich, *Master of the Return* (San Diego: Harcourt Brace Jovanovich, 1988), 156–57.

45. Ibid.

46. Fishman, *Jewish Life and American Culture*, 65.

47. For more on education for Jewish women, please see Devora Weissman, "Bais Yaakov: A Historical Model for Jewish Feminists," in *The Jewish Woman: New Perspectives*, ed. Elizabeth Koltun (New York: Schocken, 1976), 139–48; Shoshana Zolty, *And All Your Children Shall Be Learned: Women and the Study of Torah in Jewish Law and History* (Northvale, N.J.: J. Aronson, 1993).

48. Fishman, *A Breath of Life*, 170.

49. Anita Diamant, *The Red Tent* (New York: St. Martin's Press, 1997), Judith A. Kates and Gail Twersky Reimer, *Reading Ruth: Contemporary Women Reclaim a Sacred Story* (New York: Ballantine Books, 1994).

50. Fishman, "Negotiating Egalitarianism," 177.

51. Ibid., 176.

52. I believe this passage may actually be Abraham's nod to Chaim Potok's *The Chosen*, as this could easily be a description of a scene between Danny and Reuven.

53. Elaine M. Kauvar, "An Interview with Chaim Potok," *Contemporary Literature* 27, no. 3 (1986): 313.

54. For more on this shift, please see Jonah Steinberg, "From a 'Pot of Filth' to a 'Hedge of Roses' (and Back): Changing Theorizations of Menstruations in Judaism," in *Women, Gender, Religion: A Reader*, ed. Elizabeth A. Castelli (New York: Palgrave, 2001).

55. Jody Myers and Jane Rachel Litman, "The Secret of Jewish Femininity: Hiddenness, Power, and Physicality in the Theology of Orthodox Women in the Contemporary World," in *Gender and Judaism: The Transformation of Tradition*, ed. T. M. Rudavsky (New York: New York University Press, 1995).

56. Allegra Goodman, *Total Immersion: Stories* (New York: Harper and Row, 1989), 264–65.

57. Zuckerman, *Strife in the Sanctuary*, 189.

58. Ibid., 188.

59. Anne Richardson Roiphe, *Lovingkindness: A Novel* (New York: Summit Books, 1987), 271.

60. Ibid., 166.

61. Rachel Biale, *Women and Jewish Law: The Essential Texts, Their History, and Their Relevance for Today* (New York: Schocken Books, 1995), ix.

3. The New Jewish Gothic

1. Susan J. Palmer, "Frontiers and Families: The Children of Island Pond," in *Children of New Religions*, ed. Susan J. Palmer and Charlotte Hardman (New Brunswick: Rutgers University Press, 1999), 155.

2. For similarly themed "awakening" works from the late nineteenth century, please see Kate Chopin, *The Awakening* (Chicago: H. S. Stone and Company, 1899); Charlotte Perkins Gilman, *The Yellow Wallpaper*, Feminist Press Reprint No. 3 (1899; New York: Feminist Press, 1973); Henrik Ibsen, *A Doll's House*, trans. and intro. William Archer (London: T. F. Unwin, 1889).

3. "Nebbish": literally weak, timid, or ineffective. For more on the subject of Jewish masculinities, see Paul Breines, *Tough Jews: Political Fantasies and the Moral Dilemma of American Jewry* (New York: Basic Books, 1990); Harry Brod, *The Making of Masculinities* (Boston: Allen and Unwin, 1987); Brod, *A Mensch Among Men: Explorations in Jewish Masculinity* (Freedom, Calif.: Crossing Press, 1988).

4. Daniel Boyarin, *Unheroic Conduct: The Rise of Heterosexuality and the Invention of the Jewish Man* (Berkeley: University of California Press, 1997), 5. As Gail Bederman explains, gender is an ongoing historical, ideological process, not an intrinsic set of traits or values. Gail Bederman, *Manliness and Civilization: A Cultural History of Gender and Race in the United States, 1880–1917* (Chicago: University of Chicago Press, 1995).

5. Boyarin's work attempts to reverse this perception, to see these characteristics as positive ones; see Boyarin, *Unheroic Conduct*. Also see Matti Bunzl, "Jews, Queers, and Other Symptoms: Recent Work in Jewish Cultural Studies," *GLQ: A Journal of Lesbian and Gay Studies* 6, no. 2 (2000): 321–41.

6. Noah J. Efron, "Trembling with Fear: How Secular Israelis See the Ultra-Orthodox, and Why," *Tikkun* 6 (1991): 16.

7. The Jewish rite of circumcision has long been discussed and debated as a form of castration. For discussions of this practice, please see Lawrence A. Hoffman, *Covenant of Blood: Circumcision and Gender in Rabbinic Judaism* (Chicago: University of Chicago Press, 1996); Elizabeth Wyner Mark, *The Covenant of Circumcision: New Perspectives on an Ancient Jewish Rite* (Hanover, N.H.: University Press of New England for Brandeis University Press, 2003); Eric Kline Silverman, *From Abraham to America: A History of Jewish Circumcision* (Lanham, Md.: Rowman and Littlefield, 2006).

8. A 2007 Israeli film, David Volach's *My Father My Lord*, examines a similarly oppressive haredi environment, albeit through a tragic story about a young boy sacrificed for his father's adherence to Jewish law.

9. Parallels have been made with African Americans after slavery; see Bonnie Morris, "Agents or Victims of Religious Ideology? Approaches to Locating Hasidic Women in Feminist Studies," in *New World Hasidim: Ethnographic Studies of Hasidic Jews in America*, ed. Janet S. Belcove-Shalin (Albany: State University of New York Press, 1995), 168.

10. In addition to *Bread Givers*, other examples include Rose Cohen, *Out of the Shadow* (1918) and Henry Roth, *Call it Sleep* (1934).

11. E. Anthony Rotundo, *American Manhood: Transformations in Masculinity from the Revolution to the Modern Era* (New York: BasicBooks, 1993), 168.

12. Sylvia Barack Fishman, *Jewish Life and American Culture* (Albany: State University of New York Press, 2000), 43.

13. From the Yiddish *"lernen."* One refers to studying in a yeshiva as "learning." This phraseology has made its way into the Modern Orthodox lexicon, yet another example of the haredization of orthodoxy.

14. Samuel Heilman, *Sliding to the Right: The Contest for the Future of American Jewish Orthodoxy* (Berkeley: University of California Press, 2006), 146.

15. It is far easier for the full-time scholar to exist in Israel, where learning in a yeshiva is subsidized by the government.

16. This complementary but unequal relationship between men and women is seen frequently in conservative religious communities, such as the Church of Jesus Christ of Latter-Day Saints or the International Society for Krishna Consciousness. Women are necessary for assisting men to achieve a higher state

17. Jeanne Boydston, *Home and Work: Housework, Wages, and the Ideology of Labor in the Early Republic* (New York: Oxford University Press, 1990), xviii.

18. Heilman, *Sliding to the Right*, 143.

19. For some readings on the "gaze" of the Other, please see Beryl Wright, "Back Talk: Recoding the Body," *Callaloo* 19, no. 2 (1996): 397–413; Raz Yosef, *Beyond Flesh: Queer Maculinities and Nationalism in Israeli Cinema* (New Brunswick, N.J.: Rutgers University Press, 2004).

20. Described and debated in the Mishnah, *"sotah"* is a rite where a woman is shamed publicly because of suspicion of adultery.

21. E. J. Kessler, "Reading Books on the Sly, a Chasidic Girl Plots Escape," *Forward*, July 28, 1995, 9.

22. Naomi Ragen, *Sotah* (New York: HarperCollins, 1993), 125.

23. Erich Segal, *Acts of Faith* (New York: Bantam Books, 1992), 141.

24. *Kollel*: Boys attend yeshiva through high school and college. Married men who choose to (and can afford to) continue their "learning" attend *kollel*, often teaching younger classes in order to subsidize their income (much like Mendel in *A Price Above Rubies*).

25. Hella Winston, *Unchosen: The Hidden Lives of Hasidic Rebels* (Boston: Beacon Press, 2005), 32.

26. Dan Levin, "A Display of Disapproval That Turned Menacing," *New York Times*, December 16, 2007.

27. Winston, *Unchosen*, 3.

28. Kathleen M. Brown, *Good Wives, Nasty Wenches, and Anxious Patriarchs: Gender, Race, and Power in Colonial Virginia* (Chapel Hill: University of North Carolina Press, 1996), 99.

29. Bertram Wyatt-Brown, *Southern Honor: Ethics and Behavior in the Old South* (New York: Oxford University Press, 1982), 114.

30. Katrinka Blickle, "In Short—Fiction: Jephte's Daughter," *New York Times Book Review*, April 2, 1989, 28.

31. Naomi Ragen did not appreciate this review. "Ragen . . . had not read reviews of her books since a *New York Times* reviewer hailed *Jephte's Daughter* as a new genre of Jewish Gothic. 'As if I had made the whole thing up,' fumes Ragen" (Shelly Kleiman, "Author's Novels Evoke World of the Ultra-Orthodox," *Canadian Jewish News*, available through http://www.naomiragen.com/Articles/orthoworld.htm).

32. These fantasies of the harem are described in detail in Judy Mabro, *Veiled Half-Truths: Western Travelers' Perceptions of Middle Eastern Women* (London: I. B. Tauris, 1996), a collection of travel writing regarding women in the Middle East. Laura Mulvey, *Visual and Other Pleasures* (Basingstoke: Macmillan, 1989), argues that these fantasies and fetishes are male projections.

33. Thomas Grant, "Hostage to Innocence: The Captivity Melodrama from Colonial Massachusetts to Contemporary Lebanon," in *The American Columbiad: Discovering America, Inventing the United States* (Amsterdam: VU University Press, 1996).

34. Ibid., 246.

35. Joy S. Kasson, *Marble Queens and Captives: Women in Nineteenth-Century American Sculpture* (New Haven, Conn.: Yale University Press, 1990).

36. David Biale, "Israeli Secularists' Revenge," *Tikkun* (July 2000).

37. Representations of Jews in the twentieth century have ranged from overtly anti-Semitic depictions to representations perpetuated by Jews themselves. The Jewish Mother and the Jewish American Princess were both created and popularized by Jewish men. Paula Hyman's work has argued that Jewish men have produced negative images of Jewish women in order to distance themselves from "the Jew," and in this case, the typical Jew is a woman. See Paula Hyman, *Gender and Assimilation in Modern Jewish History: The Roles and Representation of Women* (Seattle: University of Washington Press, 1995). Also see Sander Gilman, *The Jew's Body* (New York: Routledge, 1991) and *Jewish Self-Hatred* (Baltimore, Md.: Johns Hopkins University Press, 1990).

38. For more on the captivity genre, see Michelle Burnham, *Captivity and Sentiment: Cultural Exchange in American Literature, 1682–1861* (Hanover, N.H.: University Press of New England for Dartmouth College, 1997); Christopher Castiglia, *Bound and Determined: Captivity, Culture-Crossing, and White Womanhood from Mary Rowlandson to Patty Hearst* (Chicago: University of Chicago Press, 1996); Gary L. Ebersole, *Captured by Texts: Puritan to Postmodern Images of Indian Captivity* (Charlottesville: University Press of Virginia, 1995).

39. Argued by Kate Ferguson Ellis and cited by Kari J. Winter, *Subjects of Slavery, Agents of Change: Women and Power in Gothic Novels and Slave Narratives, 1790–1865* (Athens: University of Georgia Press, 1992), 18.

40. Ibid., 18–19.

41. Maria Monk claimed in her *Awful Disclosures* that she escaped the convent in order to save her child. See Rebecca Reed and Maria Monk, *Veil of Fear: Nineteenth-Century Convent Tales*, intro. Nancy Lusignan Schultz (West Lafayette, Ind.: NotaBell Books, 1999).

42. Noah J. Efron, *Real Jews: Secular Versus Ultra-Orthodox and the Struggle for Jewish Identity in Israel* (New York: Basic Books, 2003), 170.

43. Ibid.

44. Michael Chabon, *The Yiddish Policemen's Union: A Novel* (New York: HarperCollins, 2007), 23.

45. Efron, *Real Jews*.

46. Noah J. Efron, "A Political Fantasy for Our Time," *Midstream* 48, no. 2 (2002): 13–16.

47. Any real anxiety about Jewish power tends to come from non-Jewish, right-wing militia folks who are trying to retain white power. And these "Jews" that white supremacists are worried about are secular Jews who "run Hollywood and the banks." These "Jews" of anti-Semitic lore are not the small haredi factions who—on the whole—avoid involvement in American politics and culture. But the dominant groups of American Jews are still very worried about these Jews.

48. Comparisons can be made to sealed marriages in the Church of Jesus Christ of Latter-Day Saints.

49. In Judaism, children are only considered illegitimate if they are born to a married woman and a man who is not her husband. Children born out of premarital relationships are not illegitimate, nor are children born to married *men* outside of marriage.

50. Carey Goldberg, "Fathers' Tactic in Divorce Wars: Jewish Custom Is Revived as Leverage Against Wives," *New York Times*, May 27, 1995.

51. Naomi Grossman, "Women Unbound: Breaking the Chains of Jewish Divorce Law," *Lilith* 18, no. 3 (1993): 8; Devora C. Hammer, "Confessions of an Agunah Activist," *Lilith* (Winter 2003): 20; Judith Plaskow, "Judith Plaskow's Un-Orthodox Take on the Feminism and Orthodoxy Conference," *Lilith* 22, no. 2 (1997): 4; Sarah Blustain, "Rabbis Demand a 'Public Outcry' On Agunot," *Lilith* 23, no. 2 (1998): 5.

52. In Lawrence Foster, *Religion and Sexuality: The Shakers, the Mormons, and the Oneida Community* (Urbana: University of Illinois Press, 1984), within the Oneida Perfectionists the control has been over *men's* bodies. This case is an exception.

53. Anson D. Shupe, *Six Perspectives on New Religions: A Case Study Approach* (New York: E. Mellen Press, 1981), 214.

54. Calev Ben-David, "One for Herself," *Jerusalem Post*, December 21, 2001.

55. Dan Izenberg, "Naomi Ragen Sued for Plagiarism—Again," *Jerusalem Post*, September 1, 2007, http://www.jpost.com/servlet/Satellite?pagename=JPost/JPArticle/ShowFull&cid=1188392510984.

56. Ben-David, "One for Herself."

57. Etgar Lefkovitz, "Haredi Youths Assail Woman on Bus," *Jerusalem Post*, October 21, 2007.

58. See Allegra Goodman, *Kaaterskill Falls: A Novel* (New York: Dial Press, 1998); and Pearl Abraham, *Giving up America* (New York: Riverhead Books, 1998) as examples of ambivalent sentiment in fiction about the haredi community.

59. Chabad is an outreach organization of the Lubavitcher Hasidic movement, geared toward increasing observance among secular Jews. Chabad Houses are often found near college campuses. Or Sameach has similar outreach methods.

4. Muggers in Black Coats

1. Anne Richardson Roiphe, *Lovingkindness: A Novel* (New York: Summit Books, 1987), 11.

2. Blanche d'Alpuget, "A Daughter Lost to Faith," *New York Times Book Review*, August 30, 1987, 9.

3. According to some right-wing Jews, the Modern Orthodox are "pretenders to the crown of Torah rather than its authentic spokesmen and interpreters" (Eli D. Clark, "Orthodoxy Lurches to the Right," *Moment* [June 1996]: 47).

4. For more information on the Orthodox move from city to suburbs, see Etan Diamond, *And I Will Dwell in Their Midst: Orthodox Jews in Suburbia* (Chapel Hill: University of North Carolina Press, 2000); and Sol Gittleman, *From Shtetl to Suburbia: The Family in Jewish Literary Imagination* (Boston: Beacon Press, 1978).

5. Tova Mirvis, *The Outside World* (New York: Knopf, 2004), 41.

6. Samuel Heilman, *Sliding to the Right: The Contest for the Future of American Jewish Orthodoxy* (Berkeley: University of California Press, 2006), 119.

7. Pearl Abraham, *Giving up America* (New York: Riverhead Books, 1998).

8. Hella Winston, *Unchosen: The Hidden Lives of Hasidic Rebels* (Boston: Beacon Press, 2005), 56.

9. Allegra Goodman, "Long-Distance Client," *New Yorker*, July 11, 2005, http://www.newyorker.com/archive/2005/07/11/050711fi_fiction.

10. Dara Horn, *In the Image: A Novel* (New York: Norton, 2002), 67.

11. Heilman, *Sliding to the Right*, 103.

12. Goodman, "Long-Distance Client."

13. Allegra Goodman, *Kaaterskill Falls: A Novel* (New York: Dial Press, 1998).

14. Because of the havoc this can wreak upon familial relationships, Aish HaTorah—an Orthodox outreach organization—offers a class called "How to Keep Kosher and Keep Your Parents" (Gabrielle Birckner, "When Children Go Frum," *Moment* [December 2001]: 253).

15. Lis Harris, *Holy Days: The World of a Hasidic Family* (New York: Simon and Schuster, 1985), 208.

16. Murray Herbert Danzger, *Returning to Tradition: The Contemporary Revival of Orthodox Judaism* (New Haven, Conn.: Yale University Press, 1989), 80.

17. For more on children in new religious movements, please see Susan J. Palmer and Charlotte Hardman, *Children in New Religions* (New Brunswick, N.J.: Rutgers University Press, 1999).

18. Eileen Barker, "Religious Movements: Cult and Anti-Cult Since Jonestown," *Annual Review of Sociology* 12 (1986): 331.

19. Ibid., 335

20. David G. Bromley, "A Tale of Two Theories: Brainwashing and Conversion as Competing Political Theories," in *Misunderstanding Cults: Searching for Objectivity in a Controversial Field*, ed. Thomas Robbins and Benjamin David Zablocki (Toronto: University of Toronto Press, 2001), 318–48.

21. Noah J. Efron, *Real Jews: Secular Versus Ultra-Orthodox and the Struggle for Jewish Identity in Israel* (New York: Basic Books, 2003), 104.

22. Philip Roth, *The Counterlife* (New York: Farrar Straus Giroux, 1986), 80.

23. Mary B. W. Tabor, "Boy, 15, in Religious Tug-of-War Meets with Parents after 2 Years," *New York Times*, March 1, 1994.

24. Mary B. W. Tabor, "Kidnapped or Converted?" *New York Times*, August 2, 1992; Joseph P. Fried, "Mother Tells of Pressures on Jewish Son by a Rabbi," *New York Times*, October 12, 1994; Michael Lesher, "The Rabbi and the Runaway," *New York Jewish Week*, June 28, 1996.

25. Tabor, "Kidnapped or Converted?" 43.

26. Joseph P. Fried, "Orthodox Rabbi Found Guilty of Kidnapping a Jewish Youth," *New York Times*, November 21, 1994.

27. Tabor, "Kidnapped or Converted?" 37.

28. Jonathan Mark, "Kidnapping Trial in New York: A Battle Over Jewish Souls," *Jewish Advocate*, March 4, 1993.

29. Debra Nussbaum Cohen, "Behind the Headlines: Case of Haredi Rabbi Who Kidnapped Boy Highlights Secular-Orthodox Tensions," *Jewish Telegraphic Agency*, November 17, 1994, 6.

30. Lesher, "The Rabbi and the Runaway."

31. Joseph P. Fried, "Following Up," *New York Times*, April 1, 2001.

32. Elaine Grudin Denholtz, *The Zaddik: The Battle for a Boy's Soul* (New York: Prometheus Books, 2001).

33. Ibid., 16.

34. Please see Jean-Marie Abgrall, *Soul Snatchers: The Mechanics of Cults* (New York: Algora, 2000); Ted Patrick and Tom Dulack, *Let Our Children Go!* (New York: Dutton, 1976); Anson D. Shupe and David G. Bromley, *Anti-Cult Movements in Cross-Cultural Perspective* (New York: Garland, 1994); Anson D. Shupe, David G. Bromley, and Donna L. Oliver, *The Anti-Cult Movement in America: A Bibliography and Historical Survey*, Sects and Cults in America 2 (New York: Garland, 1984).

35. Denholtz, *The Zaddik*, 14.

36. Ibid., 16.

37. These types of sensationalized exposés of the haredi community are common in Israel, where the bitterness between religious and secular Jews, *dati* and *lo dati*, is open and publicized.

38. Adam Dicker, "Elian Saga Could Mar Return of Children: U.S. Probing 21 Custody Cases Involving Israel, Signer of '80 Extradition Pact," *New York Jewish Week*, April 28, 2000.

39. Joseph Berger, "Holy Hypocrites?" *Moment* 25, no. 1 (2000): 55.

40. Sylvia Barack Fishman, *Jewish Life and American Culture* (Albany: State University of New York, 2000) 185.

41. Allegra Goodman, *The Family Markowitz* (New York: Farrar Straus and Giroux, 1996), 187–88.

42. Efron, *Real Jews*, 104.

43. Shiva: The seven-day mourning period following the death of a family member.

44. Philip Roth, *Operation Shylock: A Confession* (New York: Simon and Schuster, 1993), 47.

45. Tresa Grauer, "'A Drastically Bifurcated Legacy': Homeland and Identity in Contemporary Jewish American Literature," in *Divergent Jewish Cultures: Israel and America*, ed. Deborah Dash and S. Ilan Troen Moore (New Haven, Conn.: Yale University Press, 2001), 241.

46. Ibid., 242.

47. Naomi Sokoloff, "Imagining Israel in American Jewish Fiction: Anne Roiphe's *Lovingkindness* and Philip Roth's *The Counterlife*," *Studies in American Jewish Literature* (1991): 71.

48. Sylvia Barack Fishman, "Jewish Identity in American Fiction," in *Envisioning Israel: The Changing Ideals and Images of North American Jews*, ed. Allon Gal (Jerusalem: Hebrew University Press, 1996), 292.

49. Anne Richardson Roiphe, "The Whole Truth," *Tikkun* (July/August 1989): 86.

50. Jonathan D. Sarna, "A Projection of America as it Ought to Be: Zion in the Mind's Eye of American Jews" *Envisioning Israel: The Changing Ideals and Images*

of North American Jews, ed. Allon Gal (Jerusalem: Hebrew University Press, 1996), 41.

51. Fishman, *Jewish Life and American Culture*, 13.
52. Sue Fishkoff, *The Rebbe's Army: Inside the World of Chabad-Lubavitch*, 1st ed. (New York: Schocken Books, 2003), 51.
53. Richardson, "Social Context."
54. Jonathan D. Sarna, *American Judaism: A History* (New Haven, Conn.: Yale University Press, 2004), 370.
55. "Bintel Brief: Lisa Loeb Says Don't Call Your Daughter's Boyfriend a 'Parasite,'" *Forward*, January 14, 1998, http://www.forward.com/blogs/bintel-blog/12452/, accessed January 18, 2008.
56. d'Alpuget, "A Daughter Lost to Faith," 9.

CONCLUSION:
THEY ARE US IN OTHER CLOTHES

1. Chaim Grade, David Brandes, and Joseph Telushkin, *The Quarrel*, dir. Eli Cohen (Honey and Apple Productions, 1991).
2. This visual gag can be seen in at least two films, *Frisco Kid* (1979) and *Witness* (1985).
3. Thomas Friedmann, "Back to Orthodoxy: The New Ethic and Ethnics in American Jewish Literature," *Contemporary Jewry* 10, no. 1 (1989): 75–76.
4. Tova Mirvis, *The Outside World* (New York: Knopf, 2004), 159.
5. Anne Richardson Roiphe, *Lovingkindness: A Novel* (New York: Summit Books, 1987), 26–27.
6. Wendy Shalit, "The Observant Reader," *New York Times*, January 30, 2005.
7. Philip Roth, "Writing About Jews," *Commentary* (December 1963), reprint, in Philip Roth, *Reading Myself and Others* (New York: Vintage Books, 2001), 193–211.

BIBLIOGRAPHY

Aarons, Victoria. "The Covenant Unraveling: The Pathos of Cultural Loss in Allegra Goodman's Fiction." *Shofar* 22, no. 3 (2004): 12–25.

Abecassis, Eliette. *Kadosh*. Dir. Amos Gitai. MP Productions, 1999.

Abgrall, Jean-Marie. *Soul Snatchers: The Mechanics of Cults*. New York: Algora, 2000.

Abraham, Pearl. *Giving up America*. New York: Riverhead Books, 1998.

——. *The Romance Reader*. New York: Riverhead Books, 1995.

Abramov, Tehillah. *The Secret of Jewish Femininity*. New York: Targum Press, 1988.

Allen, Woody, and Marshall Brickman. *Annie Hall*. Dir. Woody Allen. United Artists, 1977.

Alter, Robert. *After the Tradition; Essays on Modern Jewish Writing*. New York,: Dutton, 1969.

Ammerman, Nancy Tatom. *Baptist Battles: Social Change and Religious Conflict in the Southern Baptist Convention*. New Brunswick, N.J.: Rutgers University Press, 1990.

——. *Bible Believers: Fundamentalists in the Modern World*. New Brunswick, N.J.: Rutgers University Press, 1987.

Amy, Lori. "Contemporary Travel Narratives and Old Style Politics: American Women Reporting after the Gulf War." *Women's Studies International Forum* 22, no. 5 (1999): 525–41.

Anolik, Ruth Bienstock. "Appropriating the Golem, Possessing the Dybbuk: Female Retellings of Jewish Tales." *Modern Language Studies* 31, no. 2 (2001): 39–55.

Antler, Joyce, ed.. *America and I: Short Stories by American Jewish Women Writers*. Boston: Beacon Press, 1990.

——. *The Journey Home: Jewish Women and the American Century*. New York: Free Press, 1997.

——. *Talking Back: Images of Jewish Women in American Popular Culture*. Hanover, N.H.: University Press of New England for Brandeis University Press, 1998.

Arweck, Elisabeth. "The Insider/Outsider Problem in the Study of New Religious Movements." In *Theorizing Faith: The Insider/Outsider Problem in the Study of Ritual*, ed. Elisabeth Arweck and Martin Stringer, 115–32. Birmingham, U.K.: University of Birmingham Press, 2002.

Avery, Evelyn. "Religion and Rebellion: Jewish American Women Writers in the '90s." *Modern Jewish Studies* (2001): 44–54.

Aviad, Janet O'Dea. *Return to Judaism: Religious Renewal in Israel*. Chicago: University of Chicago Press, 1983.

Avrech, Robert J. *A Stranger Among Us*. Dir. Sidney Lumet. Touchstone Pictures, 1992.

Barbuto, Domenica M. *American Settlement Houses and Progressive Social Reform: An Encyclopedia of the American Settlement Movement*. Phoenix, Ariz.: Oryx Press, 1999.

Barker, Eileen. *New Religious Movements: A Practical Introduction*. London: H.M.S.O., 1989.

——. "Religious Movements: Cult and Anti-Cult Since Jonestown." *Annual Review of Sociology* 12 (1986): 329–46.

Bauman, Zygmunt. *Modernity and Ambivalence*. Ithaca, N.Y.: Cornell University Press, 1991.

Bederman, Gail. *Manliness and Civilization: A Cultural History of Gender and Race in the United States, 1880–1917*. Chicago: University of Chicago Press, 1995.

Bekker, Karen. "Rally: National Day for Agunah Rights." *Lilith* 20, no. 2 (1995): 7.

Belcove-Shalin, Janet S. "Home in Exile: Hasidim in the New World." In *New World Hasidim: Ethnographic Studies of Hasidic Jews in America*, ed. Janet S. Belcove-Shalin, 205–36. Albany: SUNY Press, 1995.

——. Introduction to *New World Hasidim: Ethnographic Studies of Hasidic Jews in America*, ed. Janet S. Belcove-Shalin, 1–30. Albany: SUNY Press, 1995.

——, ed. *New World Hasidim: Ethnographic Studies of Hasidic Jews in America*. Albany: State University of New York Press, 1995.

Ben-David, Calev. "One for Herself." *Jerusalem Post*, December 21, 2001.

Berger, Joseph. "Holy Hypocrites?" *Moment* 25, no. 1 (2000): 50–55, 98–99.

Biale, David. "Israeli Secularists' Revenge." *Tikkun* 15 (July 2000): 69–75.

Biale, David, Michael Galchinsky, and Susannah Heschel. *Insider/Outsider: American Jews and Multiculturalism*. Berkeley: University of California Press, 1998.

Biale, Rachel. *Women and Jewish Law: The Essential Texts, Their History, and Their Relevance for Today*. New York: Schocken Books, 1995.

Biema, David V. "Sparse at Seder." *Time*, April 28, 1997, 67.

"Bintel Brief: Lisa Loeb Says Don't Call Your Daughter's Boyfriend a 'Parasite.'" *Forward*, January 14, 1998. http://www.forward.com/blogs/bintel-blog/12452/. Accessed January 18, 2008.

Birckner, Gabrielle. "When Children Go Frum." *Moment* (December 2001): 247–53.

Blau, Eleanor. "Traditions of Jewry Pervade Filming of 'Chosen.'" *New York Times*, November 20, 1980.

Blickle, Katrinka. "In Short—Fiction: Jephte's Daughter." *New York Times Book Review*, April 2, 1989, 28.

Bloom, Stephen G. *Postville: A Clash of Cultures in Heartland America*. New York: Harcourt, 2000.

Bluefarb, Sam. *The Escape Motif in the American Novel: Mark Twain to Richard Wright*. Columbus: Ohio State University Press, 1972.

Blustain, Sarah. "Rabbis Demand a 'Public Outcry' on Agunot." *Lilith* 23, no. 2 (1998): 5.

Boyarin, Daniel. *Unheroic Conduct: The Rise of Heterosexuality and the Invention of the Jewish Man*. Berkeley: University of California Press, 1997.

Boydston, Jeanne. *Home and Work: Housework, Wages, and the Ideology of Labor in the Early Republic*. New York: Oxford University Press, 1990.

Boym, Svetlana. *The Future of Nostalgia*. New York: Basic Books, 2001.

Brasher, Brenda E. *Godly Women: Fundamentalism and Female Power*. New Brunswick, N.J.: Rutgers University Press, 1998.

——. "Women of the Wall: Claiming Sacred Ground at Judaism's Holy Site." Review of Chesler and Haut, *Women of the Wall*. *Nashim* (Fall 2003): 241.

Breines, Paul. *Tough Jews: Political Fantasies and the Moral Dilemma of American Jewry*. New York: Basic Books, 1990.

Breslauer, S. Daniel. *Meir Kahane, Ideologue, Hero, Thinker: An Exposition and Evaluation*. Lewiston, N.Y.: E. Mellen Press, 1986.

——. *Mordecai Kaplan's Thought in a Postmodern Age*. Atlanta: Scholars Press, 1994.

Brod, Harry. *The Making of Masculinities*. Boston: Allen and Unwin, 1987.

——. *A Mensch Among Men: Explorations in Jewish Masculinity*. Freedom, Calif.: Crossing Press, 1988.

Bromley, David G. "A Tale of Two Theories: Brainwashing and Conversion as Competing Political Theories." In *Misunderstanding Cults: Searching for Objectivity in a Controversial Field*, ed. Thomas Robbins and Benjamin David Zablocki, 318–48. Toronto: University of Toronto Press, 2001.

Bromley, David G., and Anson D. Shupe. *Strange Gods: The Great American Cult Scare*. Boston: Beacon Press, 1981.

Bronner, Leila Leah. "From Veil to Wig: Jewish Women's Hair Covering." *Judaism: A Quarterly Journal of Jewish Life and Thought* 42, no. 4 (1993): 465–78.

Brown, Kathleen M. *Good Wives, Nasty Wenches, and Anxious Patriarchs: Gender, Race, and Power in Colonial Virginia.* Chapel Hill: University of North Carolina Press, 1996.

Brown, Michael. "Biblical Myth and Contemporary Experience: The Akedah in Modern Jewish Literature." *Judaism* 31, no. 1 (Winter 1982): 99–112.

Brown, Michael, and Bernard Lightman. *Creating the Jewish Future.* Walnut Creek, Calif.: AltaMira Press, 1990.

Buchbinder, Anita. "Three Generations Later: The Contemporary Mother-Daughter Dyad as Reflected in Jewish-American Women's Literature." Ph.D. diss., Indiana University of Pennsylvania, 1999.

Budick, E. Miller. *Ideology and Jewish Identity in Israeli and American Literature.* Albany: State University of New York Press, 2001.

Bunzl, Matti. "Jews, Queers, and Other Symptoms: Recent Work in Jewish Cultural Studies." *GLQ: A Journal of Lesbian and Gay Studies* 6, no. 2 (2000): 321–41.

——. *Symptoms of Modernity: Jews and Queers in Late-Twentieth-Century Vienna.* Berkeley: University of California Press, 2004.

Burnham, Michelle. *Captivity and Sentiment: Cultural Exchange in American Literature, 1682–1861.* Hanover, N.H.: University Press of New England for Dartmouth College, 1997.

Burstein, Janet. *Writing Mothers, Writing Daughters: Tracing the Maternal in Stories by American Jewish Women.* Urbana: University of Illinois Press, 1996.

Cantor, Aviva. *Jewish Women/Jewish Men: The Legacy of Patriarchy in Jewish Life.* San Francisco: HarperSanFrancisco, 1995.

Caplan, Eric. *From Ideology to Liturgy: Reconstructionist Worship and American Liberal Judaism.* Cincinnati: Hebrew Union College Press, 2002.

Carson, Mina Julia. *Settlement Folk: Social Thought and the American Settlement Movement, 1885–1930.* Chicago: University of Chicago Press, 1990.

Castelli, Elizabeth A., and Rosamond C. Rodman. *Women, Gender, Religion: A Reader.* New York: Palgrave, 2001.

Castiglia, Christopher. *Bound and Determined: Captivity, Culture-Crossing, and White Womanhood from Mary Rowlandson to Patty Hearst.* Chicago: University of Chicago Press, 1996.

Cattan, Nacha. "Survey Shows Conservative Judaism's Numbers Dropping." *Forward,* September 19, 2003, 1, 21.

Certeau, Michel de. *The Practice of Everyday Life.* Berkeley: University of California Press, 1984.

Chabon, Michael. *The Yiddish Policemen's Union: A Novel.* New York: HarperCollins, 2007.

Chametzky, Jules. *Jewish American Literature: A Norton Anthology.* New York: Norton, 2001.

Chesler, Phyllis, and Rivka Haut. *Women of the Wall: Claiming Sacred Ground at Judaism's Holy Site.* Woodstock, Vt.: Jewish Lights, 2003.

Cheyette, Bryan. *Between "Race" and Culture: Representations of "the Jew" in English and American Literature.* Stanford, Calif.: Stanford University Press, 1996.

Cheyette, Bryan, and Laura Marcus. *Modernity, Culture, and "the Jew."* Stanford, Calif.: Stanford University Press, 1998.

Chidester, David. "Saving the Children by Killing Them: Redemptive Sacrifice in the Ideologies of Jim Jones and Ronald Reagan." *Religion and American Culture* 1, no. 2 (1991): 177–201.

Chiswick, Carmel Ullman. "Economic Adjustment of Immigrants: Jewish Adaptation to the United States." In *Jews in America: A Contemporary Reader,* ed. Roberta Rosenberg and Chaim I. Waxman, 16–27. Hanover, N.H.: University Press of New England for Brandeis University Press, 1999.

Chopin, Kate. *The Awakening.* Chicago: H. S. Stone and Company, 1899.

Clark, Eli D. "Orthodoxy Lurches to the Right." *Moment* (June 1996): 29–35, 58–59.

Cohen, Debra Nussbaum. "Behind the Headlines: Case of Haredi Rabbi Who Kidnapped Boy Highlights Secular-Orthodox Tensions." *Jewish Telegraphic Agency,* November 17, 1994, 6.

Cohen, Joseph, and Yehuda Amichai. *Voices of Israel: Essays on and Interviews with Yehuda Amichai, A. B. Yehoshua, T. Carmi, Aharon Applefeld, and Amos Oz.* Albany: State University of New York Press, 1990.

Cohen, Rose. *Out of the Shadow: A Russian Jewish Girlhood on the Lower East Side.* Ithaca, N.Y.: Cornell University Press, 1995.

Cohen, Sarah Blacher. *From Hester Street to Hollywood: The Jewish-American Stage and Screen.* Bloomington: Indiana University Press, 1983.

Cohen, Steven Martin. *Content or Continuity? Alternative Bases for Commitment.* New York: American Jewish Committee, 1990.

Cohen, Steven Martin, and Arnold M. Eisen. *The Jew Within: Self, Family, and Community in America.* Bloomington: Indiana University Press, 2000.

Crocker, Ruth. *Social Work and Social Order: The Settlement Movement in Two Industrial Cities, 1889–1930.* Urbana: University of Illinois Press, 1992.

Cunningham, Frank R. *Sidney Lumet: Film and Literary Vision.* Lexington, Ky.: University Press of Kentucky, 1991.

d'Alpuget, Blanche. "A Daughter Lost to Faith." *New York Times Book Review*, August 30, 1987, 9.

Danzger, Murray Herbert. *Returning to Tradition: The Contemporary Revival of Orthodox Judaism*. New Haven, Conn.: Yale University Press, 1989.

Daum, Oren, and Menachem Rudavsky. *A Life Apart: Hasidism in America*. New York: First Run/Icarus Films, 1997.

Davidman, Lynn. *Tradition in a Rootless World: Women Turn to Orthodox Judaism*. Berkeley: University of California Press, 1991.

Davidman, Lynn and Janet Stocks. "Varieties of Fundamentalist Experience: Lubavitch Hasidic and Fundamentalist Christian Approaches to Contemporary Family Life." In *New World Hasidim: Ethnographic Studies of Hasidic Jews in America*, ed. Janet S. Belcove-Shalin, 107–33. Albany: SUNY Press, 1995.

Davis, Allen Freeman. *Spearheads for Reform: The Social Settlements and the Progressive Movement, 1890–1914*. New York: Oxford University Press, 1967.

Denholtz, Elaine Grudin. *The Zaddik: The Battle for a Boy's Soul*. New York: Prometheus Books, 2001.

Diamant, Anita. *The Red Tent*. New York: St. Martin's Press, 1997.

Diamond, Etan. *And I Will Dwell in Their Midst: Orthodox Jews in Suburbia*. Chapel Hill: University of North Carolina Press, 2000.

Dicker, Adam. "Elian Saga Could Mar Return of Children: U.S. Probing 21 Custody Cases Involving Israel, Signer of '80 Extradition Pact." *New York Jewish Week*, April 28, 2000.

Diner, Hasia R., and Beryl Lieff Benderly. *Her Works Praise Her: A History of Jewish Women in America from Colonial Times to the Present*. New York: Basic Books, 2002.

Don-Yehiya, Eliezer. "The Book and the Sword: The Nationalist Yeshivot and Political Radicalism in Israel." In *Accounting for Fundamentalisms: The Dynamic Character of Movements*, ed. Martin E. Marty and R. Scott Appleby, 264–302. Chicago: University of Chicago Press, 1994.

Dundes, Alan. *The Shabbat Elevator and Other Sabbath Subterfuges: An Unorthodox Essay on Circumventing Custom and Jewish Character*. Lanham, Md.: Rowman and Littlefield, 2002.

Ebersole, Gary L. *Captured by Texts: Puritan to Postmodern Images of Indian Captivity*. Charlottesville: University Press of Virginia, 1995.

Efron, Noah J. "Men in Black: The Politics of Jewish Identity in Israel." *Tikkun* 18, no. 5 (September–October 2003): 25–27.

——. "A Political Fantasy for Our Time." *Midstream* 48, no. 2 (2002): 13–16.

——. *Real Jews: Secular Versus Ultra-Orthodox and the Struggle for Jewish Identity in Israel*. New York: Basic Books, 2003.

——. "Trembling with Fear: How Secular Israelis See the Ultra-Orthodox, and Why." *Tikkun* 6 (1991): 15–22, 88–90.

Ehrlich, Avrum M. *The Messiah of Brooklyn: Understanding Lubavitch Hasidism Past and Present*. Jersey City, N.J.: KTAV, 2004.

Eisen, Arnold M. *The Chosen People in America: A Study in Jewish Religious Ideology*. Bloomington: Indiana University Press, 1983.

——. *Rethinking Modern Judaism: Ritual, Commandment, Community*. Chicago: University of Chicago Press, 1998.

——. *Taking Hold of Torah: Jewish Commitment and Community in America*. Bloomington: Indiana University Press, 1997.

Ellenson, David Harry. *After Emancipation: Jewish Religious Responses to Modernity*. Cincinnati: Hebrew Union College Press, 2004.

El-Or, Tamar. *Educated and Ignorant: Ultraorthodox Jewish Women and Their World*. Boulder, Colo.: Lynne Rienner Publishers, 1994.

El-Or, Tamar, and Haim Watzman. *Next Year I Will Know More: Literacy and Identity Among Young Orthodox Women in Israel*. Detroit: Wayne State University Press, 2002.

Etkes, I., and Tauber Institute for the Study of European Jewry. *The Besht: Magician, Mystic, and Leader*. Waltham, Mass.: Brandeis University Press/Hanover. N.H.: University Press of New England, 2005.

Fein, Leonard J. *Israel: Politics and People*. Boston: Little Brown, 1968.

——. *Politics in Israel*. Boston: Little Brown, 1967.

——. *Reform Is a Verb*. New York: Union of American Hebrew Congregations, 1972.

——. *Where Are We? The Inner Life of America's Jews*. New York: Harper and Row, 1988.

Fessenden, Tracy. *Culture and Redemption: Religion, the Secular, and American Literature*. Princeton, N.J.: Princeton University Press, 2006.

Fishkoff, Sue. "Black Hat Blitz." *Moment* (August 2000): 46–53, 85–88.

——. *The Rebbe's Army: Inside the World of Chabad-Lubavitch*. New York: Schocken Books, 2003.

Fishman, Aryei. *Judaism and Collective Life: Self and Community in the Religious Kibbutz*. London: Routledge, 2002.

Fishman, Sylvia Barack. *A Breath of Life: Feminism in the American Jewish Community*. New York: Free Press, 1993.

——. *Double or Nothing? Jewish Families and Mixed Marriage*. Hanover, N.H.: University Press of New England, 2004.

———. *Follow My Footprints: Changing Images of Women in American Jewish Fiction.* Hanover, N.H.: University Press of New England for Brandeis University Press, 1992.

———. "I of the Beholder: Jews and Gender in Film and Popular Culture." Paper presented at the Hadassah Research Institute on Jewish Women, Waltham, Mass., May 1998.

———. "Jewish Identity in American Fiction." In *Envisioning Israel: The Changing Ideals and Images of North American Jews*, ed. Allon Gal, 271–292. Jerusalem: Hebrew University Press, 1996.

———. *Jewish Life and American Culture.* Albany: State University of New York Press, 2000.

———. "Negotiating Egalitarianism and Judaism: American Jewish Feminisms and Their Implications for Jewish Life." In *Jews in America: A Contemporary Reader*, ed. Roberta Rosenberg and Chaim I. Waxman, 163–90. Hanover, N.H.: Brandeis University Press, 1999.

Foster, Lawrence. *Religion and Sexuality: The Shakers, the Mormons, and the Oneida Community.* Urbana: University of Illinois Press, 1984.

Fox, Margalit. "Chaim Potok, 73, Dies; Novelist Illumined the World of Hasidic Judaism." *New York Times*, July 24 2002.

Franchot, Jenny. *Roads to Rome: The Antebellum Protestant Encounter with Catholicism.* Berkeley: University of California Press, 1994.

Freedman, Samuel G. "The Battle Over Reform Judaism." Salon.com, May 1 ,1999. http://www.salon.com/news/feature/1999/05/01/jews/. Accessed June 11 2005.

———. *Jew Vs. Jew: The Struggle for the Soul of American Jewry.* New York: Simon and Schuster, 2000.

———. "Yeshivish at Yale." *New York Times*, May 24, 1998.

Freundel, Barry. *Contemporary Orthodox Judaism's Response to Modernity.* Jersey City, N.J.: KTAV, 2004.

Fried, Joseph P. "Following Up." *New York Times*, April 1, 2001.

———. "Mother Tells of Pressures on Jewish Son by a Rabbi." *New York Times*, October 12, 1994.

———. "Orthodox Rabbi Found Guilty of Kidnapping a Jewish Youth." *New York Times*, November 21, 1994.

Friedman, Menachem. "Habad as Messianic Fundamentalism: From Local Particularism to Universal Jewish Mission." In *Accounting for Fundamentalisms: The Dynamic Character of Movements*, ed. Martin E. Marty and R. Scott Appleby, 328–57. Chicago: University of Chicago Press, 1994.

——. "Haredim Confront the Modern City." In *Studies in Contemporary Jewry II*, ed. Peter Y. Medding, 74–96. Bloomington: Indiana University Press, 1986.

Friedman, Robert I. *The False Prophet: Rabbi Meir Kahane—from FBI Informant to Knesset Member*. Brooklyn: Lawrence Hill Books, 1990.

Friedman, Thomas L. "America in the Mind of Israel." *New York Times*, May 25, 1986.

Friedmann, Thomas. "Back to Orthodoxy: The New Ethic and Ethnics in American Jewish Literature." *Contemporary Jewry* 10, no. 1 (1989): 68–77.

Fuchs, Esther. *Israeli Mythogynies: Women in Contemporary Hebrew Fiction*. Albany: State University of New York Press, 1987.

Furman, Andrew. *Contemporary Jewish American Writers and the Multicultural Dilemma: The Return of the Exiled*. Syracuse, N.Y.: Syracuse University Press, 2000.

——. *Israel Through the Jewish-American Imagination: A Survey of Jewish-American Literature on Israel, 1928–1995*. Albany: State University of New York Press, 1997.

Gal, Allon, ed.. *Envisioning Israel: The Changing Ideals and Images of North American Jews*. Jerusalem: Hebrew University Press, 1996.

Gillman, Neil. *Conservative Judaism: The New Century*. New York: Behrman House, 1993.

Gilman, Charlotte Perkins. *The Yellow Wallpaper*. Feminist Press Reprint No. 3. 1899. New York: Feminist Press, 1973.

Gilman, Sander. *Jewish Self-Hatred*. Baltimore, Md.: Johns Hopkins University Press, 1990.

——. *The Jew's Body*. New York: Routledge, 1991.

Gittleman, Sol. *From Shtetl to Suburbia: The Family in Jewish Literary Imagination*. Boston: Beacon Press, 1978.

Givens, Terryl. *The Viper on the Hearth: Mormons, Myths, and the Construction of Heresy*. New York: Oxford University Press, 1997.

Glazer, Miriyam. "Male and Female, King and Queen: The Theological Imagination of Anne Roiphe's *Lovingkindness*." *Studies in American Jewish Literature* 10, no. 1 (Spring 1991): 81–92.

Glazer, Nathan. *American Judaism*. Chicago: University of Chicago Press, 1957.

Goldberg, Carey. "Fathers' Tactic in Divorce Wars: Jewish Custom Is Revived as Leverage Against Wives." *New York Times*, May 27, 1995.

Goldberg, Harvey E. "Coming of Age in Jewish Studies, or Anthropology Is Counted in the Minyan." *Jewish Social Studies* 4, no. 3 (1998): 29–65.

Goldman, Karla. *Beyond the Synagogue Gallery: Finding a Place for Women in American Judaism*. Cambridge, Mass.: Harvard University Press, 2000.

Goldschmidt, Henry. *Race and Religion Among the Chosen Peoples of Crown Heights.* New Brunswick, N.J.: Rutgers University Press, 2006.

Goldsmith, Emanuel S., Mel Scult, and Robert M. Seltzer. *The American Judaism of Mordecai M. Kaplan.* New York: New York University Press, 1990.

Goldstein, Rebecca. *The Dark Sister.* New York: Viking, 1991.

——. *The Late-Summer Passion of a Woman of Mind.* New York: Farrar Straus and Giroux, 1989.

——. *Mazel.* New York: Viking, 1995.

——. *The Mind-Body Problem: A Novel.* New York: Random House, 1983.

——. *Properties of Light: A Novel of Love, Betrayal, and Quantum Physics.* Boston: Houghton Mifflin, 2000.

——. *Strange Attractors.* New York: Viking, 1993.

Goodman, Allegra. *The Family Markowitz.* New York: Farrar Straus and Giroux, 1996.

——. *Kaaterskill Falls: A Novel.* New York: Dial Press, 1998.

——. "Long-Distance Client." *New Yorker,* July 11, 2005. http://www.newyorker.com/archive/2005/07/11/050711fi_fiction.

——. *Paradise Park: A Novel.* New York: Dial Press, 2001.

——. *Total Immersion: Stories.* New York: Harper and Row, 1989.

Gover, Yerach. *Zionism: The Limits of Moral Discourse in Israeli Hebrew Fiction.* Minneapolis: University of Minnesota Press, 1994.

Grade, Chaim, David Brandes, and Joseph Telushkin. *The Quarrel.* Dir. Eli Cohen. Honey and Apple Productions, 1991.

Grant, Thomas. "Hostage to Innocence: The Captivity Melodrama from Colonial Massachusetts to Contemporary Lebanon." In *The American Columbiad: Discovering America, Inventing the United States,* 239–48. Amsterdam: VU University Press, 1996.

Grauer, Tresa. " 'A Drastically Bifurcated Legacy': Homeland and Identity in Contemporary Jewish American Literature." In *Divergent Jewish Cultures: Israel and America,* ed. Deborah Dash and S. Ilan Troen Moore, 238–255. New Haven, Conn.: Yale University Press, 2001.

——. "Identity Matters: Contemporary Jewish American Writing." In *The Cambridge Companion to Jewish American Literature,* ed. Hana Wirth-Nesher and Michael Kramer, 269–84. Cambridge: Cambridge University Press, 2003.

Grebstein, Sheldon. "The Phenomenon of the Really Jewish Best Seller: Potok's the Chosen." *Studies in American Jewish Literature* 1, no. 1 (1975): 23–31.

Greenberg, Blu. *How to Run a Traditional Jewish Household.* New York: Simon and Schuster, 1983.

——. *On Women and Judaism: A View from Tradition.* Philadelphia: Jewish Publication Society of America, 1981.

Greenstein, Amy Lila. "The Betrothal Fiasco." *Lilith* 20, no. 3 (September 1995): 4.

Griffith, R. Marie. *God's Daughters: Evangelical Women and the Power of Submission.* Berkeley: University of California Press, 1997.

Gross, Netty C., and Yossi Klein Halevi. "Religious Revival." *The Jerusalem Report,* July 11, 1996, 14–18.

Grossberg, Lawrence, Cary Nelson, and Paula A. Treichler. *Cultural Studies.* New York: Routledge, 1992.

Grossman, Naomi. "Women Unbound: Breaking the Chains of Jewish Divorce Law." *Lilith* 18, no. 3 (1993): 8.

Gurock, Jeffrey S. *American Jewish Life, 1920–1990.* American Jewish History 4. New York: Routledge, 1997.

——. *American Jewish Orthodoxy in Historical Perspective.* Hoboken, N.J.: KTAV, 1996.

——. *From Fluidity to Rigidity: The Religious Worlds of Conservative and Orthodox Jews in Twentieth-Century America*, David W. Belin Lecture in American Jewish Affairs 7. Ann Arbor: University of Michigan Jean and Samuel Frankel Center for Judaic Studies, 1998.

——. *The History of Judaism in America: Transplantations, Transformations, and Reconciliations.* American Jewish History 5. New York: Routledge, 1998.

Gurock, Jeffrey S., and Jacob J. Schacter. *A Modern Heretic and a Traditional Community: Mordecai M. Kaplan, Orthodoxy, and American Judaism.* New York: Columbia University Press, 1997.

Hadden, Jeffrey K., and Anson D. Shupe. *Secularization and Fundamentalism Reconsidered.* Religion and the Political Order 3. New York: Paragon House, 1989.

Halkin, Hillel. "In Orthodoxy, Ritual Trumps Morality." *Jerusalem Post*, May 27, 2005.

Hallam, Elizabeth, and Brian V. Street. *Cultural Encounters: Representing 'Otherness.'* London: Routledge, 2000.

Hammer, Devora C. "Confessions of an Agunah Activist." *Lilith* (Winter 2003): 20.

Hammer, Joshua. *Chosen by God: A Brother's Journey.* New York: Hyperion, 1999.

Harap, Louis. *The Image of the Jew in American Literature: From Early Republic to Mass Immigration.* Philadelphia: Jewish Publication Society of America, 1974.

——. *In the Mainstream: The Jewish Presence in Twentieth-Century American Literature, 1950s–1980s.* New York: Greenwood Press, 1987.

Harap, Louis, and American Jewish Archives. *Creative Awakening: The Jewish Presence in Twentieth-Century American Literature, 1900–1940s.* New York: Greenwood Press, 1987.

——. *Dramatic Encounters: The Jewish Presence in Twentieth-Century American Drama, Poetry, and Humor and the Black-Jewish Literary Relationship.* New York: Greenwood Press, 1987.

Harris, Lis. *Holy Days: The World of a Hasidic Family.* New York: Simon and Schuster, 1985.

Hartman, Shari. "Identity and Storytelling in Leah Morton's *I Am a Woman—and a Jew* and Anne Roiphe's *Lovingkindness.*" Master's thesis, University of South Alabama, 2002.

Hasson, Shlomo. *The Struggle for Hegemony in Jerusalem: Secular and Ultra-Orthodox Urban Politics.* Jerusalem: Floersheimer Institute for Policy Studies, 2002.

Hasson, Shlomo, Amiram Gonen, and Floersheimer Institute for Policy Studies. *The Cultural Tension Within Jerusalem's Jewish Population.* Jerusalem: Floersheimer Institute for Policy Studies, 1997.

Haught, James A. *Holy Hatred: Religious Conflicts of the '90s.* Amherst, N.Y.: Prometheus Books, 1995.

Havazelet, Ehud. *Like Never Before.* New York: Farrar Straus Giroux, 1998.

Heilman, Samuel, and Menachem Friedman. "Religious Fundamentalism and Religious Jews: The Case of the Haredim." In *Fundamentalisms Observed*, ed. Martin E. Marty and R. Scott Appleby, 197–264. Chicago: Chicago University Press, 1991.

Heilman, Samuel C. *Defenders of the Faith: Inside Ultra-Orthodox Jewry.* Berkeley: University of California Press, 2000.

——. Foreword to *New World Hasidim: Ethnographic Studies of Hasidic Jews in America*, ed. Janet S. Belcove-Shalin, xi–xv. Albany: State University of New York Press, 1995.

——. "How Did Fundamentalism Manage to Infiltrate Contemporary Orthodoxy?" Paper presented at the Association for Jewish Studies, Boston 2003.

——. "Quiescent and Active Fundamentalisms: The Jewish Cases." In *Accounting for Fundamentalisms: The Dynamic Character of Movements*, ed. Martin E. Marty and R. Scott Appleby, 173–96. Chicago: University of Chicago Press, 1994.

——. *Sliding to the Right: The Contest for the Future of American Jewish Orthodoxy.* Berkeley: University of California Press, 2006.

Heilman, Samuel C., and Steven Martin Cohen. *Cosmopolitans and Parochials: Modern Orthodox Jews in America.* Chicago: University of Chicago Press, 1989.

Henry, Marilyn. "The War of the Messiah Heats Up." *The Jerusalem Post*, August 30, 1996.

Hertzberg, Arthur. *The Jews in America: Four Centuries of an Uneasy Encounter: A History.* New York: Simon and Schuster, 1989.

Herzl, Theodor. *The Jewish State.* Trans. Sylvie d'Avigdor. New York: Dover, 1988.

Heschel, Abraham Joshua. *God in Search of Man: A Philosophy of Judaism.* Northvale, N.J.: Jason Aronson, 1987.

Heschel, Abraham Joshua, and Fritz A. Rothschild. *Between God and Man: An Interpretation of Judaism from the Writings of Abraham Joshua Heschel.* New York: Free Press Paperbacks, 1997.

Heschel, Susannah. "Imagining Judaism in America." In *The Cambridge Companion to Jewish American Literature,* ed. Hana Wirth-Nesher and Michael Kramer, 31–49. Cambridge: Cambridge University Press, 2003.

——. *On Being a Jewish Feminist: A Reader.* New York: Schocken Books, 1983.

Hobsbawm, Eric. "Inventing Traditions." In *The Invention of Tradition,* ed. Eric Hobsbawm and T. Ranger Hobsbawm, 1–14. Cambridge: Cambridge University Press, 1983.

Hoffman, Lawrence A. *Covenant of Blood: Circumcision and Gender in Rabbinic Judaism.* Chicago: University of Chicago Press, 1996.

Horn, Dara. *In the Image: A Novel.* New York: Norton, 2002.

Howe, Irving. "Immigrant Chic." *New York,* May 12, 1986, 76.

——. Introduction to *Jewish American Stories,* ed. Irving Howe. New York: Mentor, 1977.

Hunter, James Davison. *Culture Wars: The Struggle to Define America.* New York: Basic Books, 1991.

Hutchison, William R. *Religious Pluralism in America: The Contentious History of a Founding Ideal.* New Haven, Conn.: Yale University Press, 2003.

Hyman, Paula. *Gender and Assimilation in Modern Jewish History: The Roles and Representation of Women.* Seattle: University of Washington Press, 1995.

——. "Where Do We Go from Here? Feminism and Changing Gender Expectations and Roles in Jewish Communal Life." In *Creating the Jewish Future,* ed. Michael Brown and Bernard Lightman, 185–98. Walnut Creek, Calif.: AltaMira Press, 1999.

Hyman, Paula, Deborah Dash Moore, and American Jewish Historical Society. *Jewish Women in America: An Historical Encyclopedia.* New York: Routledge, 1998.

Ibsen, Henrik. *A Doll's House.* Trans. and intro. William Archer. London: T. F. Unwin, 1889.

Izenberg, Dan. "Naomi Ragen Sued for Plagiarism—Again." *Jerusalem Post,* September 1, 2007. http://www.jpost.com/servlet/Satellite?pagename=JPost/JPArticle/ShowFull&cid=1188392510984.

Jaffe, Azriela. *What Do You Mean, You Can't Eat in My Home? A Guide to How Newly Observant Jews and Their Less-Observant Relatives Can Still Get Along.* New York: Schocken Books, 2005.

Joselit, Jenna Weissman. *New York's Jewish Jews: The Orthodox Community in the Interwar Years.* Bloomington: Indiana University Press, 1990.

——. *The Wonders of America: Reinventing Jewish Culture, 1880–1950.* New York: Hill and Wang, 1994.

Kahane, Meir. *Israel: Revolution or Referendum.* Secaucus, N.J.: Barricade Books, 1990.

——. *Listen World, Listen Jew.* 3rd ed. Jerusalem: Institute for the Publication of the Writings of Rabbi Meir Kahane, 1995.

——. *The Story of the Jewish Defense League.* Radnor, Penn.: Chilton, 1975.

——. *Why Be Jewish? Intermarriage, Assimilation, and Alienation.* Miami Beach, Fla.: Copy Service, 1977.

Kamenetz, Roger. "Has Jewish Renewal Made It into the Mainstream?" *Moment* (December 1994): 42–49.

——. *The Jew in the Lotus: A Poet's Rediscovery of Jewish Identity in Buddhist India.* San Francisco: HarperSanFrancisco, 1994.

Kaplan, Edward K., and Samuel H. Dresner. *Abraham Joshua Heschel: Prophetic Witness.* New Haven, Conn.: Yale University Press, 1998.

Kaplan, Mordecai Menahem. *The Jewish Reconstructionist Papers.* New York: Behrman's Jewish Book House, 1936.

——. *Judaism as a Civilization: Toward a Reconstruction of American-Jewish Life.* Philadelphia: Jewish Publication Society of America and the Reconstructionist Press, 1981.

Kaplan, Mordecai Menahem, and Mel Scult. *Communings of the Spirit: The Journals of Mordecai M. Kaplan.* Detroit: Wayne State University Press and the Reconstructionist Press, 2001.

Kasson, Joy S. *Marble Queens and Captives: Women in Nineteenth-Century American Sculpture.* New Haven, Conn.: Yale University Press, 1990.

Kates, Judith A., and Gail Twersky Reimer. *Reading Ruth: Contemporary Women Reclaim a Sacred Story.* New York: Ballantine Books, 1994.

Katz, Jacob. *Emancipation and Assimilation: Studies in Modern Jewish History.* Farnborough, U.K.: Gregg, 1972.

——. *A House Divided: Orthodoxy and Schism in Nineteenth-Century Central European Jewry.* Hanover, N.H.: University Press of New England, 1998.

——. *Jewish Emancipation and Self-Emancipation.* Philadelphia: Jewish Publication Society, 1986.

———. "Orthodoxy in Historical Perspective." *Studies in Contemporary Jewry* 2 (1986): 3–17.

———. *Toward Modernity: The European Jewish Model.* New Brunswick, N.J.: Transaction Books, 1987.

Katz, Jacob, and Bernard Dov Cooperman. *Tradition and Crisis: Jewish Society at the End of the Middle Ages.* New York: New York University Press, 1993.

Kaufman, Carol Goodman. "Open Our Communal Eyes to Spousal Abuse." *Forward*, November 21, 2003, 9.

Kaufman, David. *Shul with a Pool: The "Synagogue-Center" in American Jewish History.* Hanover, N.H.: University Press of New England, 1999.

Kaufman, Debra R. "Engendering Orthodoxy: Newly Orthodox Women and Hasidism." In *New World Hasidim: Ethnographic Studies of Hasidic Jews in America*, ed. Janet S. Belcove-Shalin, 135–60. Albany: SUNY Press, 1995.

———. *Rachel's Daughters: Newly Orthodox Jewish Women.* New Brunswick, N.J.: Rutgers University Press, 1991.

Kauvar, Elaine M. "An Interview with Chaim Potok." *Contemporary Literature* 27, no. 3 (1986): 291–317.

Kaye, Evelyn. *The Hole in the Sheet: A Modern Woman Looks at Orthodox and Hasidic Judaism.* Secaucus, N.J.: L. Stuart, 1987.

Kellerman, Aharon. *Society and Settlement: Jewish Land of Israel in the Twentieth Century.* Albany: State University of New York Press, 1993.

Kempley, Rita. "Faith and Irony: 'The Chosen's' Affectionate Slice of Jewish Life." *Washington Post*, September 10, 1982.

Kent, Deborah. *Jane Addams and Hull House.* Cornerstones of Freedom. Chicago: Childrens Press, 1992.

Kessler, E. J. "Reading Books on the Sly, a Chasidic Girl Plots Escape." *Forward*, July 28, 1995, 9.

Kingsolver, Barbara. *The Poisonwood Bible.* London: Faber and Faber, 2000.

Kleiman, Shelly. "Author's Novels Evoke World of the Ultra-Orthodox." *Canadian Jewish News.* Available through http://www.naomiragen.com/Articles/orthoworld.htm.

Koltun, Elizabeth. *The Jewish Woman: New Perspectives.* New York: Schocken Books, 1976.

Landau, David. *Piety and Power: The World of Jewish Fundamentalism.* New York: Hill and Wang, 1993.

Laurentis, Arthur. *The Way We Were.* Dir. Sydney Pollack. Columbia Pictures, 1973.

Lawrence, Bruce B. *Defenders of God: The Fundamentalist Revolt Against the Modern Age.* Columbia: University of South Carolina Press, 1995.

Lefkovitz, Etgar. "Haredi Youths Assail Woman on Bus," *Jerusalem Post*, October 21, 2007.

Lesher, Michael. "The Rabbi and the Runaway." *New York Jewish Week*, June 28, 1996.

Levin, Dan. "A Display of Disapproval That Turned Menacing." *New York Times*, December 16, 2007.

Levine, Stephanie Wellen. *Mystics, Mavericks, and Merrymakers: An Intimate Journey Among Hasidic Girls*. New York: New York University Press, 2003.

Levinthal, Israel Herbert. *Point of View: An Analysis of American Judaism*. London: Abelard-Schuman, 1958.

Levitt, Laura. *Jews and Feminism: The Ambivalent Search for Home*. New York: Routledge, 1997.

Libowitz, Richard. *Mordecai M. Kaplan and the Development of Reconstructionism*. New York: E. Mellen Press, 1983.

Liebman, Charles S., and Steven M. Cohen. "Jewish Liberalism Revisited." In *Jews in America: A Contemporary Reader*, ed. Roberta Rosenberg and Chaim I. Waxman, 197–200. Hanover, N.H.: Brandeis University Press, 1999.

Lilker, Shalom. *Kibbutz Judaism: A New Tradition in the Making*. Darby, Penn.: Cornwall Books, 1982.

Linzer, Judith. *Torah and Dharma: Jewish Seekers in Eastern Religions*. Northvale, N.J.: Jason Aronson, 1996.

Loeb, Laurence D. "Habad and Habban: '770's' Impact on a Yemenite Jewish Community in Israel." In *New World Hasidim: Ethnographic Studies of Hasidic Jews in America*, ed. Janet S. Belcove-Shalin, 69–85. Albany: State University of New York Press, 1995.

Lowenstein, Linda, ed. *Paper Plates: When Part of Your Family Keeps Kosher*. Northvale, N.J.: Jason Aronson, 2003.

Lurie, Alison. *Imaginary Friends*. New York: Coward-McCann, 1967.

Mabro, Judy. *Veiled Half-Truths: Western Travellers' Perceptions of Middle Eastern Women*. London: I. B. Tauris, 1996.

Magida, Arthur J. "Targeting Skeptics." *Moment* (June 1998): 53–57, 72–73, 78–82.

Mark, Elizabeth Wyner. *The Covenant of Circumcision: New Perspectives on an Ancient Jewish Rite*. Hanover, N.H.: University Press of New England for Brandeis University Press, 2003.

Mark, Jonathan. "Kidnapping Trial in New York: A Battle Over Jewish Souls." *Jewish Advocate*, March 4, 1993.

Marsden, George. *Fundamentalism and American Culture*. Oxford: Oxford University Press, 1982.

Marty, Martin E., R. Scott Appleby, and American Academy of Arts and Sciences. *Accounting for Fundamentalisms: The Dynamic Character of Movements*. Chicago: University of Chicago Press, 1994.

———. *The Fundamentalism Project*. Chicago: University of Chicago Press, 1991.

———. *Fundamentalisms and Society: Reclaiming the Sciences, the Family, and Education*. Fundamentalism Project 2. Chicago: University of Chicago Press, 1993.

———. *Fundamentalisms and the State: Remaking Polities, Economies, and Militance*. Fundamentalism Project 3. Chicago: University of Chicago Press, 1993.

———. *Fundamentalisms Comprehended*. Chicago: University of Chicago Press, 1995.

———. *Fundamentalisms Observed*. Chicago: University of Chicago Press, 1991.

Maslin, Simeon. "Who Are the Authentic Jews?" *Reform Judaism* (Summer 1996), http://reformjudaismmag.net/696sm.html.

McCarthy, Mary. *Memories of a Catholic Girlhood*. New York: Harcourt Brace, 1957.

McRobbie, Angela. "The Politics of Feminist Research." *Feminist Review* 12 (1982): 46–57.

Meijers, Daniel. *Hasidic Groups and Other Religions Collectivities in Orthodox Judaism*. Amsterdam: Free University Press, 1986.

Mergui, Raphaël, and Philippe Simonnot. *Israel's Ayatollahs: Meir Kahane and the Far Right in Israel*. London: Saqi Books, 1987.

Merkin, Daphne. "Trouble in the Tribe: How Jewish Do American Jews Want to Be?" *New Yorker*, September 11, 2000.

———. "Why Potok Is Popular." *Commentary* 61, no. 2 (1976): 73–75.

Merkle, John C. *Abraham Joshua Heschel: Exploring His Life and Thought*. New York: Collier Macmillan, 1985.

———. *The Genesis of Faith: The Depth Theology of Abraham Joshua Heschel*. New York: Collier Macmillan, 1985.

Meyer, Adam. "Putting the 'Jewish' Back in 'Jewish American Fiction': A Look at Jewish American Fiction from 1977 to 2002 and an Allegorical Reading of Nathan Englander's 'The Gilgul of Park Avenue.'" *Shofar* 22, no. 3 (2004): 104–20.

Meyer, Michael A. *Judaism Within Modernity: Essays on Jewish History and Religion*. Detroit: Wayne State University Press, 2001.

Miller, Daisy Sophia. "Serpentine Advances in Sacred Space: Representations of the Shakers in American Literature." Ph.D. diss., State University of New York at Stony Brook, 2000.

Miller, Risa. *Welcome to Heavenly Heights*. New York: St. Martin's Press, 2003.

Mintz, Jerome R. *Hasidic People: A Place in the New World*. Cambridge, Mass.: Harvard University Press, 1992.

——. *Legends of the Hasidim: An Introduction to Hasidic Culture and Oral Tradition in the New World.* Northvale, N.J.: Jason Aronson, 1995.

Mirvis, Tova. *The Ladies Auxiliary.* New York: Norton, 1999.

——. *The Outside World.* New York: Knopf, 2004.

Mittelberg, David. *Strangers in Paradise: The Israeli Kibbutz Experience.* New Brunswick, N.J.: Transaction Books, 1988.

Moelis, Joan M. "Writing Selves: Constructing American Jewish Feminine Literary Identity." Ph.D. diss., University of Massachusetts–Amherst, 1996.

Moore, Donald J. *The Human and the Holy: The Spirituality of Abraham Joshua Heschel.* New York: Fordham University Press, 1989.

Moore, R. Laurence. *Selling God: American Religion in the Marketplace of Culture.* New York: Oxford University Press, 1994.

Morris, Bonnie. "Agents or Victims of Religious Ideology? Approaches to Locating Hasidic Women in Feminist Studies." In *New World Hasidim: Ethnographic Studies of Hasidic Jews in America,* ed. Janet S. Belcove-Shalin, 161–80. Albany: State University of New York Press, 1995.

Mulvey, Laura. *Visual and Other Pleasures.* Basingstoke: Macmillan, 1989.

Myers, Jody, and Jane Rachel Litman. "The Secret of Jewish Femininity: Hiddenness, Power, and Physicality in the Theology of Orthodox Women in the Contemporary World." In *Gender and Judaism: The Transformation of Tradition,* ed. T. M. Rudavsky, 51–80. New York: New York University Press, 1995.

Nadata, Saul. "Yale's Jewish Students Keep Faith and Thrive." *New York Times,* September 14, 1997.

Nadell, Pamela Susan. *American Jewish Women's History: A Reader.* New York: New York University Press, 2003.

——. *Women Who Would Be Rabbis: A History of Women's Ordination, 1889–1985.* Boston: Beacon Press, 1998.

Nadell, Pamela Susan, and Jonathan D. Sarna. *Women and American Judaism: Historical Perspectives.* Hanover, N.H.: University Press of New England, 2001.

Neusner, Jacob. *Judaism: An Introduction.* London: Penguin, 2002.

Ozick, Cynthia. *The Pagan Rabbi, and Other Stories.* Syracuse, N.Y.: Syracuse University Press, 1995.

——. *The Puttermesser Papers.* New York: Knopf, 1997.

Pagliarini, Marie Anne. "The Pure American Woman and the Wicked Catholic Priest: An Analysis of Anti-Catholic Literature in Antebellum America." *Religion and American Culture* 9, no. 1 (1999): 97–128.

Palgi, Michal. *Sexual Equality: The Israeli Kibbutz Tests the Theories*. Norwood, Penn.: Norwood Editions, 1983.

Palmer, Susan J. "Frontiers and Families: The Children of Island Pond." In *Children of New Religions*, ed. Susan J. Palmer and Charlotte Hardman, 153–71. New Brunswick, N.J.: Rutgers University Press, 1999.

——. *Moon Sisters, Krishna Mothers, Rajneesh Lovers: Women's Roles in New Religions*. Women and Gender in North American Religions. Syracuse, N.Y.: Syracuse University Press, 1994.

Palmer, Susan J., and Charlotte Hardman. *Children in New Religions*. New Brunswick, N.J.: Rutgers University Press, 1999.

Patrick, Ted, and Tom Dulack. *Let Our Children Go!* New York: Dutton, 1976.

Perez, Loida Maritza. *Geographies of Home*. New York: Viking, 1999.

Peskowitz, Miriam. "Engendering Jewish Religious History." *Shofar* 14, no. 1 (1995): 8–34.

Peskowitz, Miriam, and Laura Levitt. *Judaism Since Gender*. New York: Routledge, 1997.

Philologos. "A New Mixed Marriage?" *Forward*, May 28, 2004.

Plaskow, Judith. "Judith Plaskow's Un-Orthodox Take on the Feminism and Orthodoxy Conference." *Lilith* 22, no. 2 (1997): 4.

Poll, Solomon. "The Charismatic Leader of the Hasidic Community: The Zaddiq, the Rebbe." In *New World Hasidim: Ethnographic Studies of Hasidic Jews in America*, ed. Janet S. Belcove-Shalin, 257–75. Albany: State University of New York Press, 1995.

——. "The Sacred-Secular Conflict in the Use of Hebrew and Yiddish among the Ultra-Orthodox Jews of Jerusalem." *International Journal of the Sociology of Language* 24 (1980): 109–25.

Pollack, Eileen. *Paradise, New York: A Novel*. Philadelphia: Temple University Press, 1998.

Potok, Chaim. *The Chosen*. New York: Fawcett Crest, 1967.

——. *Davita's Harp*. New York: Knopf, 1985.

——. *My Name Is Asher Lev*. New York: Knopf, 1972.

——. *The Promise*. New York: Knopf, 1969.

Pratt, Mary Louise. *Imperial Eyes: Travel Writing and Transculturation*. London: Routledge, 1992.

Quindlen, Anna. *Object Lessons*. New York: Fawcett Columbine, 1997.

Rabinowicz, Tzvi. *Hasidism: The Movement and Its Masters*. Northvale, N.J.: Jason Aronson, 1988.

——. *Hasidism in Israel: A History of the Hasidic Movement and Its Masters in the Holy Land*. Northvale, N.J.: Jason Aronson, 2000.

Radway, Janice A. *Reading the Romance: Women, Patriarchy, and Popular Literature*. Chapel Hill: University of North Carolina Press, 1991.

Ragen, Naomi. *Chains Around the Grass*. New Milford, Conn.: The Toby Press, 2002.

——. "Egged and the Taliban." August 1, 2004. http://www.naomiragen.com/Column %20Archive/EggedAndTheTaliban.htm.

——. *Jephte's Daughter*. New York: Warner Books, 1989.

——. *The Sacrifice of Tamar*. New York: Crown, 1994.

——. *Sotah*. New York: HarperCollins, 1993.

Ravitzky, Aviezer. "The Contemporary Lubavitch Hasidic Movement: Between Conservatism and Messianism." In *Accounting for Fundamentalisms: The Dynamic Character of Movements*, edited by Martin E. Marty and R. Scott Appleby, 303–27. Chicago: University of Chicago Press, 1994.

——. *Messianism, Zionism, and Jewish Religious Radicalism*. Chicago: University of Chicago Press, 1996.

——. "Religious and Secular Jews in Israel: A Culture War?" In *Creating the Jewish Future*, ed. Michael Brown and Bernard Lightman, 80–100. Walnut Creek, Calif.: AltaMira Press, 1990.

Rayman, Paula M. *The Kibbutz Community and Nation Building*. Princeton, N.J.: Princeton University Press, 1981.

Reed, Rebecca, and Maria Monk. *Veil of Fear: Nineteenth-Century Convent Tales*. Intro. Nancy Lusignan Schultz. West Lafayette, Ind.: NotaBell Books, 1999.

Reich, Tova. *The Jewish War: A Novel*. New York: Pantheon Books, 1995.

——. *Mara: A Novel*. Syracuse, N.Y.: Syracuse University Press, 2001.

——. *Master of the Return*. San Diego: Harcourt Brace Jovanovich, 1988.

Richardson, James T. "Social Context of New Religions: From 'Brainwashing' Claims to Child Sex Abuse Accusations." In *Children in New Religions*, ed. Susan J. Palmer, 172–86. New Brunswick, N.J.: Rutgers University Press, 1999.

Rifkind, Donna. "Defenders of the Faith." *Weekly Standard*, December 18, 1995, 41.

Robbins, Thomas, and Benjamin David Zablocki. *Misunderstanding Cults: Searching for Objectivity in a Controversial Field*. Toronto: University of Toronto Press, 2001.

Roiphe, Anne Richardson. *1185 Park Avenue: A Memoir*. New York: Free Press, 1999.

——. *Lovingkindness: A Novel*. New York: Summit Books, 1987.

——. *The Pursuit of Happiness: A Novel*. New York: Summit Books, 1991.

——. "The Whole Truth." *Tikkun* (July/August 1989): 86–88.

Roller, Alyse Fisher. *The Literary Imagination of Ultra-Orthodox Jewish Women: An Assessment of a Writing Community.* Jefferson, N.C.: McFarland, 1999.

Rosenberg, Roberta and Chaim I. Waxman, ed. *Jews in America: A Contemporary Reader.* Hanover, N.H.: University Press of New England for Brandeis University Press, 1999.

Rosenberg, Warren. *Legacy of Rage: Jewish Masculinity, Violence, and Culture.* Amherst: University of Massachusetts Press, 2001.

Rosenfeld, Alvin H. "Promised Land(S): Zion, America, and American Jewish Writers." *Jewish Social Studies* 3, no. 3 (1997): 111–32.

Ross, Tamar. "Can the Demand for Change in the Status of Women Be Halakhically Legitimated." *Judaism: A Quarterly Journal of Jewish Life and Thought* 42, no. 4 (1993): 478–92.

——. *Expanding the Palace of Torah: Orthodoxy and Feminism.* Lebanon, N.H.: University Press of New England for Brandeis University Press, 2004.

Rotem, Yehudit. *Distant Sisters: The Women I Left Behind.* Philadelphia: Jewish Publication Society, 1997.

Roth, Henry. *Call It Sleep.* New York: Avon Books, 1934.

Roth, Philip. *The Counterlife.* New York: Farrar Straus Giroux, 1986.

——. "Eli the Fanatic." In *Goodbye, Columbus, and Five Short Stories* 247–98. Boston: Houghton Mifflin, 1959.

——. *Goodbye, Columbus, and Five Short Stories.* Boston,: Houghton Mifflin, 1959.

——. *The Human Stain.* Boston: Houghton Mifflin, 2000.

——. *Operation Shylock: A Confession.* New York: Simon and Schuster, 1993.

——. *Portnoy's Complaint.* New York: Random House, 1969.

——. "Writing About Jews." *Commentary* (December 1963). Reprint, in *Writing About Myself and Others*, 193–211. New York: Vintage Books, 2001.

Rothman, Paul. *Full Circle: The Ideal of a Sexually Egalitarian Society on the Kibbutz.* New York: Filmakers Library, 1994.

Rotundo, E. Anthony. *American Manhood: Transformations in Masculinity from the Revolution to the Modern Era.* New York: BasicBooks, 1993.

Royal, Derek Parker. "Unfinalized Moments in Jewish American Narrative." *Shofar* 22, no. 3 (2004): 1–11.

Ruby, Walter. "Reform vs. Conservative." *Moment* (April 1996): 30–39, 67.

Rudavsky, David. *Modern Jewish Religious Movements: A History of Emancipation and Adjustment.* New York: Behrman House, 1979.

Rudavsky, Tamar. *Gender and Judaism: The Transformation of Tradition.* New York: New York University Press, 1995.

Ruttenberg, Danya. *Yentl's Revenge: The Next Wave of Jewish Feminism*. Seattle: Seal Press, 2001.

Sacks, Jonathan. *One People? Tradition, Modernity, and Jewish Unity*. London: Littman Library of Jewish Civilization, 1993.

Said, Edward. *Culture and Imperialism*. New York: Knopf, 1993.

———. *Orientalism*. New York: Pantheon Books, 1978.

Sarna, Jonathan D. *American Judaism: A History*. New Haven, Conn.: Yale University Press, 2004.

———. "A Projection of America as It Ought to Be: Zion in the Mind's Eye of American Jews." In *Envisioning Israel: The Changing Ideals and Images of North American Jews*, ed. Allon Gal, 41–59. Jerusalem: Hebrew University Press, 1996

Sawicki, Tom. "Answered Prayers." *The Jerusalem Report*, February 8, 1996, 12–16.

Schechter, Erik, and Amotz Asa-El. "The Anglo Difference: Contributions of English-Speaking Jews to Israel." *Jerusalem Post*, October 2, 2003.

Schecter, Eric. "The Battle for Jewish Souls." *The Jerusalem Report*, February 14, 2000, 18–21.

Schlissel, Lillian, Byrd Gibbens, and Elizabeth Hampsten. *Far from Home: Families of the Westward Journey*. New York: Schocken Books, 1989.

Schultz, Nancy Lusignan. *Fear Itself: Enemies Real and Imagined in American Culture*. West Lafayette, Ind.: Purdue University Press, 1999.

Schwartz, Margery Isis. *What's Up with the Hard Core Jewish People? An Irreverent yet Informative Approach to Judaism and Religious Devotion from a Reform Jewish Mother's Perspective*. [Bangor, Maine]: Booklocker.com, 2006.

Segal, Erich. *Acts of Faith*. New York: Bantam Books, 1992.

Selengut, Charles. "By Torah Alone: Yeshiva Fundamentalism in Jewish Life." In *Accounting for Fundamentalisms: The Dynamic Character of Movements*, ed. Martin E. Marty and R. Scott Appleby, 236–63. Chicago: University of Chicago Press, 1994.

Shaffir, William. "Boundaries and Self-Presentation among the Hasidim: A Study in Identity Maintenance." In *New World Hasidim: Ethnographic Studies of Hasidic Jews in America*, ed. Janet S. Belcove-Shalin, 31–68. Albany: State University of New York Press, 1995.

Shalit, Wendy. "The Observant Reader." *New York Times*, January 30, 2005.

Shalvi, Alice. "Alice Shalvi." In *Half the Kingdom: Seven Jewish Feminists*, ed. Francine Zuckerman. Montreal: Vehicule Press, 1992.

Shapiro, Haim, and Andy Court. "Police Rout Worshippers with Tear Gas. Extremists Attack Women Holding Fast of Esther Prayer at Wall." *Jerusalem Post*, March 21, 1989.

Shenhav, Sharon. "The Agunah: An Ancient Problem in Modern Dress." *Women's League for Conservative Judaism* 64, no. 4 (1994): 18.

Shupe, Anson D. *Six Perspectives on New Religions: A Case Study Approach.* New York: E. Mellen Press, 1981.

Shupe, Anson D., and David G. Bromley. *Anti-Cult Movements in Cross-Cultural Perspective.* New York: Garland, 1994.

Shupe, Anson D., David G. Bromley, and Donna L. Oliver. *The Anti-Cult Movement in America: A Bibliography and Historical Survey.* Sects and Cults in America 2. New York: Garland, 1984.

Shupe, Anson D., William A. Stacey, and Lonnie R. Hazlewood. *Violent Men, Violent Couples: The Dynamics of Domestic Violence.* Lexington, Mass.: Lexington Books, 1987.

Silber, Michael K. "The Emergence of Ultra-Orthodoxy: The Invention of a Tradition." In *The Uses of Tradition: Jewish Continuity in the Modern Era*, ed. Jack Wertheimer, 5–84. Cambridge, Mass.: Harvard University Press, 1992.

Silverman, Eric Kline. *From Abraham to America: A History of Jewish Circumcision.* Lanham, Md.: Rowman and Littlefield, 2006.

Sivan, Emmanuel, and Menachem Friedman. *Religious Radicalism and Politics in the Middle East.* Albany: State University of New York Press, 1990.

Sklare, Marshall. *Conservative Judaism: An American Religious Movement.* New ed. New York: Schocken Books, 1972.

——. "Intermarriage and the Jewish Future." *Commentary* (1964): 46–52.

Smith, Dinitia. "An Author's Hasidic Roots Become Her Inspiration." *New York Times*, February 8, 2005.

Smith, Jonathan Z. *Relating Religion: Essays in the Study of Religion.* Chicago: University of Chicago Press, 2004.

Smith, Tovia, and Bob Edwards. "Yale Religious Controversy." Report on *Morning Edition*, NPR, September 24, 1997.

Socolovsky, Maya. "Land, Legacy, and Return: Negotiating a Post-Assimilationist Stance in Allegra Goodman's *Kaaterskill Falls.*" *Shofar* 22, no. 3 (2004): 26–42.

Sokoloff, Naomi. "Imagining Israel in American Jewish Fiction: Anne Roiphe's *Lovingkindness* and Philip Roth's *The Counterlife.*" *Studies in American Jewish Literature* (1991): 65–80.

Soloveitchik, Haym. "Migration, Acculturation, and the New Role of Texts in the Haredi World." In *Accounting for Fundamentalisms: The Dynamic Character of Movements*, ed. Martin E. Marty and R. Scott Appleby, 197–235. Chicago: University of Chicago Press, 1994.

——. "Rupture and Reconstruction: The Transformation of Contemporary Orthodoxy." In *Jews in America: A Contemporary Reader*, ed. Roberta Rosenberg and Chaim I. Waxman, 320–76. Hanover, N.H.: University Press of New England for Brandeis University Press, 1999.

Soroff, Linda Begley. *The Maintenance and Transmission of Ethnic Identity: A Study of Four Ethnic Groups of Religious Jews in Israel*. Lanham, Md.: University Press of America, 1995.

Steinberg, Jonah. "From a 'Pot of Filth' to a 'Hedge of Roses' (and Back): Changing Theorizations of Menstruations in Judaism." In *Women, Gender, Religion: A Reader*, ed. Elizabeth A. Castelli, 369–88. New York: Palgrave, 2001.

Stone, Russell A., and Walter P. Zenner. *Critical Essays on Israeli Social Issues and Scholarship*. Books on Israel 3. Albany: State University of New York Press, 1994.

Tabor, Mary B. W. "Boy, 15, in Religious Tug-of-War Meets with Parents after 2 Years." *New York Times*, March 1, 1994.

——. "Kidnapped or Converted?" *New York Times*, August 2, 1992.

Telushkin, Joseph. *Jewish Literacy: The Most Important Things to Know About the Jewish Religion, Its People, and Its History*. New York: HarperCollins, 2001.

Trinh, T. Minh-Ha. *Woman, Native, Other: Writing Postcoloniality and Feminism*. Bloomington: Indiana University Press, 1989.

"Uproar at Wailing Wall." *Herald*, December 2, 1988.

Uris, Leon. *Exodus*. Garden City, N.Y.: Doubleday, 1958.

Uris, Leon, and Dalton Trumbo. *Exodus*. Dir. Otto Preminger. MGM, 1960.

Viorst, Milton. *What Shall I Do with This People? Jews and the Fractious Politics of Judaism*. New York: The Free Press, 2002.

Warner, Hoyt Landon. *Reforming American Life in the Progressive Era*. New York: Pitman, 1971.

Waxman, Chaim Isaac. "The Haredization of American Orthodox Jewry." *Jerusalem Letter/Viewpoints*, no. 376 (1998): 1–5.

——. *Israel as a Religious Reality*. Northvale, N.J.: Jason Aronson, 1994.

——. "Israel in American Jewish Life." In *Jews in America: A Contemporary Reader*, ed. Roberta Rosenberg and Chaim I. Waxman, 212–25. Hanover, N.H.: University Press of New England for Brandeis University Press, 1999.

Weaver-Zercher, David. *The Amish in the American Imagination*. Baltimore, Md.: Johns Hopkins University Press, 2001.

Weiss, J. G., Ada Rapoport-Albert, and Institute of Jewish Studies. *Hasidism Reappraised*. Portland, Ore.: Vallentine Mitchell, 1996.

Weissman, Devora. "Bais Yaakov: A Historical Model for Jewish Feminists." In *The Jewish Woman: New Perspectives*, ed. Elizabeth Koltun, 139–48. New York: Schocken, 1976.

Wertheimer, Jack. *A People Divided: Judaism in Contemporary America*. Waltham, Mass.: Brandeis University Press, 1997.

——. "Religious Movements in Collision: A Jewish Culture War?" In *Jews in America: A Contemporary Reader*, ed. Roberta Rosenberg and Chaim I. Waxman, 377–91. Hanover, N.H.: University Press of New England for Brandeis University Press, 1999.

——. *The Uses of Tradition: Jewish Continuity in the Modern Era*. Cambridge, Mass.: Harvard University Press, 1992.

"Whose Western Wall?" *Jerusalem Post*, March 22, 1989.

Willis, Ellen. "Next Year in Jerusalem: A Personal Account." *Rolling Stone*, April 21, 1977, 64–76.

Winston, Hella. *Unchosen: The Hidden Lives of Hasidic Rebels*. Boston: Beacon Press, 2005.

Winter, Kari J. *Subjects of Slavery, Agents of Change: Women and Power in Gothic Novels and Slave Narratives, 1790–1865*. Athens: University of Georgia Press, 1992.

Winterson, Jeanette. *Oranges Are Not the Only Fruit*. London: Pandora Press, 1985.

Wirth-Nesher, Hana. "From Newark to Prague: Roth's Place in the American Jewish Literary Tradition." In *What Is Jewish Literature?* ed. Hana Wirth-Nesher, 216–29. Philadelphia: Jewish Publication Society, 1994.

Wirth-Nesher, Hana, and Michael P. Kramer, eds. *The Cambridge Companion to Jewish American Literature*. Cambridge: Cambridge University Press, 2003.

Wisse, Ruth R. *The Modern Jewish Canon*. New York: The Free Press, 2000.

Wright, Beryl. "Back Talk: Recoding the Body." *Callaloo* 19, no. 2 (1996): 397–413.

Wuthnow, Robert. *The Restructuring of American Religion: Society and Faith Since World War II*. Princeton, N.J.: Princeton University Press, 1988.

——. *The Struggle for America's Soul: Evangelicals, Liberals, and Secularism*. Grand Rapids, Mich.: W. B. Eerdmans, 1989.

Wyatt-Brown, Bertram. *Southern Honor: Ethics and Behavior in the Old South*. New York: Oxford University Press, 1982.

Yakin, Boaz. *A Price Above Rubies*. Dir. Boaz Yakin: Miramax, 1998.

Yehoshua, A. B. "Mr. Mani and the Akedah." *Judaism* (2001).

Yezierska, Anzia. *Bread Givers: A Novel*. 1925. New York: Persea Books, 1999.

Yosef, Raz. *Beyond Flesh: Queer Maculinities and Nationalism in Israeli Cinema*. New Brunswick, N.J.: Rutgers University Press, 2004.

Zolty, Shoshana. *And All Your Children Shall Be Learned: Women and the Study of Torah in Jewish Law and History.* Northvale, N.J.: Jason Aronson, 1993.

Zuckerman, Phil. *Strife in the Sanctuary: Religious Schism in a Jewish Community.* Walnut Creek, Calif.: AltaMira Press, 1999.

INDEX